W9-BMW-975

Prima's Official Guide to Seagate Crystal Reports™ 7

**Jill K. Howe and Scott M. Spanbauer
of The BridgeBuilder Company
with Karen Mayer**

A Division of Prima Publishing

A Division of Prima Publishing

Prima Publishing and colophon are registered trademarks of Prima Communications, Inc., Rocklin, California 95677.

Publisher: Stacy L. Hiquet
Associate Publisher: Nancy Stevenson
Marketing Manager: Judi Taylor
Managing Editor: Dan J. Foster
Senior Acquisitions Editor: Deborah F. Abshier
Senior Editor: Kelli R. Crump
Assistant Project Editor: Estelle Manticas
Technical Editor: Kathryn Hunt
Development and Copy Editor: Jennifer Starbuck
Interior Design and Layout: Scribe Tribe
Cover Design: Prima Design Team
Indexer: Sharon Hilgenberg

ISBN: 0-7615-1656-6

Library of Congress Catalog Card Number: 98-66121

Printed in the United States of America

99 00 01 02 03 BB 10 9 8 7 6 5 4 3 2 1

CONTENTS AT A GLANCE

CONTENTS

ACKNOWLEDGMENTS

We would like to thank the staff at Prima Publishing for their much appreciated editorial assistance. We would also like to thank Seagate Software for their support in this project. Finally, we would like to thank our spouses and co-workers for their patience as two "computer people" became "writers" for a while at the expense of many evenings and weekends.

–Jill K. Howe and Scott M. Spanbauer of The BridgeBuilder Company

As I am the sum of my past experiences, those experiences could not have culiminated in my contribution to this book without the support of some really special people. I appreciate this opportunity to acknowledge the following friends: Marcia Sawyer, who was my mentor when I was a young technical writer; Bill Robertson and Stan Hime for giving me the chance to prove myself; my "sister," Kathy Mayer, for believing in me even if I didn't; my mom, Myrna Hudson, for showing unwavering support for me in all of my endeavors (however wacky some of them have been); my brother, Kirk Hudson, for recognizing my interests and talents before I did and encouraging me in the direction of software development; and to my dad, Walter W. Hudson, for always being there when I need him.

–Karen Mayer

Jill K. Howe is a Seagate Software Certified Trainer in both Seagate Crystal Reports and Seagate Info. She works for The BridgeBuilder Company (www.bridgebuilder.com) from her home in Seattle, Washington. Jill travels across North America delivering training for Seagate Software and The BridgeBuilder Company clients.

Scott M. Spanbauer, a Seagate Software Certified Trainer and Consultant, is founder and CEO of The BridgeBuilder Company, a professional computer consulting and training firm with offices in Charlotte and Raleigh, North Carolina and Cincinnati, Ohio. The BridgeBuilder Company writes custom training materials, creates Computer Based Training (CBT) software, and provides extensive training and consulting across the country for large and small companies. In addition to being one of the first Seagate Certified Training Partners, the firm also supports and provides consulting for the two leading Customer Relationship Management (CRM) software packages, GoldMine and SalesLogix.

Karen Mayer is a software engineer in Phoenix, Arizona. She graduated with a B.A. in Russian from Florida State University and studied Mandarin at the National Taiwan Normal University in Taipei, Taiwan. In 1998, she co-founded Phoenix Area Rottweiler Rescue, Inc., and became a foster parent. At various times in her life, she has been a technical writer, linguist, English teacher, and martial arts instructor, and has enjoyed scuba diving, martial arts, boxing, body building, sky diving, and dog training.

INTRODUCTION

Prima's *Official Guide to Seagate Crystal Reports 7* is targeted at a large array of business report designers and users. This book will get you started with basic report design if you're completely new to Seagate Crystal Reports, and will also lead you through complex report design and the advanced features and components of the product. It is meant to supplement training and serve as a comprehensive reference.

It is organized in such a way that you can follow the chapters in order and learn to design reports step by step. Each part contains chapters that build on the previous chapters to help you learn the process of designing reports. You can choose which of the later chapter topics will serve your needs and skip any that do not apply to your business needs.

What's in This Book

Prima's Official Guide to Seagate Crystal Reports 7 is organized in five major parts, with each part containing chapters covering specific topics. Read through the following sections to learn more about what this book covers.

Part I: Introducing Seagate Crystal Reports

This first part covers how to begin using Seagate Crystal Reports. It covers basic concepts with lots of instruction to help the beginner become comfortable writing basic reports, and the intermediate user find the easiest way to create them.

- **Chapter 1—An Overview of Seagate Crystal Reports.** Explains how the program is set up, how to navigate through the menus and toolbars, and some basic information regarding the structure of reports. This chapter familiarizes you with the interface and prepares you to start designing reports.

- **Chapter 2—Creating Your First Seagate Crystal Report.** Gets right to designing reports. You can follow the tutorial and design a report using a Report Expert and the Custom option, both step by step. This chapter also discusses a few other options available for designing reports. The goal is for you to design a few basic reports and begin to get a feel for how the tool works.

Part II: Adding to Your Seagate Crystal Reports

This part covers several of the topics touched on in Chapter 2 in much more detail. Part II gives step-by-step instructions, and provides extra information and hints as to how to use the functionality that Seagate Crystal Reports provides to meet your specific needs.

- **Chapter 3—Connecting to and Linking Data.** Discusses ways to connect to your specific data and provides examples and discussion regarding linking concepts. Contains steps and instructions to walk you though this sometimes complex area of report design.

- **Chapter 4—Selecting Records.** Covers record selection in more depth than in Chapter 2. Record selection is a basic yet extremely powerful tool used to filter records from your database to appear on a report.

- **Chapter 5—Standard Report Elements: Sorts, Groups, and Totals.** Explains and instructs you on how to add sorts, groups, and totals to your reports for better organization. This chapter also covers the new Running Total Expert.

- **Chapter 6—The Power of Formulas.** Discusses the usefulness of formulas and provides examples of how to create simple formulas to get you started. The chapter also covers If-Then-Else formulas and the use of variables.

- **Chapter 7—Formatting Your Report.** Covers formatting options for your reports, including both field formatting and section formatting. This chapter uses the If-Then-Else type of formula introduced in Chapter 6 in conditional formatting, and demonstrates the new Highlighting Expert.

Part III: Advanced Reporting Topics

Once you get to this part, you'll have a feel for designing basic reports; the sections in this chapter introduce you to advanced features and functions. These advanced reports use familiar methods—Experts and dialog boxes.

- **Chapter 8—Creating Advanced Reports.** Tackles creating and using subreports, cross-tab reports, and the drill down capability in summary reports. These functions all add pizzazz to basic reports, making them function the way you want them to, and adding to the readability and organization of your data.

- **Chapter 9—Adding Graphs and Maps for Better Data Analysis.** Covers creating and integrating graphs and maps into your reports—two excellent tools for looking at your data pictorially.

- **Chapter 10—Advanced Database Concepts.** Discusses the SQL Designer and Crystal Dictionaries—two alternate ways to interact with your data source.

- **Chapter 11—Creating Ad Hoc Reports with Seagate Query.** Covers the new query tool that allows you to design queries from either your Windows environment or the Web.

- **Chapter 12—OLAP Reporting.** Covers OLAP technology—what it is and how to use Seagate Crystal Reports to design reports off cube instances.

Part IV: Using Seagate Crystal Reports with Other Tools

This part covers some basic interactions between Seagate Crystal Reports—a popular and versatile product within the Windows environment—and other tools and software programs. It also includes a helpful chapter about managing reporting projects.

- **Chapter 13—Integrating Seagate Crystal Reports with Other Products.** Includes a brief discussion of Visual Studio member Visual Basic, along with exporting and compiling options to other formats. The chapter also covers designing reports off of a popular spreadsheet, Microsoft Excel.

- **Chapter 14—Integrating Seagate Crystal Reports with the Internet.** Covers the basics of setting up and using Seagate Crystal Reports with your Internet and intranet services.

- **Chapter 15—The Benefits of Seagate Info.** Describes features included with Seagate Info, in addition to the features of Seagate Crystal Reports. Read this chapter to help determine whether to deploy Seagate Info within your organization.

- **Chapter 16—Managing Report Development Projects.** The book concludes with helpful information and advice for starting a reporting project. Reporting can be very basic or very complex depending on what information you use, where it comes from, and the final format needed.

Part V: Appendixes

Appendix A shows you how to set up an ODBC Data Source while Appendix B discusses how to get help. A comprehensive glossary is also included near the back of the book.

Finding More Information

Throughout this book you will see sample reports presented in the figures along with exercises that will help you master Seagate Crystal Reports. The sample reports are available on both The BridgeBuilder Company Web site at www.bridgebuilder.com and the Prima Tech Web site at www.prima-tech.com/scr7. In addition to the sample reports, example formulas, other activities, helpful resource information, and tips and resources to support you in your use of Seagate Crystal Reports and Seagate Info are available as well.

What's New in Version 7

Seagate Crystal Reports (SCR) 7 has many new and exciting features:

- **New Summary Functions.** SCR has made nine new summary functions available when inserting summary fields and when writing formulas.

- **Running Total Expert.** Running Totals can now be created using an Expert. Any summary function can be used and the totals can be evaluated for each record, on change of field, on change of group, or based on a formula.

- **Highlighting Expert.** Number and currency fields can now be highlighted using an Expert rather than conditional formulas. Formatting options available with the Expert include Background, Border, and Font.

- **New CRPE (Crystal Report Print Engine) Functions**. New functions are available for developers using the runtime Crystal Report Print Engine in custom applications.

- **Parameter Fields**. Version 7 has many enhancements for using Parameter fields. Pick lists and masking can be used, ranges can be set, and mandatory prompting can be applied to an input field.

- **Charting**. Charting has more features and options built into the Expert. Additionally, an Analyzer view can be used to manipulate and modify the chart.

- **Map Expert**. This new Expert allows you to insert a geographical map into your report and manipulate that map to meet your needs. The Map Expert supports an Analyzer view for editing the map.

- **Cross-tabs**. Cross-tabs have gained many useful options, including suppressing empty rows, columns, and totals, and conditional formatting with the new CurrentFieldValue function. Row headers can be repeated on pages, and there are enhanced page break features.

- **Field Clipping**. Field clipping is now an option for number and currency fields. If the value of a field exceeds the space allotted for that field on a report, the field reads ####, alerting you that the value has been cut off. This function can be turned on or off in the Format Editor.

- **Object Size and Position Dialog Box**. This dialog box allows you to type in the exact position and dimension of a field or other object on your report.

- **Formula Editor**. The Formula Editor is enhanced by the additions of bookmarks, search and replace, undo/redo, function sorting for easier navigation, the ability to work on several formulas at once, and the ability to customize settings.

- **Seagate Query**. With Web-enabled report design capabilities, this new query tool lets you create ad hoc reports with basic formatting and graphing abilities.

- **Field Mapping**. This function opens a dialog box automatically when SCR detects a change in your data source, allowing you to map existing fields in a report to new fields in the database.

- **On Demand Subreports**. SCR now allows you to decide if you want a subreport to always appear in the Preview tab, or if you want the subreport data hidden until specifically called for. You can preview the subreport simply by double-clicking the subreport name using drill-down functionality.

- **Hyperlinks**. Using the Tool Tip Text conditional formula icon you can enter a link that shows up in the Preview tab when your pointer rests over a field.

- **Crystal Reports Web Server**. New features in version 7 include multithreaded job handling, support for the CGI Web application standard, and more efficient handling of large numbers of requests.

- **Report Exporting**. SCR now supports exporting directly to an application.

- **Document Import Tool**. Use this tool to convert ASCII text reports into SCR.

- **Server-Side Processing**. Processing can be pushed to the server by having grouping performed on the server. This cuts down on connection time to the server, transfer time to the client, and memory demands.

- **SQL Expressions**. SCR supports directly entered SQL statements. An editor similar to the Formula Editor allows you to create new expressions and insert them on your report like database fields.

- **ActiveX Report Designer Component**. A new ActiveX designer for Visual Basic allows you to design reports from within the Visual Basic IDE.

Conventions Used in This Book

The text assumes that you are knowledgeable in a Windows environment. You will find that most dialog boxes or commands can be reached through any of the following three ways: A main menu command, a toolbar button, or a shortcut menu command. The book focuses on menu commands and the toolbars, but if you like shortcut menus do take advantage of them.

Also note that you can rest the pointer over almost any object in the Crystal Report Designer and a bubble will appear with a text description of that object. This goes for the toolbar buttons as well. Just be patient—sometimes it takes a moment for the text to appear.

Each chapter will walk you through completing tasks, giving you hints and tips along the way. The instructions are as generic as possible, so that you can follow the steps as many times as you need, filling in your own data.

Many times exact search words for the online Help files are referenced in places where the online Help augments the discussion. The online Help is quite good in Seagate Crystal Reports, and scrolling through topics will help you become aware of all it can do.

Special Elements

Throughout the book, you will find several special elements that will make this book easier to use:

Tips are short hints that provide shortcuts or recommendations on the best way to use a feature.

Notes provide further information on how a feature works or on its uses or limitations.

As you might expect, cautions tell you what to watch out for when using a feature.

SIDEBARS

You'll see sidebars throughout the text that provide exercises and also discussions about how you can best use a particular feature.

Ready, Set, Go!

Good luck using one of the best report writer programs available! You'll find *Prima's Official Guide to Seagate Crystal Reports 7* useful for a brand new user of Seagate Crystal Reports and as a reference and great source of extra information for the more experienced report writer.

PART I

Introducing Seagate Crystal Reports

An Overview of Seagate Crystal Reports

- Getting Started

- Getting a
  Head Start with
  Report Experts

- Custom Reports

- Connecting a
  Report to a
  Data Source

- Crystal Report
  Designer:
  Basic Concepts

T his first chapter introduces you to some of the basics of Seagate Crystal Reports (SCR). You'll learn about how Seagate Crystal Reports works, and how to navigate it and find what you need. You'll also see a sample report that ships and automatically installs with the software. When you finish with Chapter 1, you should be comfortable with the design interface as well. In Chapter 2, you'll put the concepts and ideas presented in Chapter 1 into practice by designing two reports.

Getting Started

You first need to install Seagate Crystal Reports on your computer. The software includes installation instructions and requirements.

You may create an icon, or *shortcut*, on your desktop for the Crystal Report Designer, or you can access the application from the Seagate Crystal Reports program group on your Windows Start menu, as shown in Figure 1.1.

You will learn more about the other applications in the Seagate Crystal Reports program group in later chapters. For now, open the Crystal Report Designer from your Windows program group.

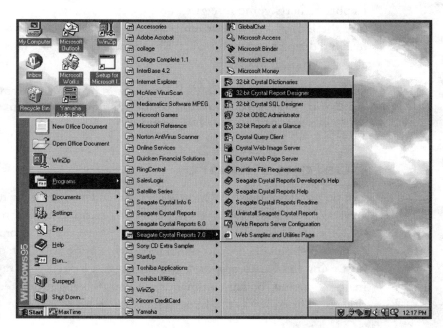

Figure 1.1
Notice that the software installation includes many other items

The Crystal Report Designer is the focus of most of this book.

When you start a new report using Seagate Crystal Reports, you have four choices:

- Report Expert
- Custom
- Another Report
- Document Import Tool

Initially, you'll learn about the Report Expert and Custom methods of starting a report. Then the basic components of a report and some common terminology are covered. In Chapter 2, you'll actually design two reports, one using an Expert and the other using the Custom option.

Getting a Head Start with Report Experts

Report Experts are templates you can use to walk through designing a report. Report Experts come in eight flavors, each containing a series of tabs that give the Expert a wizard or template-like feel. Each tab contains prompting text and dialog box functionality. Keep in mind that some tabs are only available in certain Experts.

Many new users find the Experts to be a great way to start a report. An Expert walks you through report design and prompts you for the most important elements of a report.

Custom Reports

You do not have to use a Report Expert when creating a new report. Seagate Crystal Reports also gives you the ability to design reports through the Custom option. Using the Custom option, you have the functionality of all the Experts combined, plus additional formatting options. When designing a report using the Custom option, you design and format your report using the main menu and toolbar commands, instead of being prompted for information for your report as the Experts do.

Once you have designed a report using an Expert, you can make further modifications using any of the toolbars or menus. Experts and the Custom option are almost interchangeable, with the exception of formatting. When you use an Expert, you must pick from one of ten style formats provided by SCR in order to preview the report, and then you can customize. When you design a report using the Custom option, you have complete freedom and control over all of the formatting from the start.

Connecting a Report to a Data Source

Throughout this book, the information included in reports is referred to as *data*. Typically, this data resides in a repository called a database, data source, or data warehouse. Seagate Crystal Reports provides three options for connecting to your data. Within each of the three basic connection types, many more options ensure that SCR can read your specific data. The three connection types include:

- **Data File**. For databases such as Access, Paradox, FoxPro, and more.

- **SQL\ODBC**. For structured query language (SQL) databases, such as Oracle and SQL Server; and for any database accessed through an ODBC connection.

- **Dictionary\Query**. For any database for which a data dictionary has been defined, or for which a query has been designed to extract a subset of the data.

 Open Database Connectivity (ODBC) is a language software programs use to communicate with many types of databases. Seagate Crystal Reports includes the ODBC Administrator, which you can use to help choose and load certain database drivers that might be necessary to connect to your data source. See Appendix A, "Setting Up an ODBC Data Source," for more information.

The type of data source you use determines the type of connection to use. The flexible nature of Seagate Crystal Reports provides compatibility with almost any data source. Chapter 2 introduces the different types of data sources. More information follows in Chapter 3 to help you decide which connection works best with your data source.

Figure 1.2

The Select Expert, like many other dialog boxes, makes designing your report easier.

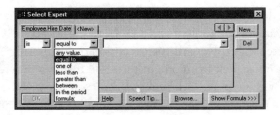

Selecting Records to Include on a Report

Most data sources contain much more information than you need on one report. As you design your report, you can select the particular information you want on your report. This process is called *record selection*. You have the ability to select exactly which records you want on your report, using one or many criteria. For example, you may need to run a Human Resources report that documents all employees hired after a certain date. Therefore, you would set the selection criteria so any employee in your database hired after the date you specify shows up on the report.

The Select Expert is provided to help you set the selection criteria, and it also gives you the ability to customize selection criteria using a formula (see Figure 1.2). Experts such as the Select Expert consist of dialog boxes that contain drop-down lists and other options that assist you in designing reports.

Many dialog boxes and Experts in Seagate Crystal Reports help you design reports with ease. These functional Experts differ from Report Experts. Report Experts are *wizards* that walk you through creating a new report. SCR sometimes refers to functional dialog boxes that help you set up certain features in a report as Experts—like the Select Expert.

Design Tab Sections

One of the main work areas within the Crystal Report Designer application is the Design tab. The Design tab consists of multiple sections that help you place information on your report where you want it to print.

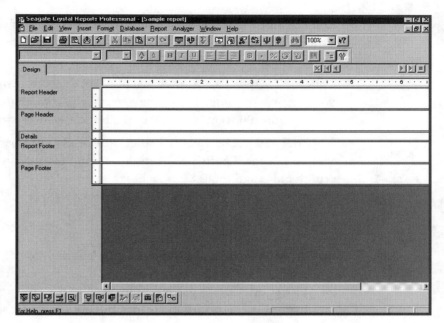

Figure 1.3
The Design tab has five sections by default.

Basic Report Sections

A basic report consists of five sections, as shown in Figure 1.3. These sections cannot be deleted nor the order changed, though their size can be manipulated. However, the sections can be hidden or suppressed and formatted to meet your needs. More sections can be added to the basic five, as needed.

- **Report Header.** The Report Header prints once per report, at the top of the first page. In this section you can place a report title, date, or any other information you want to print first on your report. You can even put a graph in the Report Header section, and size it to use the whole first page of your report, if you like.

- **Page Header.** The Page Header section prints once at the top of every page of your report. You can place page numbers in this section, or any other information that you want to print at the top of every page. For some reports, you may want the title to print in the page header, or maybe a company logo or company confidential message.

- **Details.** In the Details area, you insert most of the database fields to print on the report. This section repeats once for every record the report pulls from the database.

- **Page Footer.** The Page Footer area prints at the bottom of every page of your report. You might insert page numbers, comments, or any other information you want to repeat at the bottom of every page.

- **Report Footer.** The Report Footer area prints once per report at the very end of the report. This section is a good place for notes about the report and grand totals.

Other Sections

You can add more sections to your reports. In addition to the five basic sections, you will often insert *group* sections. SCR helps you sort and organize data on a report by creating groups. When you add a group to your report, SCR automatically inserts Group Header and Group Footer sections. These sections print *nested* around the Details section, as shown in Figure 1.4. Unless

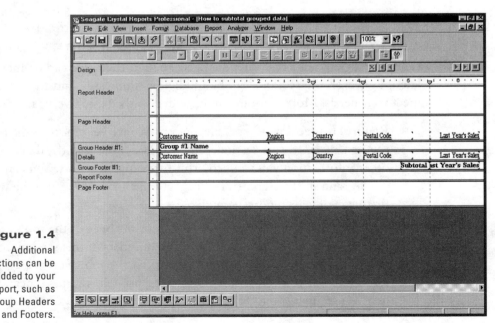

Figure 1.4

Additional sections can be added to your report, such as Group Headers and Footers.

you turn the option off, SCR automatically inserts the Group Name field into the Group Header section. And, when you insert subtotals and other summaries on your report, SCR places these fields in the Group Footer area, right under the Details field being totaled or summarized.

 Each section can be split into multiple sections, such as a Page Header b or Details b section. These sections serve many different purposes and will be covered in Chapter 7, "Formatting Your Report."

Crystal Report Designer: Basic Concepts

It's time to get your hands dirty. Now, you will open a sample report, look at the Design tab that you read about earlier, and maneuver around a bit to begin getting a feel for how SCR works. To open a sample or existing report:

1. Open the Crystal Report Designer, if it is not open already.

 2. On the Welcome dialog box, click the Open Report button. If you do not see the Welcome dialog box, click either the Open button on the toolbar or choose File, Open.

 When you first open SCR, several dialog boxes may open. If you have not yet registered your software, a registration dialog box appears. For now, click Register Later to move on. If the Welcome dialog box did not appear, it has been turned off. You can turn it back on so that it shows up every time you open the Report Designer by choosing Help, Welcome Dialog and then selecting the Show Welcome Dialog at Startup check box.

3. In the Open dialog box, with the Crystal Reports directory open, select the report named "sgt07," and click Open. This opens a very simple sample report (see Figure 1.5).

 This sample report is used in the upcoming section as a reference. You do not need to have this report open or your computer turned on if you prefer to follow the figures.

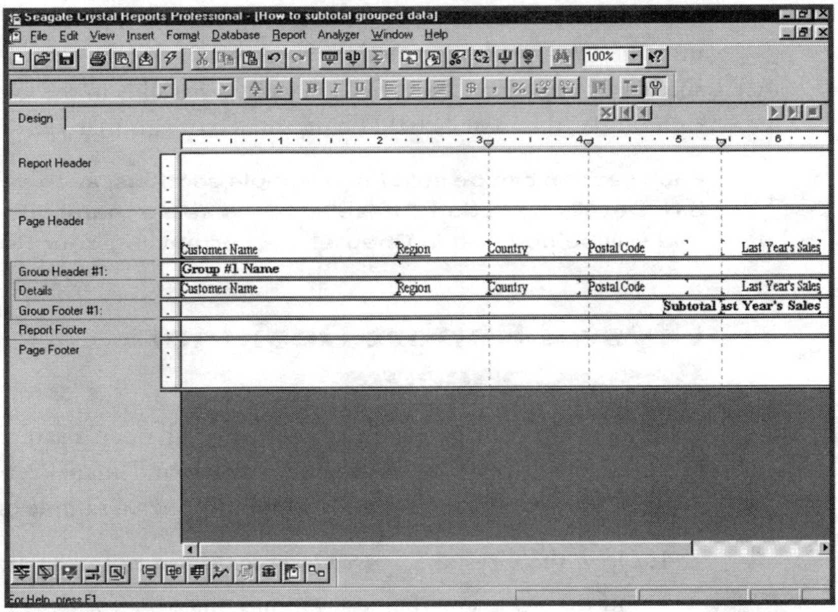

Figure 1.5
Sample report
sgt07.rpt shows
the different
sections of the
Design tab.

Toolbars and More

By default, SCR displays a menu bar and two toolbars across the top of the Crystal Report Designer, and one toolbar across the bottom. Clicking any of the menus opens lists containing the actions and functions you use when designing and running reports. The toolbars contain buttons duplicating many of the common menu commands. The toolbar buttons offer a quicker way to open a dialog box or apply an option.

SCR places toolbars in the locations shown in Figure 1.5 by default. By dragging the toolbars, you can move them wherever you prefer in the application window. Use the View, Toolbars command to turn toolbars on and off.

Throughout this book, menu commands and the related toolbar buttons are pointed out. You can choose which method to use. You will notice that for almost every tool, SCR provides two or three different ways to invoke the function or open the dialog box. You can use the main menu or the toolbar, and many times you can use shortcut menus that open when you right-click in the proper area. For example, if you want to insert a subtotal on your report, you can click a toolbar button, choose the Insert, Summary menu command, or right-click with the pointer over the field you want to summarize. SCR gives you complete functionality using whichever method you like best.

The Design and Preview Tabs

As previously discussed, you conduct the majority of your report design on the Design tab. The Design tab shows the various sections of a report, such as Page Header and Details. The five default sections cannot be deleted, but you can add many more sections as you find necessary.

By looking at Figure 1.6, you can see that database fields have been added to the Details section. Column headings appear in the Page Header section, as well as a Group Name in the Group Header section and a subtotal in the Group Footer section.

Though the Design tab is the best place for working on the nuts and bolts of your report, it doesn't exactly present a true picture of what the report will

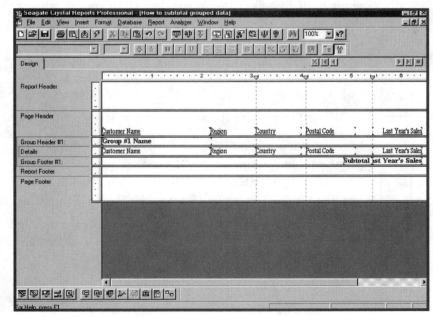

Figure 1.6

Note the sections in the sample report and the fields located in each different section.

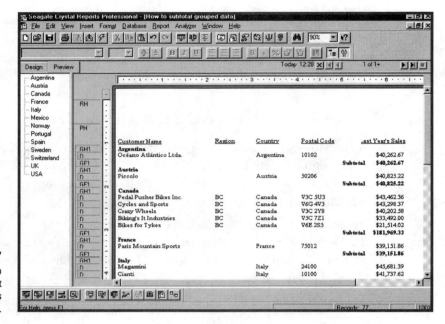

Figure 1.7

The Preview tab shows you what your report looks like with data.

look like. For this, there is the Preview tab. The act of previewing your report sends SCR to collect the report data from your database. The Preview tab shows exactly what your report would look like if you were to print it, as shown in Figure 1.7.

Now try previewing the sample report open in the Crystal Report Designer.

1. On the toolbar, click Print Preview, or choose File, Print Preview.

2. The Preview tab appears next to (on top of) the Design tab.

In the Preview tab, notice a Group Tree area at the left. This area lists all of the groups on your report and can be used for navigation through the report. The Group Tree will be blank if you have no groups in your report. You can turn the Group Tree on or off using the Group Tree toolbar button.

To go back to the Design tab, just click on the tab (see Figure 1.8). You can freely move back and forth between Design and Preview as you work on your report.

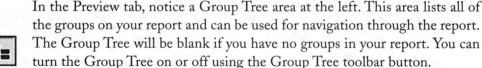

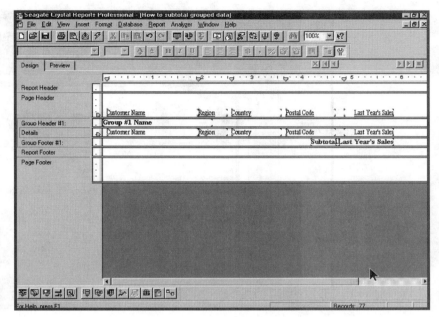

Figure 1.8

Toggle back and forth between Design and Preview by clicking the tabs.

Navigation in the Crystal Report Designer

You have already learned about the toolbars and how to preview a report. Once in the Preview tab, page controls become available in the upper right hand corner, just below the toolbars (see Figure 1.9). The page controls allow you to navigate forward or backward through your report. You can click the red X button to close the tab you are currently viewing. However, you do not need to close the tabs, you can just move among them.

The page number of the report displays between the forward and backward page controls in the X of Y format, letting you know what page you are viewing in relation to the entire report. SCR uses page-on-demand technology to count your report pages, similar to how Web pages function. SCR only previews the page you have asked for until you ask for more. This way you don't spend time waiting for a page to format and be ready for viewing if you might never look at it.

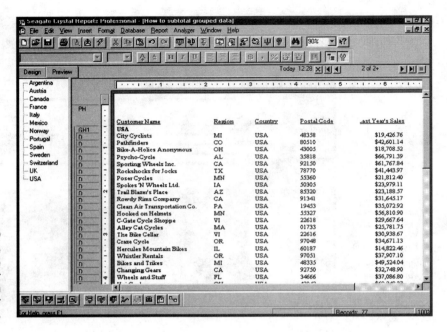

Figure 1.9

Page controls are available in the Preview tab for navigation through your report.

When you first preview a report the page numbers show up as 1 of 1+. This indicates that you are viewing page one of a report that contains more than one page.

The date and time at which you previewed your report displays to the left of the page controls (refer to Figure 1.9). This represents the date and time of your last refresh (when you last ran the report against the database to collect any and all records which meet the report's selection criteria). On the toolbar, you can click Refresh to force a refresh at any time. A refresh is similar to previewing your report for the first time in that it collects all the data from your database that meet the criteria for your report.

Chapter 2, "Previewing Your Report," covers more information regarding the differences between previewing and refreshing your report.

Making Reports Available on the Web

Publishing a Crystal report on the Web is not a new feature in version 7, but the technology enhancements make the reports more functional and give users and designers more options.

PAGE-ON-DEMAND TECHNOLOGY

Think of page-on-demand like Web pages on the Internet. If you go to the Seagate Software Web site to check for a training class in your city, you ask for only the information regarding training classes, and that specific information transfers to your computer for viewing. You do not download the entire Seagate Software Web site and then look at only what you need. SCR uses this same technology when previewing reports. You only see what you ask for, not wasting time waiting for every page of a long report to generate when you only want to check that the title is centered correctly on page one.

Crystal reports can be exported into many formats, including HTML. This exporting functionality means that you can design a report using the Crystal Report Designer, save it as an HTML file, and then place it on a Web server. Users can then navigate to that Web site and view the report.

Seagate Crystal Reports has Web viewers, which can be easily downloaded from a Web server. The Web viewer provides some preview functionality, like refreshing, drill down, sorting, and printing. Chapter 14, "Integrating Crystal Reports with the Internet," covers this topic in detail.

Summary

The Crystal Report Designer is a powerful tool for designing reports, with four methods for starting a new report: using a Report Expert, the Custom option, Another Report as a template, and the Document Import Tool. Chapter 2 discusses all four of these methods.

Once you start a new report, the Design tab provides structure to ease formatting and field placement. Powered with four toolbars and the ability to right-click for shortcut menu options, design functionality is always at your fingertips. And, the ease of navigating between the Design and Preview tabs provides instant access to see what your report really looks like at any step of the design process.

CHAPTER **2**

Creating Your First Seagate Crystal Report

- Creating a Report Using the Standard Report Expert

- The Other Experts: Creating Specific Report Types

- Other Ways to Start a Report

- Designing a Custom Report

- Linking Databases and Tables

Seagate Crystal Reports offers four methods to start a new report:

- Report Experts
- Another Report option
- Document Import Tool
- Custom option

All four methods will be explained in this chapter. First, you will use the Standard Report Expert, followed by sections briefly explaining each of the other Experts and the different tabs you'll encounter. Then, you'll learn about the Another Report option and Document Import Tool. Finally, you will go through the steps to design a report using the Custom option.

Creating a Report Using the Standard Report Expert

As discussed in Chapter 1, Seagate Crystal Reports has eight Report Experts to assist you in designing reports. In this chapter, you'll design two reports step by step, one using the Standard Report Expert, and another using the Custom option. You can design your reports either way. If you start a report using an Expert, you can most certainly add to it or change it using the custom options.

Opening the Crystal Report Designer and Starting a Report

First, you need to open the Crystal Report Designer and start a new report in order to use an Expert.

1. Click Start, Programs, Seagate Crystal Reports, Crystal Report Designer. The Crystal Report Designer application window opens.

2. Click New Report on the opening Welcome dialog box. If you cancel the Welcome dialog box, click File, New or the New toolbar button. The Report Gallery dialog box opens (see Figure 2.1).

3. Click Standard. The Standard Report Expert opens.

Figure 2.1
Start the Standard
Report Expert
from the
Report Gallery
dialog box.

Report Experts, similar to wizards, walk you through designing reports. Once you start an Expert, you navigate from tab to tab responding to the prompts. The information you provide creates the basis of your report. Which Report Expert you use dictates which tabs appear.

Choosing the Source of Report Data

Each tab in the Standard Report Expert prompts you to take a particular action. First, the Data tab asks what type of data source you will be using. To choose a database for your report:

 You can use many types of data sources for your reports, listed as buttons on the Experts. For now, use the Data File connection. Later chapters explore the other options.

1. From the Standard Report Expert dialog box, click Data File. The Choose Database File dialog box opens over the Data tab (see Figure 2.2).

2. Click the name of the database file that you want to use for your report, in this case the studio.dbf file, and then click Add.

Figure 2.2
Choose the
database files you
need for your
report by
selecting them
and clicking Add.

3. Repeat step 2 to add another database file, movie.dbf.

This tutorial uses two database files that ship with Seagate Crystal Reports. Seagate Software provides these files as samples to be used for report design practice.

4. Click Done to close the Choose Database File dialog box.

The two database files selected for this tutorial each contain one table. If, when designing your own reports, you work off a database file that contains multiple tables, the Select Tables dialog box opens at this point. Chapter 3 covers using the type of database which contains many tables in one database file.

If you selected more than one database file, SCR lists them on the Data tab. When you click Done on the Choose Database File dialog box, the Links tab automatically opens if you have more than one database file selected (see Figure 2.3).

If you have only one database file or table chosen, the Links tab does not appear. To go to the next tab of the Expert, simply click the tab that you want to go to. You can also click Next at the bottom of the Report Expert dialog box.

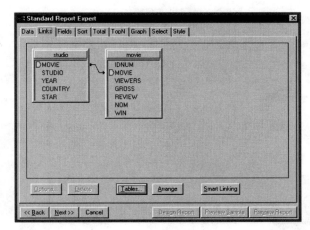

Figure 2.3

The Links tab only appears if you have chosen more than one database file for your report.

The Links Tab

If you choose two or more database files for your report, you need to link the tables and databases together in order to use information from both on your report. SCR automatically displays the Links tab, and completes the linking using Smart Linking. You'll learn about linking in detail in Chapter 3, so for now just continue on to the next tab, the Fields tab.

Selecting Fields to Print on the Report

You specify which fields to print on your report using the Fields tab. You can choose from any of the fields in the database files that you selected on the Data tab. The Database Fields list shows a tree, with all the field names listed below the database file names. By default, the tree has the first table expanded, listing the fields within that table. You can expand the second table by clicking the plus sign next to its name in the tree, as shown in Figure 2.4.

The plus and minus signs make navigating through your available database fields easier. To add fields to your report:

1. Either double-click the field you want to add to your report, or select the field and click <u>A</u>dd. The field shows up in the Report Fields list. Add fields to your report in the order in which you want them to print across your page from left to right. For this example, add the following

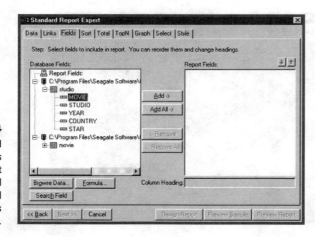

Figure 2.4

Use the plus and minus signs throughout Seagate Crystal Reports to expand and collapse lists of information.

fields to the Report Fields list: From movie.mdb, select the MOVIE, IDNUM, and GROSS fields.

 Throughout Seagate Crystal Reports you can use the arrow buttons next to or above a list box to change the order of that list's contents.

 In the lower right hand corner, the Column Heading field displays the name of the field selected in the Report Fields list. You can change this name by typing a new name in the field. This name appears as the column heading on each page of your report for that field.

2. Once you have all the fields you want on your report listed in the Report Fields list, click Next to go to the Sort tab.

Determining Sort Order

SCR helps you organize your report by sorting records into groups. You can use any field available to your report for grouping. To add a group to your report:

1. On the Sort tab, click the field on which you want to base your group from the Available Fields list (see Figure 2.5). For this example, select the YEAR field from the studio.dbf file.

2. Click Add. The field moves to the Sort Fields list.

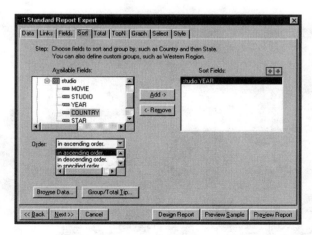

Figure 2.5

Click the field you want to base your group on from the Available Fields list and add it to the Sort Fields list.

3. With a field chosen in the Sort Fields list, select the order of your group from the Order list (under the Available Fields list).

4. Click Next to go to the Total tab.

Adding Summaries, Subtotals, and Grand Totals

In the Total tab, you can specify if you want to add any summaries or subtotals to the report and if you want a grand total at the end of the report. SCR calculates summaries and subtotals—all you need to do is specify which field you want the function to act upon and which summary function you want to use.

SCR distinguishes between subtotals and summaries. Subtotals are sum calculations; summaries are counts, averages, percentiles, and so forth. To add a subtotal or summary to your report:

1. Click the field you want to total in the Available Fields list. For this example, select the GROSS field. Click Add to move the field to the Total Fields list (see Figure 2.6).

 Chapter 7 includes detailed information regarding totaling.

2. Select which summary or subtotal function you want to perform from the drop-down list below the Total Fields list. For this example, set the function to sum.

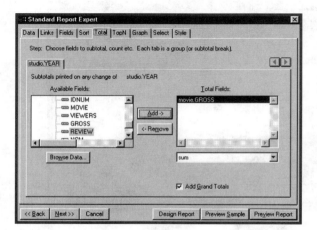

Figure 2.6
The Gross field will be totaled per Year.

Notice that you do not usually have to move a field from Available Fields to Totals Fields. Rather, SCR does this for you by evaluating the fields you chose for your report and selecting any that appear as candidates for totaling. How smart!

3. Be sure to check any fields that SCR selects for totaling. Sometimes the program may add a field that you do not want to total. To remove fields you do not want to total, select the field and click Remove.

4. Lastly, select the Add Grand Totals check box to add a grand total to the end of your report for the field selected in the Total Fields list.

For now, skip the TopN tab and the Graph tab. Chapter 5 covers TopN in detail, and Chapter 9 covers graphing. The TopN and Graph tabs that you see in the Standard Report Expert are the same as the dialog boxes you see when working with the functionality through the menu commands or toolbar buttons.

Selecting Records to Include

You specify which records from your database to print on a report using the Select tab. This tab allows you to select which records you want to see, and which to exclude. For example, you may want to run a report for only one month, not for every month. Or, you may need to run a report for only one department, not every department. SCR does not limit the number of selection criteria you can set. To define selection criteria:

1. Click on the Select tab in the Standard Report Expert dialog box to bring it to the front.

2. From the Available Fields list, select the field on which you want to base your selection criteria. For this example, select the COUNTRY field from the studio.dbf file.

3. Click Add to move the field to the Select Fields list. Below the Available Fields list, two drop-down lists appear, giving you options for setting selection criteria, as shown in Figure 2.7.

4. In the second (right-most) drop-down list, select a choice other than Any Value. A third drop-down list appears. The third drop-down list contains actual values from your database, pulled from the field on which you are basing the selection criteria.

Figure 2.7

Use the drop-down lists to further define your selection criteria.

5. From that third drop-down list, select the value that completes the selection criteria (see Figure 2.8). For this example, select studio.COUNTRY is equal to U.S.A.

> Figures 2.7 and 2.8 demonstrate how to select only records that are equal to U.S.A. for the example report. Any movies that were produced in other countries will not be on the report. Chapter 4 goes into detail about the many options available to you when setting record selection criteria.

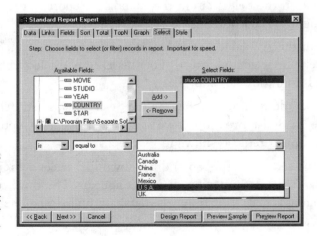

Figure 2.8

You can use the third drop-down list to select values from your database.

When you use the third drop-down list on the Select tab, every value in your database may not show up. Therefore, you can also type the value that you want to use.

Once you have set the record selection criteria, move to the last tab, Style.

Applying a Report Style

The Style tab gives you formatting options for your report, as well as the option to add a title and picture. To apply a style to your report:

1. First, pick a style from the Style list (see Figure 2.9). A sample of the formatting displays next to the Style list.

2. Add a title to your report by entering one in the Title box.

3. Add a picture or graphic file to your report by clicking the picture button. The Open dialog box appears. Locate and select the graphic file you want to add to the report and click Open. The graphic is added to your report.

 More detail about this feature can be found in Chapter 7.

Now that you have gone through all of the basic tabs of the Standard Report Expert, you are ready to preview the report you designed. Keep in mind that you can go back to any of the tabs later to make changes.

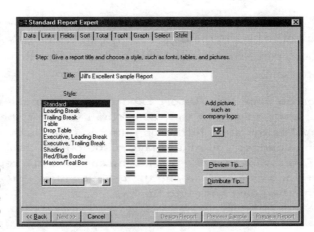

Figure 2.9
Use the Style tab to select a style and add a title to your report.

Previewing Your Report

Next, you should run your report with real data. The three options for previewing from an Expert include:

- Design Report
- Preview Sample
- Preview Report

The Design Report button opens the Design tab with your report displayed on it. This option does not collect data from your databases, but instead shows you what the Expert created with your instructions. Experienced users of Seagate Crystal Reports may like to come here before previewing to make any fine-tuning adjustments that they cannot do through the Expert.

The Preview Sample button previews your report with a sample of data from your database. The Preview Sample dialog box appears and gives you the option to preview All Records, or First *n* records. You can fill in a number for *n*. This option allows you to preview your report to see what it looks like, without having to collect *all* records that meet your report's selection criteria. This is useful if you have a very large report to run and just want to quickly preview your report to see what it looks like, without collecting 100 pages of data!

Lastly, the Preview Report option collects all records from your database meeting your report's selection criteria, and shows you the report on the Preview tab.

 By previewing your report, you see what your report looks like and how it will print. You can go back to the Expert at any time to modify your report. You can use the Report Expert button on the toolbar, or click Report Expert from the Report menu.

 caution   **When you go back to a Report Expert, you can make any changes that you want on any of the tabs. When you exit the Expert, the Expert applies the style formatting that you chose, overwriting any formatting changes you might have made on the Design tab of the report. If you want to make formatting changes to a report that you designed using an Expert, make the changes after you are sure that you will not be going back into the Expert.**

The Other Experts: Creating Specific Report Types

Report Experts come in many flavors, each of which helps you design a certain type of report. Any type of report can be created using the Custom option. The Experts help you design by giving you templates to build from.

Form Letter Report Expert: Repeating a Report with Different Data

The Form Letter Report Expert walks you through creating a form letter as a Crystal report. The Form Letter Report Expert includes the Data, Fields, Sort, Total, Select, and Form Letter tabs. The Form Letter tab allows you to create the body of your form letter (see Figure 2.10). Select the report section to which you want to add information from the Sections list. Use the fields you selected using the Fields tab and the large white area to type the body of your letter. You can incorporate database fields by selecting them and then clicking Add. This way you customize each letter with the appropriate information about each record.

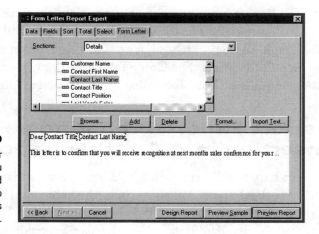

Figure 2.10

The Form Letter tab gives you space to add information to several sections of a report.

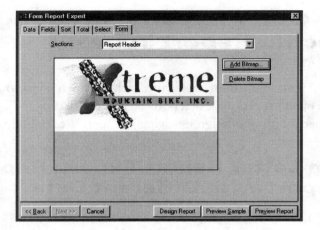

Figure 2.11
The Form tab can
be used to add
graphics to
different sections
of your form-style
report.

Form Report Expert: Making a Report Look Like a Pre-Printed Form

The Form Report Expert formats a basic form using the information you provide on the Data, Fields, Sort, Total, and Select tabs. The Form tab gives you the option to add graphic files to sections of the report (see Figure 2.11).

Cross-Tab Report Expert: Analyzing Data in a Spreadsheet

The Cross-Tab Report Expert provides the template to create a basic cross-tab report (see Figure 2.12). The Cross-Tab Report Expert contains the Data, Cross-Tab, Graph, and Select tabs. Refer to Chapter 8 for an explanation of designing Cross-Tab reports. The Cross-Tab tab in the Expert is exactly the same as the stand-alone Cross-Tab dialog box explained in Chapter 8.

Subreport Expert: Preparing a Report for Insertion into Another Report

The Subreport Expert walks you through designing both a main report and a subreport, both using Experts. When you open the Subreport Expert, you first use the Contain Subreport Expert to design the main report. This Expert has all of the tabs of the Standard Report Expert, plus a Subreport tab. When you come to the Subreport tab (see Figure 2.13), you open the Subreport Expert.

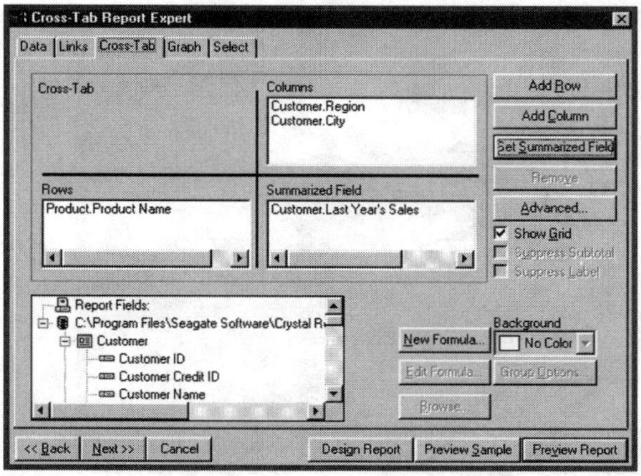

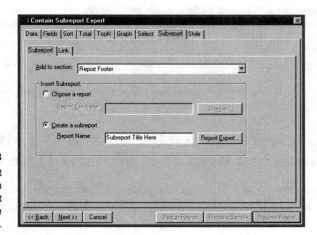

Figure 2.12
The Cross Tab
Report Expert
helps you create
Cross Tab reports.

The only real difference between the Contain Subreport Expert and Subreport Expert is that the Subreport Expert asks which section of the main report you would like to insert your subreport into. Once you complete the Subreport Expert, click OK to return to the Contain Subreport Expert, the main report. When you preview the main report, you'll also see the subreport you created.

 Chapter 8 covers subreports in detail. Depending on the complexity of the reports you wish to create, Chapter 8 will be very helpful, as subreports have many uses.

Figure 2.13
Use the Subreport
tab in the Contain
Subreport Expert
to create
your subreport.

Figure 2.14
Use the Label tab
to choose your
label style.

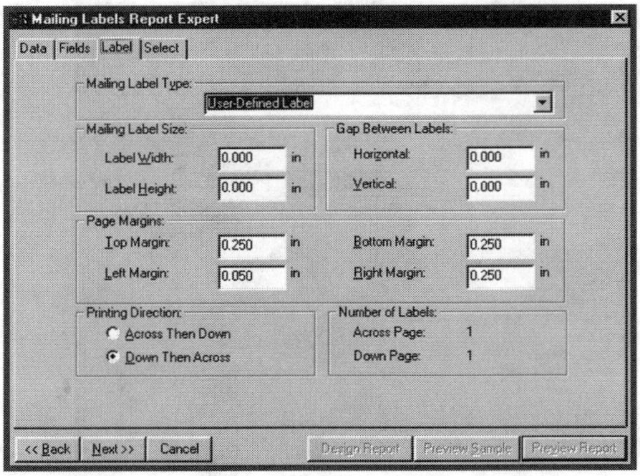

Mailing Labels Report Expert: Printing Data on Standard or Custom Labels

The Mailing Labels Report Expert makes creating mailing labels from your database easy. This Expert has just four tabs: Data, Fields, Label, and Select. You select the fields you want on your labels using the Fields tab. Using the Label tab (see Figure 2.14), you select what type of labels you are using. The Mailing Label Type list contains Avery label numbers. Or, you can set the label dimensions yourself.

If you want to print multiple database fields on one line, such as City, State, and Postal Code, you can use a formula to pull the fields together into one field. Such a formula might look like:

{tablename.City} + ", " + {tablename.Region} + "   "+ {tablename.Postal Code}

See Chapter 6 for information on how to write formulas.

Drill Down Report Expert: Combining Summaries and Details on One Report

Because some reports have a lot of detail or many groups, SCR provides the ability to hide sections, thus showing only the summary information on the

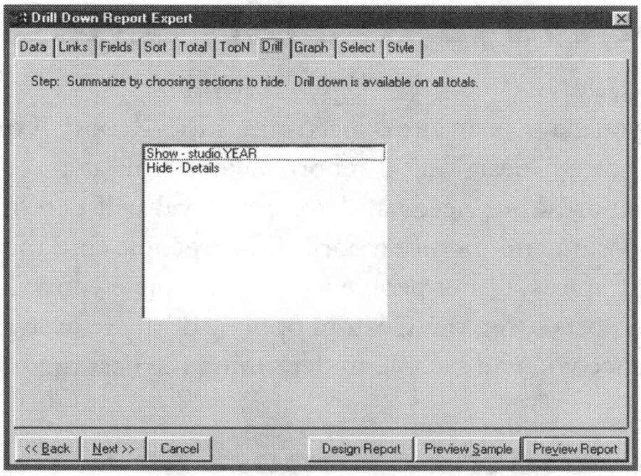

Figure 2.15
Use the Drill tab
to choose the
sections you want
users to have to
drill down to see.

main report. Drill down reports present summary information first, allowing users to double-click to drill down to lower levels of detail.

The Drill Down Report Expert adds the Drill tab to the tabs of the Standard Report Expert. Using the Drill tab, you can hide a group or detail section of the report (see Figure 2.15). By clicking a section, you toggle the section between Show and Hide. If a section has Hide in front of the name, then you will not see it when you preview the main report. In the Preview tab, however, you drill down by double-clicking a summary or group name field to view the data behind that field. Chapter 8 offers more detail on the functionality of drill down reports and how to create them.

OLAP Report Expert: Making Data Three-Dimensional

To design a report using an OLAP cube as a data source, choose the OLAP Report Expert. OLAP, on line analytical processing, is a technology used to create three-dimensional data structures called cubes. SCR has an Expert to help you design reports from these cube structures, and it is covered in detail in Chapter 12. Please refer to that chapter for full instructions and more information about OLAP.

Other Ways to Start a Report

Now that you have been introduced to all the Report Experts available to walk you through designing a report, take a look at the other options for starting a report. Your needs and comfort level will determine which tools you use to design and modify reports. Some people find that they like to use the Report Experts. Other people like the complete control and flexibility of designing reports using the Custom option. Both are user-friendly and with a little practice you will be able to determine the best method for you.

Using Another Report as a Template

Using another report as a template might just be one of the most useful features in Seagate Crystal Reports. You work hard on a report. It's great. Formatted to look just the way you want. It uses your company colors in the pie chart. And, the special fields (like page numbers and dates) are in just the right place. What a great report! Not to mention it can get the correct database files and database drivers set up over your network. Now your supervisor asks you to make five more reports using the same colors and formatting so that they can be presented side by side. You want to ask, "Do you know how long this took me to get it perfect?" Well, here is your solution. You can use the first report you designed as a template for other reports. You can use the same data files or new ones, change the title or not, add a field here, delete one there, or maintain the graph and the formatting that you need to be consistent.

To use another report as a template is as simple as clicking Another Report in the Report Gallery dialog box (see Figure 2.16) and specifying which report

Figure 2.16

Use Another Report to save time designing similar reports.

you want to use from the Open dialog box. SCR opens a copy of the template report on the Design tab, where you can make modifications and save the report with a new name.

Importing a Report with the Document Import Tool

The Document Import Tool is new to version 7 of Seagate Crystal Reports. This tool allows you to take a report designed in another report writer whose format is exported to ASCII, and convert it into a Seagate Crystal Report (see Figure 2.17).

A great example of this would be legacy reports from large mainframe databases. Open the Document Import Tool by clicking its button on the Report Gallery dialog box. This actually opens a secondary application, called Document Import Tool, complete with its own online Help system, menu bar, toolbar, and more. Using this tool, you select fields from the old report and place them in sections of a new Crystal report.

The Document Import Tool assists those that need to convert many reports in a short time. You do not need to use this tool when designing a report in SCR from scratch. For more information and instructions open the online Help from within the Document Import Tool.

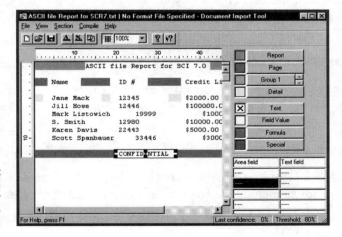

Figure 2.17
The Document Import Tool helps you convert other reports into Crystal reports.

Designing a Custom Report

Designing a custom report gives you, the designer, freedom to use all of the functionality you saw in the Experts together in one report. By designing a report using the Custom option, you have control over everything from the start. The Experts walk you through tabs that assist you in creating a report and, once on the Design tab, you can customize the report any way that you like. When you start a report using the Custom option, you bypass starting with an Expert and design your report from a blank Design tab. You must use commands found on the menu bar and toolbars to create your entire report.

Some people like the Custom option because they have complete flexibility and control from the start over what goes where. Others find it more difficult to start from a blank Design tab because SCR does not prompt for the basic elements of a report, and the designer has to remember to add them. In the next section, you will become familiar with how to design a report using the Custom option, and then you can decide which way you like best.

 Keep in mind that if you design a report using one of the Experts, you can change or add anything to the report on the Design tab using the toolbars. You have the best of both methods—starting the report using an Expert and then customizing it using the toolbars.

In the next section, you'll design the same report that you created using the Standard Report Expert but this time you'll create it step-by-step by using the Custom option. This way you can see how the two methods differ in process, yet result in the same data on the final report.

Connecting to Data

After you tell SCR that you want to start a new Custom report, you then select the database containing the information on which you want to report. To begin designing a Custom report:

1. Click New on the toolbar or choose File, New. The Report Gallery opens.

2. Click Custom from the Report Gallery dialog box. The dialog box expands to include the Report Type and Data Type buttons.

3. Click Data File. The Choose Database File dialog box opens (see Figure 2.18).

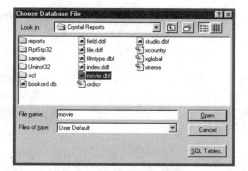

Figure 2.18
Select the database file you want to use from the Choose Database File dialog box.

4. Click the database file that you want to use in your report, in this case movie.dbf, and then click Open. Now the Design tab of the Crystal Report Designer opens along with the Insert Fields dialog box. The database file you selected appears along with the fields within that file (see Figure 2.19).

With the Design tab open, you can now start designing a report. Before you start inserting fields, however, you may want to add another database file to the

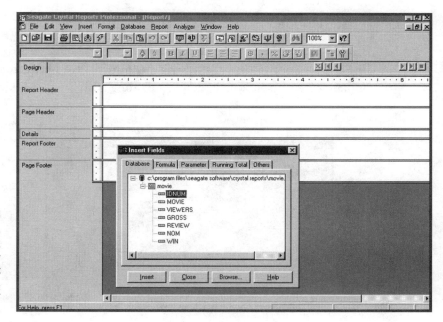

Figure 2.19
Fields in the database file, movie.dbf, appear listed in the Insert Fields dialog box, which floats over the Design tab.

report. When you design a report using the Custom option, SCR only allows you to choose one database in the Choose Database File dialog box. Therefore, you must add any additional database files after the Design tab opens.

When designing reports, you can add and remove database files at any time. In the next section, you'll add a second database file to this report. Chapter 3 has more detailed information regarding adding database files and tables to reports.

Linking Databases and Tables

To have more than one database file or table available for your report, you add the extra file and then link it to the other file. To add a second database file and link to the first:

1. Close the Insert Fields dialog box by clicking <u>C</u>lose.

2. Click <u>D</u>atabase, <u>A</u>dd Database to Report. The Choose Database File dialog box opens.

3. Click the file you want to add, and then click <u>O</u>pen. The Visual Linking Expert opens (see Figure 2.20). Crystal has linked the tables automatically using Smart Linking.

4. Click OK.

Linking takes place in the Visual Linking Expert. SCR performs Smart Linking to link your tables together via a common field between the two tables. Chapter 3 covers linking in detail, including both Smart Linking and manual

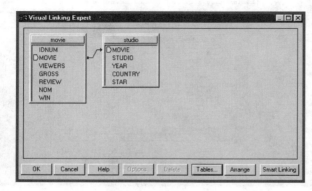

Figure 2.20
SCR's Smart Linking has linked the database files together.

linking. With the two database files or tables now linked, you can begin designing your actual report.

Some database files contain only one table, as in the sample databases used in this chapter. Other database files may contain more than one table. If you select a database file that contains more than one table from the Choose Database File dialog box, SCR first has you choose the specific tables that you want to use for your report, before opening the Crystal Report Designer. Chapter 3 uses a sample database file that contains many tables, which will help you if you are using a database file with several tables.

Inserting Fields into Your Report

The next step in creating a report from scratch involves placing database fields onto the report. To insert fields on your report, open the Insert Fields dialog box. You can use either the Insert Fields toolbar button, or click Insert, Database Field.

Click the plus sign next to the database file name (see Figure 2.21), and then click the plus sign next to the table name. This expands the list, showing the fields in the table available for your report. To add a field to your report:

In this Custom report example, use the same fields as in the report you designed using the Standard Report Expert. Start by inserting the MOVIE field from the movie.dbf file.

1. Select the field you want to insert onto your report. Next, click Insert on the Insert Fields dialog box and the field *attaches* to the pointer.

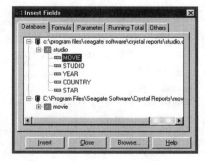

Figure 2.21
Click the plus sign to expand a file.

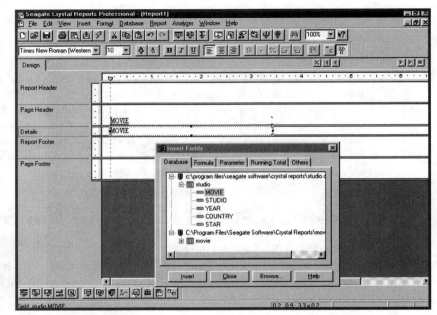

Figure 2.22
Drop a field onto
the Details
section of the
Design tab.

2. Drag the field from the Insert Fields dialog box and drop it by clicking in the Details section of your report (see Figure 2.22). Once you insert a field into the Details area, a column heading is automatically inserted into the Page Header section as a column heading for the data.

3. Insert the IDNUM and GROSS fields into the Details section from the movie.dbf file.

When inserting fields, you can also double-click the field to attach it to the pointer. You can then click anywhere on the report to place the field. You can also use the standard Windows dragging operation to select a field and place it on the report.

Notice that sometimes the field is quite large on your report. With the field selected, you can resize the field by dragging any of the four resizing handles (see Figure 2.23). To resize a field:

1. Move the pointer over one of the resizing handles. The pointer changes to a double-headed arrow.

2. Drag the resizing handle to adjust the size of the field.

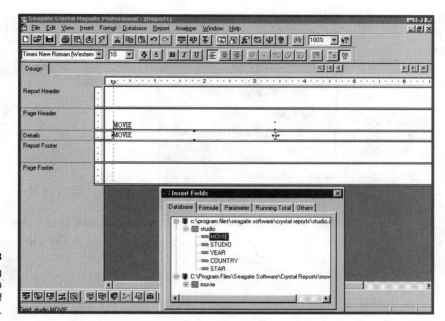

Figure 2.23
Use the resizing handles to change the size of any field.

You can resize both the field and the column heading at the same time. Select one field, hold down either the Shift or Ctrl key, and then click another field. You can select as many fields as you want at once in this way. Now, whatever action you take, such as resizing, applies to all the selected fields.

Grouping Data on Your Report

Next, you may want to group the data on your report to make it easier to read and more meaningful. If you do not group or sort your data, it appears on your report in the same order it was entered into your database. To create a group:

1. Click the Insert Group toolbar button, or click Insert, Group. The Insert Group dialog box opens (see Figure 2.24).

2. The first drop-down list allows you to select which field you want to base your group on. For this example, select the Year field for grouping from the list.

Figure 2.24

Use the Insert Group dialog box to set group criteria.

3. The second drop-down list allows you to select the order that you would like your groups to be in. For this example, select the descending order choice from the list.

4. Click OK to close the dialog box.

Notice that SCR added Group Header and Group Footer sections on either side of the Details section, as well as a group name field (see Figure 2.25).

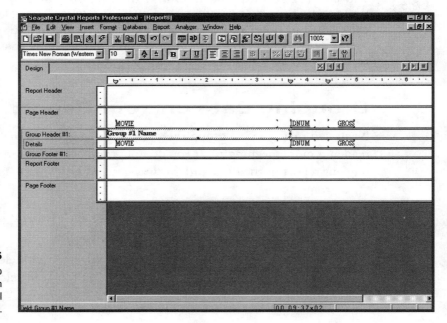

Figure 2.25

Adding a group to a report results in additional sections.

Using these sections, you can print a name at the start of each new group, and insert summary information after each group.

 More detailed information and hints to help you with grouping can be found in Chapter 5.

Sorting Records

Having the ability to sort records makes your reports much more useful and easy to read. SCR sometimes puts sorting and grouping (a type of sorting) together in the Report Experts even though you may need the individual functions to do quite different tasks. By sorting your records using the Record Sort Order dialog box, you can easily set the sort order for the fields on your report. To define the sort order:

1. Open the Record Sort Order dialog box by either clicking the Sort Order toolbar button or clicking Report, Sort Records.

2. The Record Sort Order dialog box lists the Report Fields on the left and the Sort Fields on the right (see Figure 2.26). The group you created in the last section appears here because grouping is a type of sorting.

3. Add a sort field by selecting a field in the Report Fields list and clicking Add to move the field over to the Sort Fields list. For this example, select the MOVIE field and now, within each year, the movie names will sort alphabetically.

4. Once you have a field in the Sort Fields list, you can set the sort direction by clicking Ascending or Descending.

5. Click OK to save your sort settings and exit the dialog box.

Figure 2.26
Use the Record Sort Order dialog box to sort the records on your report.

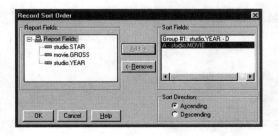

You can have as many levels of sorting as you have fields on your report.

Totaling and Subtotaling

Adding totals to your reports can be as easy as a few clicks with your mouse. Totals add value to reports and give you information that may not be in your database. To add any type of total to your report, you must select the field you want to total. To insert a total or subtotal:

1. Select the field to be totaled or subtotaled—for this example, choose the GROSS field to subtotal— and then click Insert, Subtotal to open the Insert Subtotal dialog box (see Figure 2.27).

2. If your report contains any groups, they appear in the drop-down list. Select the group level for which you want to calculate a subtotal.

3. Click OK to close the dialog box and SCR inserts the subtotal on the report in the Group Footer section, right below the field it totals.

You can add a group and a subtotal or summary in one step. If there are no groups on your report, or if you want to create a new group, select the field that you want to base your new group on from the second drop-down list. Both the group and total appear on your report when you click OK to close the dialog box.

Figure 2.27

Use the Insert Subtotal dialog box for adding subtotals to your report.

Adding Titles and Special Fields to the Report

Using the previous steps, you have created the body of your report, but it would not be complete without a title, page numbers, and a date. SCR makes it easy to add this information to your report.

Adding Text Objects

Text objects serve as mini word processors. A text object can be placed anywhere on your report—in any section, any size you want. You can then type text into the object, such as a report title, a label for a summary field, or any other information you want to print on your report. To add text to a report:

1. Click the Text Object toolbar button or Insert, Text Object.

2. The text object attaches to the pointer, acting just like it does when inserting a database field. Move the pointer over the report and click once where you want to place the text object.

3. Once you place the text object, it appears with a shaded border and blinking insertion point, indicating the object is in Edit mode and you can enter the text (see Figure 2.28). Now you can add a title to your report.

You can move this text object anywhere you want on your report and make it as big as you want using the resizing handles. Keep in mind that the section in which you place the text object determines how many times and where it prints. You'll learn about formatting text objects in Chapter 7.

Adding Special Fields

Seagate Crystal Reports contains a selection of Special Fields that you can add to your report, such as Page Number and Print Date. These fields act like database fields and are based on your computer's settings.

1. Open the Others tab of the Insert Fields dialog box, or click Insert, Special Field.

2. The Others tab has both the Group Name fields listed as well as the Special Fields. Click the plus sign next to Special Fields to expand the list (see Figure 2.29).

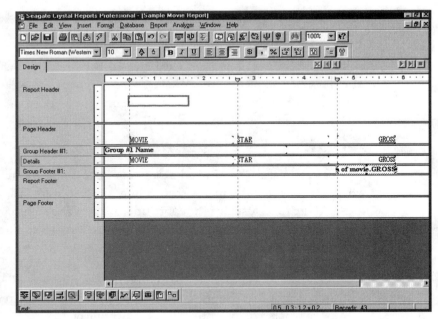

Figure 2.28
Use a text object
to add a title to
your report.

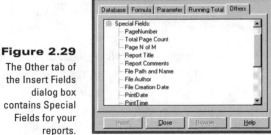

Figure 2.29
The Other tab of
the Insert Fields
dialog box
contains Special
Fields for your
reports.

3. Add special fields as you add any other field: Click the field you want to add and drag it onto your report, or click Insert. Remember that different sections print at different points in the report, so place your special fields accordingly.

If you want to use the Report Title and Report Comments fields, you need to enter information in the Document Properties dialog box (click File, Summary Info). If you enter data after you place the special fields on your report, refresh your report (Report, Refresh Report Data, or F5) and the new information displays.

Saving Your Report

 Just like in many other software programs, you can locate the directory and folder where you would like to save your report using the Save or Save As dialog boxes. Your Crystal reports have the extension .RPT. It is a good idea for you to not save your reports in the same directory as your program files. Instead, create a separate directory for all of your reports. This way, if for some reason you reinstall your software (an upgrade for example) you will not accidentally overwrite your reports.

Previewing Your Report

To collect data from your data source and preview your report, either click the Preview toolbar button, click File, Print, Preview Sample, or simply press the F5 key. This opens the Preview tab in the Crystal Report Designer. The Preview tab collects all the data for your report and formats it according to the instructions you have given on the Design tab.

SAVING OPTIONS

You can save your report with or without data. Click Save Data with Report from the File menu to turn the option on or off. A check mark appears next to the command when the option is on. By clicking File, Options, you can also change the global option on the Reporting tab. There are several reasons why you may want to save a report with or without data. You may want to turn the option on when working with a large report that takes a long time to preview. By saving data with the report, SCR does not have to re-collect *all* the records from the database each time you preview, only the *new* records. You might also save data with the report if you want to send it to someone without database access.

Other times you might want to turn this option off and not save the data. If you e-mail the report to someone you may not want the data floating around over the Internet. The file will also be much smaller without the data, thus the transmission will be quicker. You should also save a report the last time without data. This way, when a user opens the report, there will be no Preview tab full of old data and he will have to collect new data for the report.

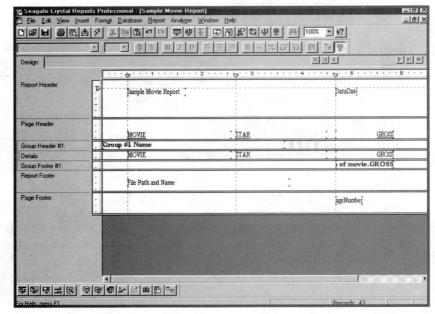

Figure 2.30

The Design tab contains the instructions for running your report.

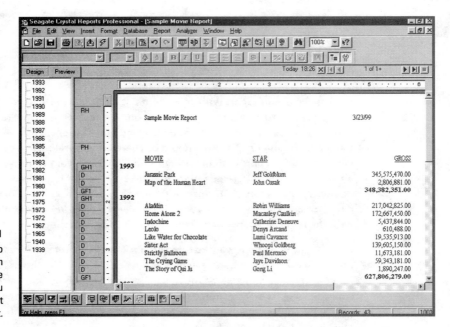

Figure 2.31

The Preview tab collects data from your data source and shows you how your report will print.

Figures 2.30 and 2.31 show the Design tab and Preview tab for the same report. Take a look to see how the elements in the Design tab translate to the various fields, objects, and other report components you see on the Preview tab.

 See Chapter 1 for more information and instructions on maneuvering in the Preview tab and between the Design and Preview tabs.

Summary

This chapter has led you through designing a basic report with the Standard Report Expert and the Custom option. You have connected to a data source and chosen tables and fields for a report. Basic grouping, sorting, and totaling were also covered. Hopefully, you now feel comfortable with the design interface and are excited to learn more about how you can use Seagate Crystal Reports to design reports specific to your needs.

The advanced chapters of this book (beginning with Chapter 8) cover tasks where more information, detail, examples, and hints are explained. You have conquered the tip of the iceberg. In the next chapters, you'll look at what is beneath the water! SCR combines a friendly interface with tons of functionality and options to help make your report meet your specific expectations.

PART II

Adding to Your Seagate
Crystal Reports

CHAPTER 3

Connecting to and Linking Data

- Determining Your Data Connection Type

- Using the Data File Connection

- Using the SQL/ODBC Connection

- Using the Dictionary or Query Connection

- Linking Tables Together

In this chapter, you will be introduced to the three main types of data connections used for designing in Seagate Crystal Reports: Data File, SQL\ODBC, and Dictionary\Query. You will first learn how to choose the right type of connection for your data. Then, linking will be covered and you will gain a basic understanding of linking tables and join types. Because linking differs slightly depending on the type of data connection you use, you can choose to review only the section that applies to the type of data source you will be using.

Determining Your Data Connection Type

It is important to know what type of data source you will be working with when designing your reports. The term *data source* refers to a repository of information. That repository might collect information from an accounting system, from an inventory system, from a call tracking system, or any number of other automated systems you or your company uses. The type of data source you use dictates how you connect to that data. SCR gives you three data connection options:

- **Data File.** Use to connect to data like Microsoft Access, Dbase, and Btrieve.

- **SQL\ODBC.** Use to connect to SQL databases such as Oracle, SQL Server, and Sybase. Also use to connect through ODBC to any kind of compatible database.

- **Dictionary\Query.** The dictionary acts as a "layer" over the database. The queries are separate from the database and act to pull out a subset of data from the database.

Depending on the type of data source you use, you connect with one of these three methods. The following three sections describe how to use each data connection type to access various data sources. If you know which data connection you need to use, feel free to read only the section pertaining to that connection type, skipping the other two.

If you're unsure of what type of data source you need to use, ask your Database Administrator. If your database cannot use the Data File connection, you need to go the "Using the SQL\ODBC Connection" section and learn how to connect that way.

When you start designing a new report, you first choose a Report Expert or the Custom button from the Report Gallery dialog box. After this, you need to choose a Data File connection type. The following steps show examples from the Custom option as opposed to a Report Expert option, as will the majority of steps in the remainder of this book. Though Report Experts simplify the process of creating a report, doing things the "manual" way will give you a more thorough tour of SCR and a better overall education.

Using the Data File Connection

Seagate Crystal Reports uses the Data File connection to connect reports to a data file type of database, such as Microsoft Access, dBase, FoxPro, Clipper, Btrieve, and Paradox. If you use this type of database for your report, choose the Data File connection. Seagate Crystal Reports has native drivers that communicate directly with your specific database when you use the Data File connection.

Sometimes a data file type database is referred to as a PC-type database. For a complete list of supported databases, see the product information on Seagate Software's Web site at www.seagatesoftware.com.

Connecting to Your Data Source Using Data File

The following section walks you through connecting to your data source using the Data File connection type. To connect to a database with the Data File connection:

1. With the Crystal Report Designer open, choose File, New or click the New Report toolbar button.

2. When you click the Custom button, the Report Gallery dialog box expands to display the Report Type and Data Type options. Choose your data type—in this case, click Data File (see Figure 3.1). The Choose Database File dialog box opens.

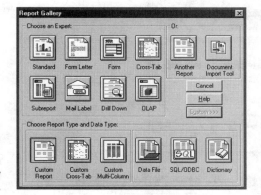

Figure 3.1
Click Data File in
the Report Gallery
dialog box.

3. Navigate through the directories to select the database you want to use (see Figure 3.2). Click Open.

Notice the **SQL** Tables button on the **Choose Database File** dialog box. You can use this button to add another database of a different type to your report. See more discussion of this topic in the "Adding and Removing Databases and Tables" section of this chapter.

4. Once you have chosen the database that you want to use, the Select Tables dialog box opens, listing all of the tables in your database.

If your database contains only one table, then the Design tab opens immediately. If you need more than the one database for your report, you can either open the Visual Linking Expert or choose **D**atabase, **A**dd Database to Report to add a second database file. See the section "Using the Visual Linking Expert" later in this chapter, as well as the "Custom Report" section of Chapter 2.

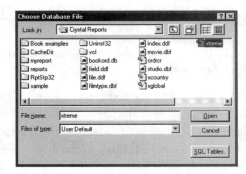

Figure 3.2
Choose the
database that you
want to use for
your report.

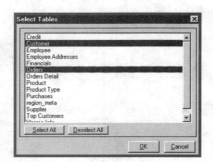

Figure 3.3

You can choose as many tables as you need for your report.

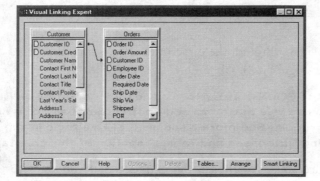

Figure 3.4

You can see the tables and links in the Visual Linking Expert.

5. Select the tables that you want to use for your report (see Figure 3.3).

You can choose more than one table at a time if you hold down either the Shift key or the Ctrl key when clicking your second and third (and so on) table names.

6. Click OK. The Visual Linking Expert opens, as shown in Figure 3.4.

The Visual Linking Expert lets you see exactly what tables you are working with and how they are linked. The Visual Linking Expert will be explained further later in this chapter.

7. Click OK in the Visual Linking Expert to close it. The Design tab displays with the Insert Fields dialog box open. You can now start designing your report using any of the fields from the tables that you chose and linked (see Figure 3.5). Scroll down in the Insert Fields dialog box to view and choose fields for your report.

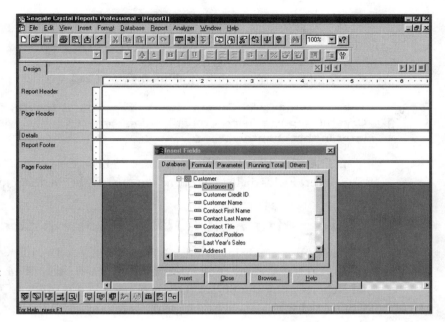

Figure 3.5
You can begin designing a report using fields from the tables you selected.

In the Database tab of the Insert Fields dialog box, you can double-click a table name to hide all of the fields in that table. Double-click again on the table name and the list of fields expands. Expanding and collapsing the list of fields for each table helps with navigation through the many tables in the Insert Fields dialog box.

Learning to Use the Data File Connection

To practice choosing a data source using the Data File connection, follow this exercise using the Xtreme.mdb sample database that shipped and installed with your Seagate Crystal Reports software. To start a report using the Xtreme.mdb database:

1. Choose File, New.

2. From the Report Gallery, click Custom. Then click the Data File button that appears in the expanded Report Gallery dialog box.

3. In the Choose Database File dialog box, click the Xtreme.mdb file and click OK. You can find the Xtreme.mdb file in Program Files/Seagate Software/Crystal Reports.

4. Holding the Ctrl key down, click the Customer and Orders tables in the Select Tables dialog box. Then click Done.

5. The Visual Linking Expert opens, showing your linked tables. Smart Linking performed the linking for you. Click OK.

 The Customer and Orders tables were linked together by Seagate Crystal Reports using Smart Linking. Smart Linking will be covered later in this chapter.

6. The Visual Linking Expert closes and the Design tab opens with the Insert Fields dialog box open. You can now begin designing your report.

Using the SQL/ODBC Connection

If you use almost any kind of database other than a data file, you need to use the SQL/ODBC connection. Most any database can connect to Seagate Crystal Reports using the SQL\ODBC connection. ODBC, or Open Database Connectivity, is a standard language developed by Microsoft Corporation that allows software programs, like Seagate Crystal Reports, to communicate with a variety of databases.

Though different, SCR combines the ODBC and SQL methods of accessing data into one option. Using this method you can access a SQL database directly or through ODBC. ODBC also allows access to many types of non-SQL databases. You may even want to use the SQL/ODBC connection type to access a data file database via ODBC, because this connection type offers additional options. Commonly, you might choose to access a data file database with ODBC because you can change the type of joins between the tables. When using the Data File connection, all links must be left as outer joins.

 For more information about table joins—or links—please see the sections "Using the Visual Linking Expert" and "Why the Link Direction Is Important" later in this chapter. These sections explain the differences between connection types and how they affect reports.

Many databases have an ODBC driver that serves as a translator of information from a specific database into the ODBC language. Seagate Crystal Reports also has an ODBC driver that translates information from Seagate Crystal Reports language into the ODBC language. The two DLL files (or two ODBC drivers) are used by the database and by Seagate Crystal Reports. In the middle, ODBC is being *spoken* by both the database and Seagate Crystal Reports. Communication actually takes place in this middle layer.

The ODBC language requires that the database have an ODBC driver to use for communicating with Seagate Crystal Reports' ODBC driver. Installing Seagate Crystal Reports also installs ODBC Administrator, which can be found in the Seagate Crystal Reports program group. Actually a Microsoft application, the ODBC Administrator contains many ODBC drivers that you can install if you do not already have one for your specific data source.

Go to Appendix A, "Setting Up an ODBC Data Source," for more information on how to set up your database to be accessed through ODBC. Note also that you must go to the ODBC Administrator to access the Help file for that application.

Connecting to Your Data Source Using SQL/ODBC

The following steps assist you in connecting to your data source using the SQL\ODBC connection. The steps assume that you are using the Custom report option. To connect to a database with the SQL/ODBC connection:

1. Start a new report and click Custom on the Report Gallery.
2. From the expanded Report Gallery dialog box, click the SQL/ODBC button (see Figure 3.6). The Log On Server dialog box opens (see Figure 3.7).

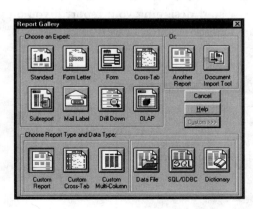

Figure 3.6
Click the SQL/ ODBC button to connect directly to a SQL database or to connect via ODBC to your data source.

Figure 3.7

Choose a data source to use for your report.

The Log On Server dialog box lists either your database or the driver that you need to use to connect to your database via ODBC. Check with your Database Administrator if you are not sure what to use. What you see listed in this dialog box depends on your network.

3. Choose the server or database name that you want to use for your report. Click OK. The Choose SQL Table dialog box opens (see Figure 3.8).

4. The Choose SQL Table dialog box lists the driver and/or data source you have chosen on the right and the tables in that data source on the left. Click one table that you want to use in your report and then click OK. You can only choose one table here. Adding more tables will be done in a later step.

Notice the Database File button on the Choose SQL Table dialog box. You can use this button to add another database of a different type to your report. See more discussion of this topic in the "Adding and Removing Databases and Tables" section of this chapter.

5. The Design tab opens with the selected table in the Insert Fields dialog box. You can now start designing your report if you only need the one table you already chose.

Figure 3.8

Choose one table from the Choose SQL Table dialog box.

If you need more than the one table, you must use the Visual Linking Expert to add and link additional tables. See the section "Adding SQL\ODBC Tables" later in this chapter for more information.

 If you cannot connect to your data source, you get any error regarding your ODBC driver or connection, or do not see your data source or driver listed in the Log On Server dialog box, you might need to install the correct driver using the ODBC Administrator application. Refer to Appendix A for more help.

Using the Dictionary or Query Connection

You may have a dictionary or query available to you when designing reports. A *dictionary* is a structured view of a database. Someone has to design the dictionary, and part of the design process involves choosing the data sources and tables, linking those tables, and choosing which fields to include in the dictionary. The same is true of a query. The query designer needs to connect to the data sources, choose and link tables, and choose which fields to include in the query.

The major differences between dictionaries and queries will be discussed in Chapters 10 and 11. For now, just consider both dictionaries and queries as means of accessing data sources where you don't have to worry about directly connecting to your data source or choosing and linking tables. To connect to a database through a dictionary or query:

1. Start a report by choosing File, New and click Custom on the Report Gallery.

2. To connect to a Dictionary or Query, click the Dictionary button in the expanded Report Gallery dialog box (see Figure 3.9). The File Open dialog box appears.

3. From the File Open dialog box, choose your Dictionary or Query file and click Open.

 If you choose the Dictionary option but want a query, edit the File Name field in the File Open dialog box, deleting the *.dct, *.dc5 and instead typing *.qry. Click OK. This brings up any query files available to you. Be sure you have selected the network directory that stores your queries!

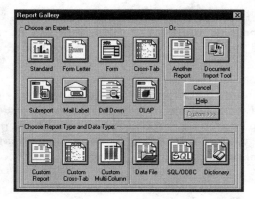

Figure 3.9
Click the
Dictionary button
for either a
dictionary
or query
data source.

4. Once you choose a dictionary or query to use as the data source for your report, the Design tab opens and you can begin designing your report.

Now you have connected to your data source and chosen tables using any one of the available three methods. If you connected via a data file or SQL/ODBC, you need to read on. You'll learn about how to link tables and why linking is important. If you connected with a Dictionary or Query you can skip the discussion on linking and go to the next chapter.

Linking Tables Together

When designing reports for your business, you most likely need to link two or more tables together in order to have all the information you need available. Most databases have many tables, each table containing a certain type of information. Figure 3.10 pictures two tables from a fictitious credit card company's database.

The company's database contains information needed for reports. In order to have information on your report from more than one table, you need to link the tables together. The fields used for linking must have something in common, such as name, length, or field type.

It is important to carefully choose the fields to use for linking. An easy way to choose a field, if there are several common fields between two tables, is to choose the field that is a unique identifier, like a social security number, bank account number, or credit card number.

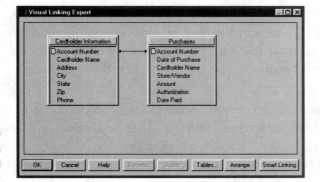

Figure 3.10

Two tables from Free Credit Bank's database.

When you link two tables together, you need the information from one table to match the corresponding information from the other table. Think about the Free Credit Bank example discussed here. Say you work for this company and need to design a report to run monthly invoices. The company has two tables that you could use, Cardholder Information and Purchases.

To design and run a report to run each cardholder's monthly bill, you might want the customer name and address, account number, date, store/vendor, and amount of each purchase (see Figure 3.11). To design this information into a report you need several fields from both the Cardholder Information and Purchases tables.

Correct linking ensures that the information the report pulls from the Cardholder Information table matches the information pulled from the Purchases table. This way, the cardholder's name printed on each bill matches the purchases listed on the bill.

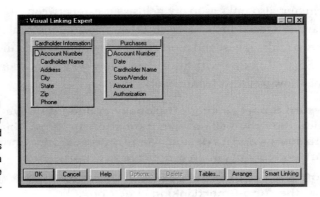

Figure 3.11

The Customer Information and Purchases tables are needed for a monthly invoice report.

Account Number is the best field to link in this example. Every cardholder has a unique Account Number, so even if two or more cardholders have the same name, they will each get their correct bill. Cardholder Name, though common between the tables, would not be the best choice because two customers might have the same name.

In the next section, Smart Linking, a function of Seagate Crystal Reports that performs linking automatically, will be covered. You will also examine the Visual Linking Expert, which allows you to manually link tables and offers many options including changing the link direction and adding additional tables and databases to a report.

Letting SCR Perform Smart Linking

Seagate Crystal Reports contains a tool called *Smart Linking* that links tables together automatically. SCR looks at the tables you have chosen for your report, evaluates the fields in them, and links the tables together using the fields that it thinks are common between the tables. By default, Smart Linking is turned on. Whenever you select multiple tables for a report or add a new table to an existing report, Smart Linking links the tables together and shows you the links in the Visual Linking Expert.

Smart Linking can be a great tool—have SCR figure out which fields to link so you don't have to worry about it! Unfortunately, Seagate Crystal Reports can't do several things vital for effective linking. SCR's Smart Linking cannot distinguish between two or more sets of linkable fields. Using the Free Credit Bank example, SCR has no way to know that linking Cardholder Name to Cardholder Name is not as good as linking Account Number to Account Number.

Smart Linking also links as many fields as it can between two tables, sometimes drawing several links between them. Most of the time, only one link between two tables is best and most efficient, but multi-field indexes are valid too. Try Smart Linking with your data. How your data source was set up determines how well this feature works for you.

You can turn Smart Linking off globally in Seagate Crystal Reports if you decide that you will not use it most of the time. This depends on your data source and its design. Many data sources cannot use Smart Linking effectively because it creates too many links.

To turn off Smart Linking, choose File, Options and click the Database tab. Clear the Auto-SmartLinking check box.

Using the Visual Linking Expert

The Visual Linking Expert is Seagate Crystal Reports' tool for linking tables. This Expert shows the tables that you added to your report and either links them for you using Smart Linking or allows you to manually link the tables. Several options are available using this Expert, including adding and deleting tables and databases and manipulating the link direction and join type.

You can invoke the Expert at any time by choosing Database-Visual Linking Expert or using the Visual Linking Expert button on the toolbar. If you have selected more than one table when using a Report Expert or the Data File connection, this Expert opens at just the right time to link your tables together. If you use a SQL/ODBC connection, you can only choose one table and then the Design tab opens. In this case, you have to open the Visual Linking Expert manually.

Adding More Tables to Your Report

You can use two methods to add more tables to your report—right from within the Visual Linking Expert, or through the main menu, which opens a dialog box that takes you to the Visual Linking Expert in an extra step or two. To add more tables to your report while in the Visual Linking Expert:

Using the Visual Linking Expert to add tables is explained in this section. In the last section of this chapter, there is discussion of how to add and remove databases and tables using the other options available from the Database menu.

1. Open the Visual Linking Expert using the toolbar button or choose Database, Visual Linking Expert.
2. Click the Tables button on the Visual Linking Expert. The Choose Tables To Use In Visual Linking dialog box opens (see Figure 3.12).
3. If you used the Data File connection to your intended data, click the Add Data File button. If you used the SQL\ODBC connection to your intended data, click the Add SQL\ODBC button. Please keep in mind that you can have two different types of data connections on the same report. This is one of SCR's strengths.

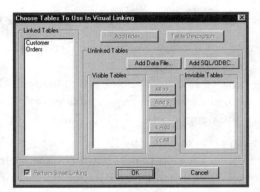

Figure 3.12
Click Add Data
File or Add
SQL\ODBC to add
a file or table to
your report.

Depending on which type of connection to data you use, follow the appropriate steps in one of the sections below, either "Adding Data File Tables" or "Adding SQL\ODBC Tables."

Adding Data File Tables

To add tables to an existing report using the Data File connection:

1. In the Choose Tables To Use In Visual Linking dialog box, click the Add Data File button. The Choose Database File dialog box opens, the same dialog box you used earlier when starting a report with the Data File connection.

2. Click the name of the database from which you want to add more tables. Then click the Add button.

3. The Select Tables dialog box opens and you can select tables by clicking them, holding the Shift or Ctrl keys to select more than one table. Click OK and the Select Tables dialog box closes, leaving the Choose Database File dialog box open. Click Done to close that dialog box as well.

4. Click OK on the Choose Tables To Use In Visual Linking dialog box (see Figure 3.13). It closes, leaving you with the Visual Linking Expert open.

5. Click OK to close the Visual Linking Expert.

 If Smart Linking is on, Seagate Crystal Reports performs table linking for you. If not on, you need to link the tables manually prior to closing the Visual Linking Expert.

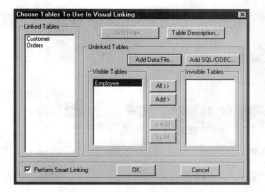

Figure 3.13

The tables that you selected in the Select Tables dialog box appear in the Visible Tables list of the Choose Tables To Use In Visual Linking dialog box.

Adding SQL\ODBC Tables

Adding a SQL\ODBC table to your report is very similar to adding a Data File table to your report, only a few of the dialog boxes differ. Again, these steps are only applicable if you choose the Custom option when starting a new report.

When you design a report using the SQL\ODBC connection to your data, you can only chose one table the first time through. Once you have the Design tab open, and before you start adding fields to your report, you may want to open the Visual Linking Expert to add more tables. To continue adding tables from a SQL/ODBC database:

1. Choose Database, Visual Linking Expert from the menu. Or, You can also click the Visual Linking Expert button on the toolbar. The Visual Linking Expert displays the table you chose earlier.

2. Click the Tables button to open the Choose Tables To Use In Visual Linking dialog box.

3. Click the Add SQL\ODBC button. The Choose SQL Table dialog box opens (see Figure 3.14).

If the Log On Server dialog box opens instead of the Choose SQL Table dialog box, choose the server that you used for this report again. Click OK and the Choose SQL Table dialog box opens.

4. Select tables by clicking them and then clicking the Add button, or by just double-clicking them. They appear listed in the Invisible Tables list

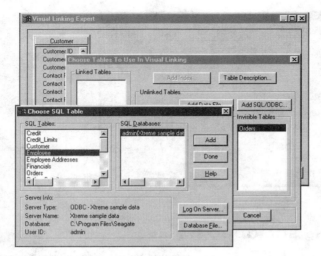

Figure 3.14
Choose tables to
add to your report
using the Choose
SQL Table
dialog box.

of the Choose Tables To Use In Visual Linking dialog box. Click Done
and the tables you chose move into the Visible Tables list.

5. Click OK in the Choose Tables To Use In Visual Linking dialog box.
The Visual Linking Expert remains open. You now need to link your
tables by clicking the Smart Linking button or manually linking them,
as explained in the next section.

Linking Tables

If you decide that Smart Linking won't work efficiently for your tables, you
need to draw the table links manually. To manipulate a link, you can select it
with a mouse click. When selected, links appear white (if you're using the
Windows Standard color scheme). You can then delete or change a link. To
link tables in the Visual Linking Expert:

 **It's useful to make the Visual Linking Expert as large as possible (maxi-
mized) so that you can arrange the tables easily. Sometimes all of
your tables won't show in the window. If you maximize the window,
then you'll have less scrolling to do.**

1. Click the field from which you want to link, in the left-hand table.

2. Drag the mouse over to the field in the table to which you want to link.

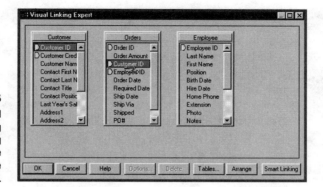

Figure 3.15
Highlight the field
you are linking
from and drag
your mouse to the
field you are
linking to.

3. Once both fields are highlighted and the pointer has changed to a 'Z' shaped arrow, let go of the mouse button (see Figure 3.15). SCR shows the link that you drew as a line between the two fields.

You can link many tables together, like running a string from one to the next to the next. You can also link one table to two other tables. Rules and options apply to the type of link that you use. These are covered in the following section.

 You might want to work with your Database Administrator (DBA) to find out how to link your tables and in which order they need to be linked. Generally, you place your main table on the left-hand side of the Visual Linking Expert and link from left to right. You can also clean up the window from time to time by clicking the Arrange button to automatically align the tables.

Why the Link Direction and Join Type Are Important

Now that you are comfortable with the concept of linking tables together, you'll explore some rules that go along with linking, as well as some different types of links.

Linking Data File Tables

When using the Data File connection and linking tables, you must link to an indexed field. An *indexed field* is a field used by the database to organize and

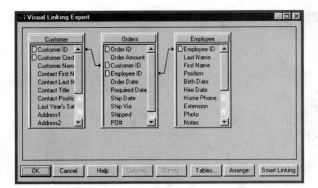

Figure 3.16

You must link to an indexed field when using the Data File connection.

sort records in order to quickly retrieve data. Indexed fields have colored icons next to them in the Visual Linking Expert, as shown in Figure 3.16. Whoever designed the database you're working with defined the fields to be indexed, and it is these fields that are the unique identifier type of fields. By noting these fields with icons, SCR makes linking easier, for the best fields to link are the indexed fields.

Some indexes may appear as white with a "#" symbol, indicating that the field belongs to a multi-field index. Database designers use multi-field indexes when records require more than one field to be uniquely identified.

When linking tables together using the Data File connection, SCR always uses a left outer join. This means that all of the records from the table on the left print on your report, regardless of whether a related record from the right-hand table exists. Conversely, if a record from the right-hand table does not have a related record in the left-hand table, it does not print on the report.

Take a look at the Free Credit Bank example used earlier. You linked the Cardholder table to the Purchases table. If you use a Data File connection for these tables, the link type is left outer join. Thus, when running a statement report, a statement prints for each Cardholder along with their purchases. However, because fields from the left-hand table, Customer Information, print even if no records in the right-hand table, Purchases, match, the report prints statements for customers with a zero balance due.

The left outer join is the only join type available when using the Data File connection. As was mentioned earlier in this chapter, however, you can connect to Data File type data sources using an ODBC driver. If you choose to connect to a data file through ODBC, you then have the ability to change the join type, as described in the section "Other Join Types."

Linking SQL\ODBC Tables

Linking tables when using the SQL\ODBC connection to your database differs slightly from using a Data File connection. First, SCR does not limit linking of tables in SQL\ODBC data sources to indexed fields. This makes linking tables very flexible. The disadvantage is that you have no hints as to the best fields to link, usually the indexed fields.

By default SCR applies the equal join type to links between tables in a SQL\ODBC data source. This means that reports only print records with equal matches. If a record from one table has no matching records from the other table, regardless of right or left, SCR does not print that record on your report.

Returning again to the Free Credit Bank example, if you connected to your database using the SQL\ODBC connection and used the default equal join type, you would only have statements for cardholders with purchases. The report would not include statements for cardholders without any purchases during the statement period, as there would be no matches in the Purchases table.

Other Join Types

Now that you know about the difference between the default join type when using a Data File connection versus a SQL\ODBC connection, you need to know that when using the SQL\ODBC connection you can change the join type. You cannot change the join when using a Data File connection.

By default, SQL\ODBC uses an equal join. SCR gives you the ability to change this join type. You have seen the left outer join, the default for data files. You can also use the opposite: the right outer join. If you use a right outer join, the report prints all the records from the right-hand table, and only matching records from the left-hand table.

Back to Free Credit Bank. If you link the Cardholder table to the Purchases table using a right outer join, your report would have every purchase made from the Purchases table, and a matching Cardholder record. If a cardholder did not have any purchases, that Cardholder record would not print. However, if for some reason a record existed in the Purchases table without a related Cardholder record, that Purchases record would still print on the report.

Other join types include:

- Greater
- Less
- Greater or Equal
- Less or Equal
- Not Equal

 Search Seagate Crystal Reports' online Help using the keyword phrase "SQL Join Types" for more information on each of these join types.

SCR gives you the ability to change the join type of a link in the Visual Linking Expert. Assess what information you want on your report, what type of data connection your report uses, and the advantages of the different join types available to you. Then follow these steps to change the join type:

1. In the Visual Linking Expert, select the link you want to change. Click the Options button, or right-click the link and choose Options. The Link Options dialog box opens (see Figure 3.17).

2. In the SQL Join Type area, select a different join type, and then click OK.

Adding and Removing Databases and Tables

Once you have a report design started, you can add and delete tables at any time. SCR offers two ways to add or remove databases and/or tables: using the Add Database to Report and Remove from Report menu commands, or using the Visual Linking Expert, which has been covered earlier in this chapter.

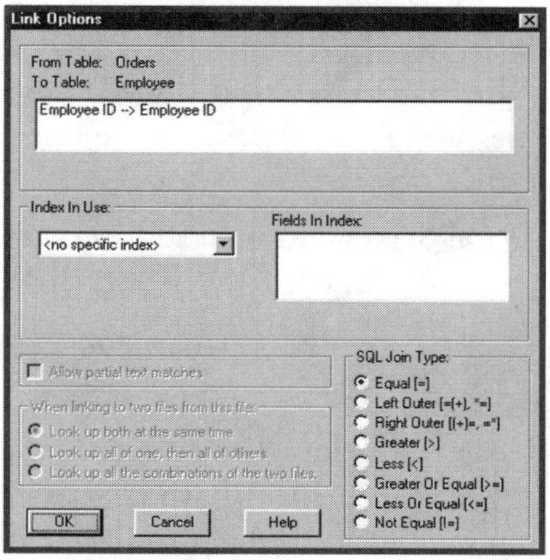

Figure 3.17

With the Link Options dialog box open you can change the type of join for your link.

Adding Databases and Tables

You can add tables to your report from either the data source you are already using, or from a different data source. The language of the Add Database to Report menu command can be confusing, because you use that command to add tables from either the existing or a new data source. Essentially, you wouldn't add a new database to your report without adding at least one table from that database. Therefore, adding a database, by default, involves adding a table. To add a table to your report, from an existing or new database:

1. Choose <u>D</u>atabase, <u>A</u>dd Database to Report. Depending on the databases your report already uses, this menu command opens either the Choose Database File dialog box or the Choose SQL Table dialog box.

2. At this point you have a number of choices. If the Choose Database File dialog box opens, you can:

   - Choose the same database as the report already uses, and click OK. The Select Tables dialog box opens.

   - Choose a new data file type database, and click OK. The Select Tables dialog box opens.

   - Click the SQL Tables button to select a SQL/ODBC type database to add to your report. Either the Log On Server or Choose SQL Table dialog box opens.

If the Choose SQL Table dialog box opens, you can:

- Select a database from those already added to your report from the SQL Databases list. Then, choose a table from the SQL Tables list and click OK.

- Click the Log On Server button to add a new SQL/ODBC type database to the report. The Log On Server dialog box opens.

- Click the Database File button to add a new data file type database to the report. The Choose Database File dialog box opens.

3. No matter what dialog box opens or what choices you make, the basic steps are the same. Select the database, whether existing or new, containing the table you want to add. From that database, select the tables you want to add. For more specific steps on the various dialog boxes that may open, see the subsections within the "Using the Visual Linking Expert" section that describe adding tables to reports.

 When you add another data source, you may experience problems with connectivity to the second data source, or to two data sources at the same time. In this case, talk to your Database Administrator for help in resolving the problem.

Removing Databases and Tables

To remove a table from your report, first be sure that you are not using that table on your report in any way and that you do not need the table to link through to another table. If you remove a table still in use, you may get an error message preventing you from removing the table. Or, you may not get an error message until you again try to run or preview the report.

Like adding a table to a report, you need to choose the Database, Remove from Report menu command to remove either a database or a table from your report. If you remove all tables from a particular database from the report, you have essentially also removed the database from the report. To remove a table:

1. Choose Database, Remove from Report. The Remove from Report dialog box opens.

2. Select the tables that you want to remove, and then click Remove.

3. When you finish removing tables, click Done.

Summary

Linking tables is an important part of successful reporting using any tool. Seagate Crystal Reports uses the same concepts as other reporting tools and databases. Hopefully, if you have used other reporting or database tools, the concept of linking is familiar. If this has all been new, it is worth your time to experiment and plan your linking based on the final information that you want on your report.

Depending on the type of data source you use, you need to choose either the Data File, SQL\ODBC, or Dictionary or Query connection to your data. Data File and SQL\ODBC connections require that you choose tables to include for use in your report and that you link those tables together if you're using more than one on a report.

If you use a SQL\ODBC connection to your data source, you have link options that allow you to manipulate the join type. This affords you more control over what information to actually include on any given report. Though you have more options when using the SQL\ODBC connection, do not completely shy away from the Data File connection, for in many instances it provides the exact type of connection that you will want to use.

Selecting Records

This chapter will explain the ins and outs of record selection. Record selection was introduced in Chapter 1 and performed using the Standard Report Expert in Chapter 2. In this chapter, you will learn in more detail how to set selection criteria, as well as how to create advanced selection criteria to meet the needs of many reports.

After completing this chapter, you will know how to use SCR's well-developed Select Expert. The Select Expert lets you pick items from lists to set up the selection criteria more easily. However, you will also learn about bypassing the lists and actually writing a formula for record selection. You might need to do this for more advanced selection criteria.

Using the Select Expert

The Select Expert is the tool to use for setting selection criteria for your report. As explained in previous chapters, you need to select which records from your data source you want to print on a report. Often, you don't want or need every record from certain tables. Rather, you will want to filter out records not applicable to the purpose of your report. By selecting only the records that you need, your report not only avoids unnecessary information, but processes much faster.

For example, if you run a report to print invoices, you might want to limit the records on your report to only charges incurred during a set date range. You would therefore set up record selection criteria to include only records that fall within the date range that you specify, such as a month billing cycle.

Another example might be a human resources report, where you need to include only records of employees who are taking part in a certain benefit plan. In this case, you would define selection criteria to filter out any employees not participating in the particular benefit plan.

SCR places no limit on the number of criteria you can set up for one report. You can use any field available within your report as the basis for selection criteria.

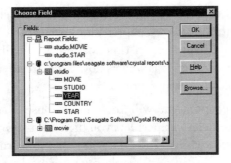

Figure 4.1
Select a field to use in record selection by clicking a field in the Choose Field dialog box.

Setting Selection Criteria

Setting selection criteria involves the Select Expert. This Expert makes setting criteria straightforward using drop-down lists. To open the Select Expert:

1. Click the Select Expert toolbar button or click Report, Select Expert. The Choose Field dialog box opens (see Figure 4.1).

If you have a field selected on your report when you open the Select Expert, that field appears as a tab in the Select Expert, bypassing the Choose Field dialog box. If you do not want to use that particular field for your selection criteria, click Del to delete the tab and then click New to open the Choose Field dialog box.

2. Scrolling if necessary, click the field on which to base your selection criteria. Click OK. The Select Expert opens with the name of the field you chose listed as a tab. Two drop-down lists appear that, by default, display *is* and *any value*, respectively (see Figure 4.2).

If you leave the selection criteria with the default values, no selection will take place. Think of setting this criteria as an English statement, such as "select all records where department 'is' 'equal to' sales."

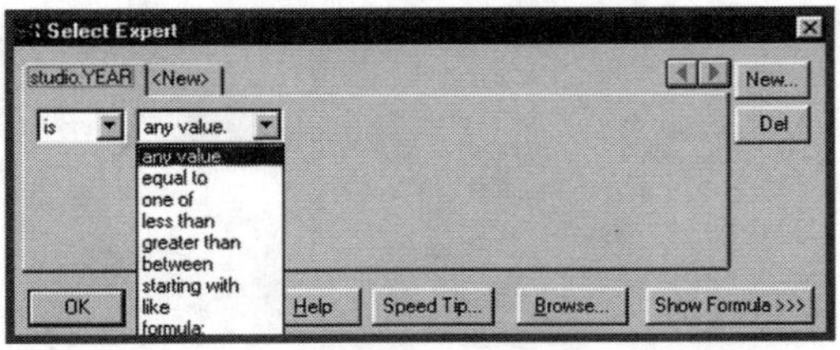

Figure 4.2
The Select Expert opens and supplies drop-down lists to help you set selection criteria.

Figure 4.3

Use the additional list—or other controls—to finish setting up your criteria statement.

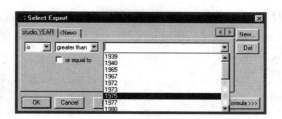

3. Select options from the drop-down lists to narrow the selection criteria. Once you select anything other than *any value* from the second list, one or possibly two more lists become available (see Figure 4.3).

 Select an option from the second (right-most) drop-down list first. After you do so, SCR adds the *is not* option to the first list. For example, say you want the selection criteria to read "...is not equal to...." First, select *equal to* from the second list, and then go back and select *is not* from the first list.

CHECKING FOR CASE SENSITIVITY

If the additional drop-down list in the Select Expert does not show the value you want to use, just type it in the box. However, note the format of the field values that do appear in the list, making certain to use the correct format and case.

Your database driver can tell whether or not your database is case sensitive. If your data is case sensitive, you must match the case (and format) of how the data exists in your database.

When using the Data File connection, your data may or may not be case sensitive. Microsoft Access has been designed to allow case insensitivity. Many others in the DB2 family of databases are case sensitive. The same is true if you are using the SQL\ODBC connection: Case sensitivity depends on options set up in the database.

To check if your data is case sensitive, choose File, Options and click the Database tab. If the Case-Insensitive SQL Data check box is selected, then your data *is not* case sensitive (your database driver checked this box when you connected to your database). If the box is cleared, then your data *is* case sensitive. The label on this check box is a bit misleading because it mentions SQL Data. But, the check box works the same for Data File and ODBC connections as well.

4. The third drop-down list contains actual field data from your data source. Type or select a value to complete the selection criteria (sometimes not every value from the field appears in the list).

 Which option you select in the second drop-down list affects the choices available. For example, choosing *less than* or *greater than* displays the Or equal to check box. Choosing *between* displays two drop-down lists with the word "and" in between. And, choosing *one of* displays a list plus Add and Delete buttons.

5. Click the New tab or button to add more selection criteria to your report. Once you have set up a tab for each criterion, click OK to close the Expert.

Your selection criteria is now set. You can go back to the Select Expert at any time to add to or change criteria. The next time you preview your report, you should notice that the records you have filtered out no longer appear.

Beyond the Select Expert: Writing Selection Formulas

As you develop a report, you often have very specific selection criteria in mind. But sometimes you may find that when you try to set up the selection criteria with the Select Expert, you can't make it work like you had in mind. You might find that the Select Expert does not offer the comparison options you need, or that the way the Select Expert links multiple selection criteria does not work for a certain report. If you do encounter this problem, don't worry. You can either edit the selection criteria formula created by the Select Expert, or even enter your own selection formula from scratch. With this feature, you have the power to manipulate selection criteria to meet your exact needs.

SCR offers two ways for you to create or modify selection formulas. First, you can expand the Select Expert dialog box to display the selection formula in a text box. Here, you could make simple changes or additions. If you want to create a selection formula from scratch or make more extensive changes and additions to a formula created by the Select Expert, then you can open the Formula Editor, which has various tools to assist you in writing the formula.

Though Chapter 6 covers formulas in detail, the following section suggests a few ways to use formulas for setting up your selection criteria. It will give you some formula examples and get your mind working over the possibilities. After you go through Chapter 6, you can refer back to this section to get ideas for selection formulas that you may need to use in your reports. Though formulas may seem complicated, once you go through Chapter 6 and come back you will have a new perspective. So read on and focus more on the possibilities rather than the actual formula language.

When to Use the Formula Editor

You may need to write formulas for your selection criteria if the options available in the Select Expert do not meet your needs. You may also want to write formulas to compensate for inconsistencies in your data, such as inconsistent case used in a database field (for example, "Smith," "smith," and "SMITH"). More ideas will come to mind once you learn about the Formula Editor and start designing reports. The next sections will explore a few common situations in which you might need to edit the selection criteria formula.

And vs. Or

When the Select Expert creates a selection criteria statement—or formula—it connects individual statements from each tab with an "and" clause (see Figure 4.4). This means that for any record to print on your report, it must match each individual criteria statement.

Figure 4.4

The record selection formula that the Select Expert creates connects each statement with an "and" clause.

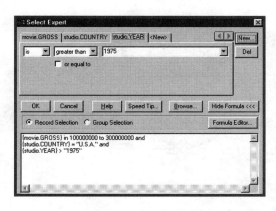

For some reports the "and" criteria doesn't select the data you want. Two examples are: One where you just change the "and" to an "or," and another where you need to cut and paste to manipulate the formula to meet your needs.

Changing And to Or

Say your report needs to contain information about all employees from two offices, as well as any other employees in the company involved in Marketing and Training, regardless of their home office. If you set up selection criteria using the Select Expert, your report would only contain information for employees that met both criteria—located at either of the two offices *and* members of either Marketing or Training, as shown in Figure 4.5.

If you click Show Formula on the Select Expert, the dialog box expands to display the complete selection formula. In the formula text box, you can change the "and" to an "or," thereby creating the selection criteria formula that you really want (see Figure 4.6).

This report now includes records that meet either criteria—employees located in either of the two offices *or* members of either the Marketing or Training departments.

Making More Extensive Changes to the Selection Formula

For this second example, imagine you need to develop a human resources report containing employees from the Training department of the Charlotte office and the Marketing department of the Cincinnati office. These two

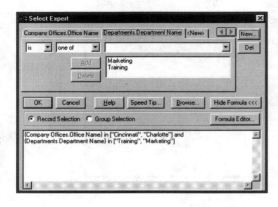

Figure 4.5

The Select Expert uses an "and" to connect the criteria you set up.

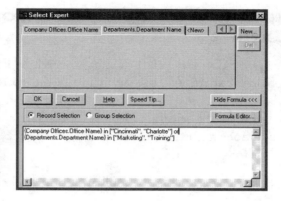

Figure 4.6

Change the "and" to an "or" to achieve the selection criteria that you need for a report.

teams are going to receive a bonus for some excellent work they did together developing a new product.

It is not possible to create the proper selection criteria using the Select Expert. The best it could do would be to print all employees in either the Training or Marketing departments in either the Charlotte or Cincinnati offices. But, you want Marketing from Cincinnati only, and Training from Charlotte only. You must edit the selection formula to change one "and" to an "or," and also move some of the statements around to accommodate the requirements. Click Show Formula in the Select Expert to modify the selection formula so that you get only the information that you want on your report (see Figure 4.7).

Use the Windows commands Ctrl+C and Ctrl+V to copy and paste in the formula box. Doing so makes changing formulas much easier.

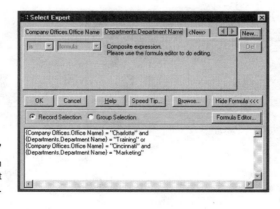

Figure 4.7

Edit the selection formula to meet your exact needs.

Opening the Formula Editor from the Select Expert

As mentioned earlier, SCR gives you the ability to open the Formula Editor right from the Select Expert. You may want to use the Formula Editor—instead of the basic formula text box on the expanded Select Expert dialog box—if you plan to write the selection formula from scratch or make extensive changes or additions to the formula created by the Select Expert. To use the Formula Editor for selection formulas:

1. Open the Select Expert using the toolbar button or click <u>R</u>eport, <u>Se</u>lect Expert.

2. With the Expert open, click Show Formula. This expands the dialog box showing the formula that SCR wrote based on any selection criteria you have already set up, as shown in Figure 4.8.

3. Click the Formula Editor button. The full Formula Editor opens with the current selection formula displayed in the formula text box, as shown in Figure 4.9. Change the formula here to have the full functionality of the Formula Editor available.

4. When finished editing or adding to the formula, click the Save and Close toolbar button to save the formula and close the Formula Editor.

5. Click the Hide Formula button to close the expanded section of the Select Expert. Notice that instead of the drop-down lists, the Expert now contains a message explaining that you have created a composite

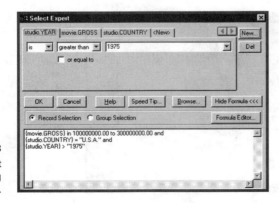

Figure 4.8

Expand the Select Expert by clicking Show Formula.

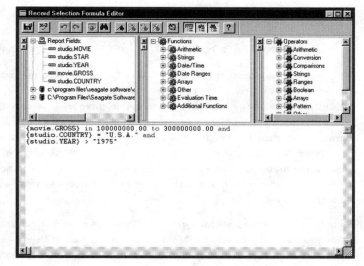

Figure 4.9

Open the Formula Editor from the Select Expert to edit the selection formula easily.

expression and that you must use the Formula Editor to do any editing. Click OK to close the Select Expert.

The composite expression message means that you can no longer use the tabs of the Select Expert to change the selection formula. However, you can still use the Select Expert to add new tabs and manipulate criteria that was not affected by the change in your formula.

Handling Null Values

Null values can be useful in selection criteria. If a field in your database has nothing entered in it, SCR considers this a null value. A null value in a field on your report prints nothing.

You can use null values to your advantage in selection criteria. If you need to include records with null values on your report, you can select the equal to option and leave the third drop-down list blank. This selection criteria statement includes all records where the specified field contains a null value.

When would you use this sort of selection criteria? Think of a financial report where you need to list all orders that have not been paid. You could set up

BASING GROUPS ON A SELECTION FORMULA

You may also realize that using the Select Expert to filter the groups on your report would be useful. For example, perhaps each group of your report sums the gross amount of money earned by each movie category (horror, action, comedy, and so forth). If you want your report to include only movie categories that have earned more than $100 million, you would set up a group selection formula to accomplish this. Note that since group selection formulas often involve a summary field (discussed more in Chapter 5), you'll probably work some on the main body of your report first, and then return to the Select Expert to add the group selection formula.

To use a selection formula for a group, in Step 1 on page 90 click Group Selection after you click Show Formula. Most of the Select Expert becomes unavailable. Click the Formula Editor button and the Formula Editor becomes available to write a selection formula for the group. Once you complete the formula, close the Formula Editor and follow the above steps just like you had set criteria for records.

Another option allows you to bypass the Select Expert and go directly to the Group Selection Formula Editor. To do so, choose Report, Edit Selection Formula, Group.

selection criteria based on the Date Paid field in your database, as shown Figure 4.10. If this field is null, you could assume that the payment has not yet been received. Therefore, you can use the Date Paid field in your record selection criteria to select only the unpaid records for your report. This report would be a great place to keep track of which customers had not yet paid their bill.

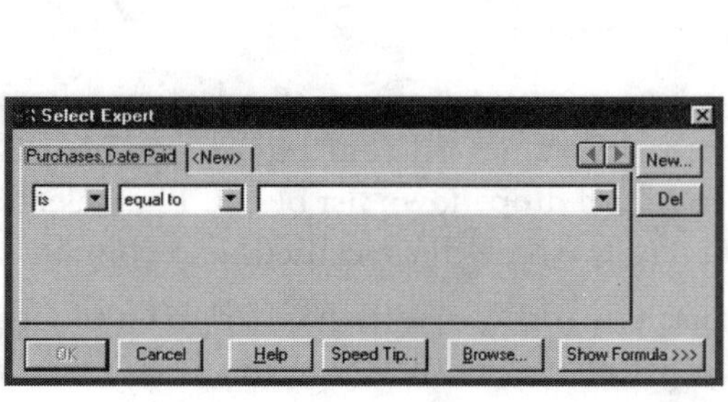

Figure 4.10

Setting selection criteria equal to null lets you pick specific records from your database for a report.

Converting Null Values to a Default

SCR gives you the option to keep the null values or convert them to the Seagate Crystal Reports default. If you keep the null values, then you can use them in your record selection criteria. If you will not be using null values in selection criteria, you might want to convert them to the SCR default: $0.00 for currency fields, 0.00 for number fields, and a blank for the other field types.

Why would you want to change null values to the default? If you have applied formatting to a field, you might want to change the null value to the default because SCR can format the default, but it cannot format a null value.

For example, your report may contain an Amount Paid field. If this field has a null value that you have not converted to the default, the field prints blank on your report. However, if you set this same report to convert null values to the SCR defaults, that same field would print $0.00.

Using Parameter Fields in Record Selection

Parameter fields allow you—and subsequent report users—to be prompted for selection criteria. You can create a parameter field, and then use it in the Select

SETTING REPORT OPTIONS FOR NULL VALUES

You can set up individual reports to convert null values to the defaults. Or, you can set a global option to change null values to the defaults for every new report you design.

For a single report, convert null values to the defaults by clicking File, Report Options, and selecting the Convert Null to Default check box. This makes the change for the current open report only.

To change this option globally, click File, Options. On the Reporting tab, select the Convert Null Field Value to Default check box. This converts null values to the default in any new reports you design.

Expert. (Chapter 8 covers creating and using parameter fields.) Basically, when you refresh a report with a parameter field in use, a prompting dialog box appears. The prompt asks the user for selection criteria values. The value the user picks or enters becomes the value the report uses in selection criteria.

For example, a basic human resources report might need to be run for each department in a company. The exact same report is desired, only one for Marketing, one for Human Resources, one for Training, and so on. Instead of creating multiple copies of the same report with slightly different selection criteria and maybe a different title, you can use a parameter field.

A parameter field in the selection criteria prompts users of the report to select the department to run the report for. Users would type the name of the department or select it from a list. The Select Expert uses the value entered by the user to determine which records to print on the report. This parameter field can also be used in the title of the report to print the name of the selected department.

Parameter fields can be used in many places in your report, starting with the selection criteria. Parameter fields used with formulas provide flexibility and the power to precisely format and control your data and how it prints on your report. After reading Chapter 6 on formulas and Chapter 8 on parameter fields, be sure to refer back to this section to help you brainstorm ideas for making the most of selection formulas.

Summary

This chapter went into more detail about using the Select Expert and gave several examples of when and why you might need to edit the formula created by the Expert. Hopefully, with the ideas presented here, you have a solid understanding that the Select Expert can be used as a tool to help you create the exact filter you need to have only the records you want on your report. Remember that if you experiment and the formula or criteria you write does not return the records you want, you can always change the criteria back to the way the Select Expert started. Click Undo several times, or simply delete all of your criteria and start over. You may need to experiment to find the right combination of criteria statements, formulas, and parameters.

CHAPTER 5

Standard Report Elements: Sorts, Groups, and Totals

- Sorting Detail Records

- Creating Groups

- Putting Groups into a Specified Order

- Creating Subtotals, Summaries, and Grand Totals

- Creating Running Totals

To finish the basics of report design, sorting, grouping, and totaling will be covered in this chapter. These basic elements of reports have Experts and functional dialog boxes to assist you—like the Select Expert you learned about in Chapter 4. In the previous chapters, you learned how to put basic information on your report; now you will learn how to sort, group, and summarize that information.

Sorting Detail Records

Sorting records on a report make the report easier to read and understand. Seagate Crystal Reports provides the Sort Order dialog box to help you sort the detail records on a report. You can have more than one level of sorting on any report. Without a sort order the records on your report print in their original order, the order in which they appear in your database.

Choosing Record Sort Order

Use the Record Sort Order dialog box to set the sort order of the records on your report. To assign a sort order to detail records:

1. Open the Record Sort Order dialog box with the Sort Order toolbar button or by clicking Report, Sort Records.

2. To designate a field to sort records by, click that field in the Report Fields list and then click Add to move the field over to the Sort Fields list (see Figure 5.1). You can also double-click a field to move it right over to the opposite list.

Figure 5.1
Use the Record Sort Order dialog box to set a sort order for the records on your report.

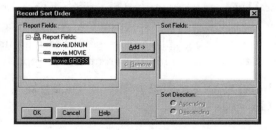

If you already have a group on your report, SCR shows the group in the Sort Fields list of the Record Sort Order dialog box. To remove or change this group, you must use the Change Group Expert.

3. You can adjust the sort direction by clicking Ascending or Descending in the Sort Direction area.

4. Add as many sort fields as you want by moving fields to the Sort Fields list. To remove fields from the Sort Fields list, select the field and click Remove.

Creating Groups

Creating groups organizes the information on your report and allows you to calculate subtotals for each group. For example, you could group by region and then city to organize the information on your report geographically. SCR does not limit the number of groups you can have on a report and offers many options for manipulating groups. When you insert a group on a report, SCR adds Group Header and Footer sections, one set for each group created. These sections allow space for the group name and subtotal fields.

Inserting One or More Groups

When inserting groups on your report, do so from the Design tab so that you can see how SCR adds the Group Header and Footer sections to your report. The following section outlines inserting one group on your report and how to change that group if need be. Repeat the same steps to add additional groups at any time while designing a report.

You can insert as many groups on a report as you need using the Insert Group dialog box. Several levels of grouping can organize vast amounts of information into more manageable pieces. Groups allow you to create summary or drill down reports, or insert a graph or cross-tab for each group. These topics are covered later in this book. To insert a group onto a report:

1. Click the Insert Group toolbar button or click Insert, Group to open the Insert Group dialog box.

Figure 5.2
Select a field to
base your group
on and the order
of the group on
the Insert Group
dialog box.

2. Use the first drop-down list to select the field you want to base your grouping on. The second drop-down list gives options for the order of the groups on your report (see Figure 5.2).

3. From the next list, select one of four options for group order: Ascending, Descending, Specified, or Original. Ascending and Descending refer to alphanumeric order. The next section, "Creating Custom Groups," covers specified order. Original order is the order that the records appear in your database, usually the order in which the data was entered.

4. Select the Keep Group Together check box to prevent groups from being split over two pages. Select the Repeat Group Header on Each New Page check box to repeat the group header section on as many additional pages as the group extends.

 If you check Keep Group Together and your first group does not fit on the first page of your report, the group skips page one and prints starting on page two, leaving the first page blank after the Page Header.

5. Click OK to close the dialog box. The Group Header and Footer sections appear on your report, with the Group Name field in the Group Header area.

 You can turn off the option that inserts the Group Name field into the Group Header section. Click File, Options and clear the Insert Group Name with Group check box on the Layout tab. If you have deleted the Group Name field from your report, you can add it again from the Others tab of the Insert Fields dialog box or by clicking Insert, Group Name Field. Move the field onto your report like you would any other field.

Figure 5.3

Use the Change
Group Expert to
select the group
you want
to change.

Once on your report, groups can be moved around. When you add a group, SCR always adds it as the lowest level group. If you want it to be at a higher level, you can drag it to where you want it in the section area to the left of the Design tab.

If you have a group on your report and you want to change it, you do not need to delete it and insert another. Instead, you can change everything about a group from the Change Group Options dialog box. To change a group field or options:

1. You have two options for opening the Change Group Options dialog box:

   Click Report, Change Group Expert, which opens the Change Group dialog box (see Figure 5.3). Select the group you want to change and click Options. The Change Group Options dialog box opens.

   OR

   In the Design tab, right-click the Group Header or Footer section of the group you want to change. A shortcut menu opens (see Figure 5.4). Click Change Group to open the Change Group Options dialog box.

Figure 5.4

Right-click the
Header or Footer
section of the
group that you
want to change to
open a shortcut
menu with the
Change Group
command.

Figure 5.5

Use the Change
Group Options
dialog box
to change the
definition or
options of a group
at any time.

2. The Change Group Options dialog box looks just like the Insert Group dialog box, except for the name. Here you can change the field you have based the group on, choose a different order, or select or clear either of the check boxes (see Figure 5.5). Click OK to close the dialog box.

Deleting a Group from Your Report

You have two ways to delete a group from your report. Click Edit, Delete Group, or select Delete Group from the shortcut menu opened from the Group Header/Footer sections. This removes both the Group Header and Footer sections and any fields contained within them.

Specified Order: Much More than Ordering Groups

Seagate Crystal Reports provides many options for creating custom groups. Specified order grouping gives you the ability to customize groups. You can change the order of your groups and also rename and set criteria for what records to include in a group. There are also many report-specific grouping needs not addressed directly by the Group Expert, but require a little creativity within SCR to work with your specific data and grouping needs.

Specified order grouping is one of the choices on the Insert Group dialog box in the group order drop-down list. Click this option to open a series of tabs and a dialog box to add and edit specified order groups. You can specify the exact order of existing groups if ascending, descending, or original order do not fit your needs. Also, you can create new groups by joining any existing groups and specifying their order.

Putting Groups into a Specified Order

If you've added a group to your report and the ascending/descending options don't meet your needs, you can use the specified order option. To change the order of existing groups:

1. With the Insert Group or Change Group Options dialog box open, select Specified Order from the group order list. This adds a Specified Order tab and opens it.

2. Select the groups that you want on your report from the Named Group list. Use the up and down arrows to the right of the group list to change the order of the groups (see Figure 5.6).

3. Select the option that meets your needs from the Others tab (see Figure 5.7). The Others tab has three options for dealing with any groups not included in the specified groups you created.

   - **Discard all others.** This option discards all groups not included in a specified group.

   - **Put all others together with the name.** This option puts all remaining groups into one group with the name "Others" or with whatever name you specify in the field box.

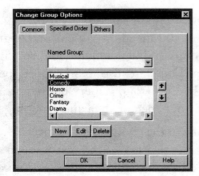

Figure 5.6

Change the order of existing groups by adding them to the Group list and adjusting the order.

Figure 5.7
Select what to do
with any groups
not included in
your named
groups using the
Others tab.

- **Leave in their own groups.** This option leaves the remaining records in their own groups and lists the groups, after the specified order groups, in original order.

4. Click OK to close the Insert Group or Change Group Options dialog box (depending on which one you used).

5. Preview your report to see the groups now in the order that you specified.

Customizing Groups

You may want or need to customize your groups. Using Specified Order grouping you can manipulate the actual name and contents of a group.

When you define a new named group, you can use an existing name or create a new name. Any of the existing groups can then be added to the new named group. You can use the Select Expert-like tabs to select which records from an existing group you want to include in the new group.

For any groups not defined or added to defined groups, the Others tab appears and provides three options for dealing with the "leftover" groups, as described in the last series of steps. To combine existing groups into new groups:

1. Navigate to the Specified Order tab in either the Insert Group or Change Group Options dialog boxes.

Figure 5.8

Set the name of a customized group and the records to be included in the group in the Define Named Group dialog box.

2. To customize an existing group, select the group from the Named Groups list and move it down into the list below. Then click Edit to open the Define Named Group dialog box.

   OR

   To create a new custom group, click New to open the Define Named Group dialog box (see Figure 5.8).

3. If you selected an existing group and clicked Edit, the name of the group appears in the Group Name box. If you clicked New, delete "untitled" from the Group Name box and type a name for your custom group. You could also type the new name in the empty Named Group box and click New.

4. Use the tabs to set which field values you want included in the specified group (refer to Figure 5.8). Note that you use the records in the field you chose for grouping, and combine these records together into one new group with the name you specified.

Though the Define Named Group dialog box has tabs that look similar to the tabs of the Select Expert, they do not have all the same functionality of the Select Expert tabs.

5. Click OK to close the Define Named Group dialog box and save the custom group that you just defined. SCR adds this group to the list on the Specified Order tab, as shown in Figure 5.9.

6. Repeat Steps 2 through 5 for each group you want to add or customize.

7. On the Others tab, click Put All Others Together With The Name to include all of the leftover records from the field into an Others group.

8. Click OK to close the dialog box. Preview your report to see the results of your custom grouping (see Figure 5.10).

Figure 5.9

All custom groups appear in the Specified Order tab. You can leave the remaining groups intact by clicking the Leave in Their Own Groups option on the Others tab.

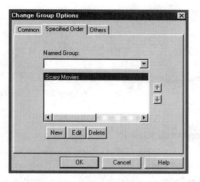

Figure 5.10

Specified Order grouping allows you to change the name and definition of some groups while leaving others as is.

Using the Group Tree

The Group Tree is a navigation tool for quickly jumping to a particular section of a report. The Group Tree appears on the left side of the Preview tab. By default, the Crystal Report Designer displays the Group Tree. You can turn the Group Tree on and off with a toolbar button. You can turn the Group Tree on and off with a toolbar button, or, if you don't want the Group Tree to display, go to the Layout tab of the Options dialog box and clear the Create Group Tree check box.

USING A FORMULA TO SORT GROUPS

Though you can use Specified Order grouping to handle many unique grouping requirements, you may find other creative ways to use SCR's features to handle the requirements for your report.

Using a formula, you can rename groups to a value that can be sorted properly. Say your database has a month field written out like "January." If you group by month, April or September will always be first, depending on whether you select ascending or descending order for your groups. As a workaround, you could write an If-Then-Else formula on which to base your grouping. The formula would be something like:

```
If {table.month field}="January" then "1" else

If {table.month field}="February" then "2" else
```

And so on for all 12 months. Then you would base your group on this formula. Since you might want the full month name listed as the group name on your report, you could suppress or delete the Group Name field (which would print the number you assigned to each month) and add the field—table.month—into the Group Header section. This prints the full name of the month for each group.

 The Group Tree lists each group on your report. If you have more than one level of grouping on a report, each group has a plus sign next to it. Click the plus sign to expand the next level of grouping in the tree, as shown in Figure 5.11.

 Disabling the Group Tree may improve the speed with which you can preview your report. Each time you preview a report, SCR creates the Group Tree. This means that SCR must read all of the groups and display them in the Group Tree. If you have many groups in a large report, or if you use formulas in your group selection criteria, it may take longer to open the Preview tab than if the Group Tree did not display by default.

The Group Tree is an excellent navigation tool for moving through your report. Since it lists all of the groups on your report, you can check that the groups you expect are present without having to go page by page through a

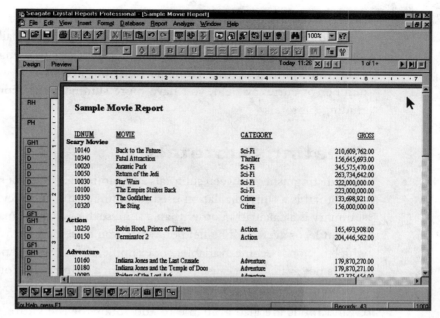

Figure 5.11

Use the Group Tree to navigate through a report to a particular group without searching page by page.

report. Also, you can navigate to the beginning of a certain group by clicking that group's name in the Group Tree, instead of scrolling page by page.

Creating Subtotals, Summaries, and Grand Totals

Use subtotals and summaries to apply a function to all the data generated in one field within a group. For example, use a summary to calculate a subtotal, average, or distinct count. Creating summaries in Seagate Crystal Reports can be as easy as clicking your mouse or as complex as writing your own formulas. This section will cover the summaries Seagate Crystal Reports makes directly available. Keep in mind, however, that if SCR doesn't offer the specific summary function you need (not likely, as it has almost 20 of them), you can always write a formula to do the summarization you want.

To calculate any kind of summary on a report, you follow the same basic steps. First, you select the field you wish to summarize. Then you open the

Insert Summary dialog box and select the summary function you want to apply to the field. SCR makes the appropriate functions available depending on what type of field you have selected. If you are working with a string field, you will have certain summary functions available. If working with a number or currency field, you have more summary function options, including subtotals.

Creating Subtotals

SCR distinguishes between subtotals and summaries in its menu commands. A subtotal is a sum calculation used for number and currency fields only. A summary is a calculation other than a sum, such as a count, maximum value, percentile, or average. The field on which you base the summary determines which options become available. For example, if you select a string field, subtotal is not available because you cannot sum a string field. You use subtotals and summaries in Group Header and Group Footer sections.

Grand totals are also available to add totals for the entire report. When inserting a grand total, you have all of the subtotal and summary functions available. See the section "Other Summary Functions" for a complete list of the available functions and where to find additional help regarding each function.

If you have selected a number or currency field, SCR gives you the option to calculate a subtotal. To insert a subtotal for a group:

1. With the field you want to subtotal selected, click Insert, Subtotal from the menu, or click the Insert Subtotal command on the field's shortcut menu. The Insert Subtotal dialog box opens (see Figure 5.12).

2. Select the group you want to subtotal from the list.

3. Click OK to close the dialog box. The subtotal field appears directly below the field it summarizes in the Group Footer section.

SCR does not insert a label for any summary fields. Use a text object next to the summary field to add a label. In the formatting chapter, Chapter 7, you will learn how to insert fields directly into text objects to have them trim automatically.

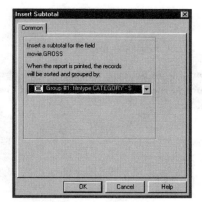

Figure 5.12

Use the Insert Subtotal dialog box to sum the selected field for a particular group.

Creating Summaries

Summaries are like subtotals, you just have many functions from which to choose. To insert a summary for a group:

1. With the field you want to summarize selected, click Insert, Summary or use the Insert Summary toolbar button. The Insert Summary dialog box opens, as shown in Figure 5.13.

2. Using the first list, select the summary function that you want to calculate for the chosen field. Nearly 20 functions are available.

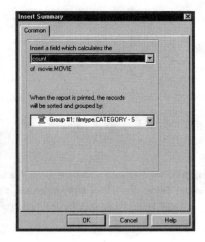

Figure 5.13

Use the Insert Summary dialog box to insert any of a large selection of summary functions.

OTHER SUMMARY FUNCTIONS

Only the sum function is offered from the Insert Subtotal dialog box. SCR offers many other summary functions in the Insert Summary or Insert Grand Total dialog boxes. Your options include:

- Sum

- Average

- Maximum

- Minimum

- Count

- Sample Variance

- Sample Standard Deviation

- Population Variance

- Population Standard Deviation

- Distinct Count

- Correlation

- Covariance

- Weighted Average

- Median

- Pth Percentile

- Nth Largest

- Nth Smallest

- Mode

- Nth Most Frequent

You can find excellent information in the online Help describing each of these functions. Search for the Summary Functions Index. Unfortunately, the index does not list all functions, so you may also need to search by the function name.

3. The second list gives you the ability to specify which group to add the subtotal or summary calculation for. If you have only one group on your report, only one group will be listed here.

4. Click OK and the summary field appears directly below the field it summarizes.

 You can insert a summary and a new group at the same time. Instead of selecting an existing group from the second list, click the field on which to base the new group. SCR then inserts the new group and summary field in one step.

Creating Grand Totals

Grand totals are totals for an entire report. They differ from subtotals and summaries, which calculate per group. All of the functions available for summarizing groups are also available for creating grand totals for the report. Like subtotals and summaries, you first select the field you want to summarize in order for the Insert Grand Total command to be available. To insert a grand total summary:

1. With a field selected, click Insert, Grand Total. You can also use the shortcut menu of the field you have selected. The Insert Grand Total dialog box opens (see Figure 5.14).

2. Select the summary function you want to calculate. Click OK to close the dialog box.

3. The summary field appears in the Report Footer section of your report, directly below the field it summarizes.

Figure 5.14

Use the Insert Grand Total dialog box to add grand totals to the Report Footer section.

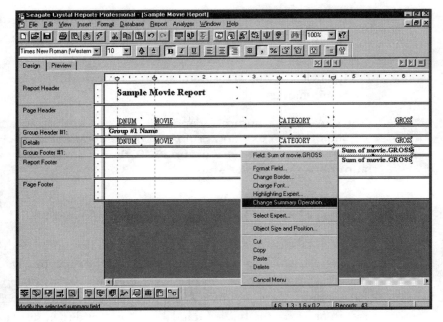

Figure 5.15
Open the shortcut menu from any summary field to change the summary operation.

Changing the Summary Operation

If you have added a summary field to your report, you can easily change the summary operation. With the summary field selected, click Change Summary Operation from the shortcut menu (see Figure 5.15). The Change Summary Operation dialog box opens, from which you can select a different summary function from the list.

Creating Running Totals

Running totals are similar to subtotals and summaries in the totaling operation used. They are different in that they calculate the accumulating total record by record, so you can see the total growing by each record.

You create Running Totals fields with the Running Total Field Expert. You could create a running total using a formula and taking advantage of the running total functions or using variables and evaluation time functions. However, the new Running Total Field Expert in version 7 makes the process much easier.

Using the Running Total Expert

Running totals require several steps, or parts, to work properly. A running total field needs to be instructed to start at zero. This is referred to as "resetting" the running total. For example, you'll need to reset the running total for each group if you want to calculate the running total for each group on a report.

Next, the running total needs to add each new record to the total before it. This second step is referred to as the actual running total. You insert this field into the Details section, thus printing the running total for each record on the report. To insert a running total:

1. Click Insert, Running Total Field. The Insert Fields dialog box opens with the Running Total tab in front. Click New to open the Create Running Total Field dialog box, as shown in Figure 5.16.

2. Type a name for the running total in the Running Total Name box.

3. Select the field for which you want to calculate a running total from the Available Tables and Fields list. Click the arrow button to move it to the Field to Summarize box.

4. Next, select a summary function from the Type of Summary list. Specify when and how often you want the running total to calculate in the Evaluate area.

Figure 5.16
Use the Create Running Total Field dialog box to create a running total for a report.

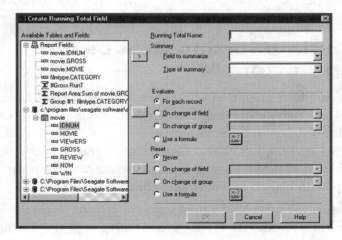

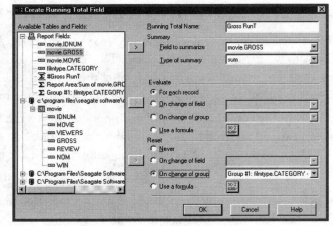

Figure 5.17

The options selected in this dialog box calculate a running total of the movie.GROSS field for each movie record. The running total resets when moving to a new category of movies.

5. Select if and when you want the running total to reset in the Reset area (see Figure 5.17). To set your running total to calculate per group, you need to reset it per group here.

6. Click OK to close the Create Running Total Field dialog box. Select the name of the running total you just created from the Running Total tab and place the field on your report.

7. Preview your report to see the running total (see Figure 5.18).

Change any aspect of your running total by clicking Edit on the Running Total tab of the Insert Fields dialog box. The running total field on your report automatically updates with any changes you make.

Limiting/Sorting Groups with Top/Bottom N

Once you have groups on your report, you may want to sort those groups based on a subtotal or other summary field. Using Specified Order grouping you learned how you can customize and combine groups, and set specific orders. Using the Top N/Sort Group Expert, you can sort your groups based on a summary field for that group, and you can have the report print only the groups with highest or lowest values in the summary field.

To begin, you must have a summary field on your report in order to use the Top N/Sort Group Expert. To sort and limit groups based on summary fields:

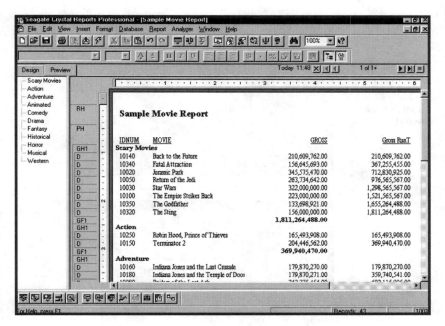

Figure 5.18
This report
contains the
running total,
GrossRunT,
defined by the
settings displayed
in Figure 5.17.

 1. Click Report, Top N/Sort Group Expert or the Top N Expert toolbar button. The Top N/Sort Group Expert opens.

2. In this Expert, a tab represents each group on your report. Select the tab for the group you want to sort.

3. From the first list box, select Sort All if you want to include all groups on your report. Select Top N if you want to include only groups with the highest values in a summary field. Or, select Bottom N if you want to include only groups with the lowest values (see Figure 5.19).

4. The second list includes each summary field on your report for the group listed on the tab, as shown in Figure 5.20. You can base a sort on one of the summary fields in the list.

5. If you selected Sort All, click either Ascending or Descending for each summary field you want to sort.

6. If you selected Top N or Bottom N, enter how many groups you want to include on your report by entering a number in the Where N Is box. If you want to include any remaining records in another group, select the

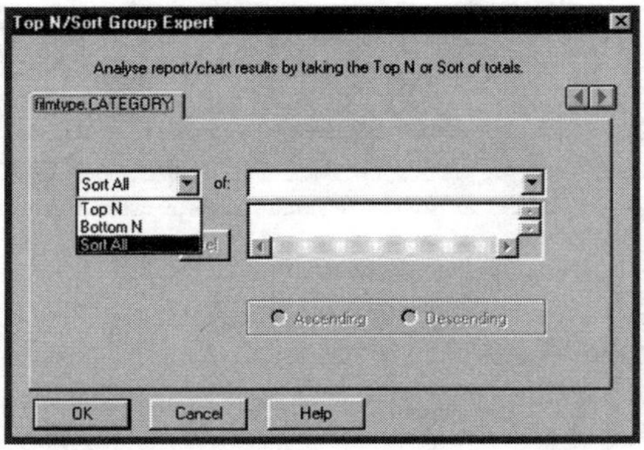

Figure 5.19

Use the Top N/
Sort Group Expert
to sort the groups
on your report
based on
summary
information for
each group.

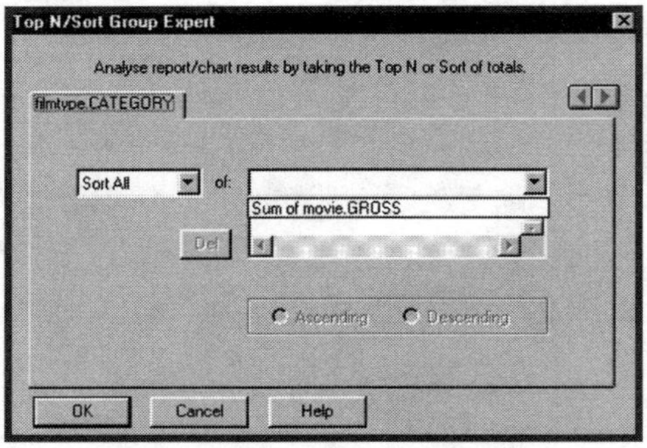

Figure 5.20

The second list
shows the
summaries you
have created on
your report.

Include Others check box and enter a name for the group (SCR supplies the name "Others" by default, but you can change it).

7. Click OK to close the Expert. Preview your report to see the effect of sorting your groups. Go back to the Top N/Sort Group Expert at any time to change or remove the sort.

Summary

In this chapter, SCR features that are commonly thought of as basic elements of report design were covered. Sorting and grouping records serve to organize information so that the report is easier to read and interpret. Summarizing information by group and for the entire report also serves an important role in managing the information on a report and getting more from it.

USING SUMMARIES TO SOLVE GROUP SORTING PROBLEMS

To ensure that your report doesn't merge information from two groups into one, you may need to group your records on a unique ID field. For example, say your report has a group for each manager, and your company has two managers named John Smith. You would need to group by a unique field like ManagerID—rather than by Manager Name—in order to ensure separate group sections for each of the two John Smiths. But, you do not want the groups sorted by that ID field, you want them sorted by last name.

Based on ManagerID, the groups would be in the numerical order of the ID numbers. And there's no direct way to tell the report to sort the groups based on a different field. However, you can use summaries to change the sort order of a group. Continuing the example, here's how you would make your report sort the manager groups by manager last name.

1. Drop the ManagerLastName field into the Details section of your report. From the field's shortcut menu, click Format Field. In the Format Editor, select the Suppress check box on the Common tab.

2. With the ManagerLastName field still selected, click the Insert Summary command from the shortcut menu. Select the maximum summary from the first list and select the ManagerID group from the second list. SCR inserts the maximum summary field in the Group Footer section.

3. Suppress the maximum summary field like you suppressed the name field in Step 1.

4. Click Top N/Sort Group Expert from the Report menu. On the tab for the ManagerID group, select Sort All from the first list box, then select the Max of ManagerLastName item from the second list box.

5. Preview your report. The manager groups now sort in order of the managers' last names.

The different grouping options help you organize your report in a meaningful way, regardless of how information was originally entered and organized in your database. As you become experienced in more advanced features of Seagate Crystal Reports, you will begin to use several features simultaneously to create reports that collect and format data exactly the way you want. Creativity working with sorts, summaries, formulas, and Top N functionality gives you many options beyond the "basics."

CHAPTER 6

The Power of Formulas

In this chapter, you will be introduced to writing Crystal formulas. You will learn how to write a formula using the Crystal Formula Language, including how to use functions provided by Seagate Crystal Reports and how to use the formulas in your reports. The goal is for you to gain a basic understanding of how to construct formulas, use functions, and integrate formulas into your reports.

What Is a Formula?

A formula is an instruction to Seagate Crystal Reports written in the Crystal formula language. Formulas provide a way to programmatically affect the data or static text in your report. They can also be used to provide additional information by performing calculations and analyses of existing data. Each field, group, or text block can use a formula to determine whether it appears on the report and what form it takes. Once you learn to use formulas as a tool, you will rely on them heavily to enhance your reports and have complete control over the data, look, and style of them as well.

What Can I Do with Formulas?

Seagate Crystal Reports has four types of formulas: field, conditional, record selection, and group selection. You write each of the four types of formulas in a similar manner, but you use them for different purposes.

- **Formula fields.** You insert formula fields into the report as fields, just like data or text fields. On the printed report, they cannot be distinguished from data or text fields. Use field formulas to perform calculations, analyze data, or print dynamic text.

- **Conditional formulas.** Use conditional formulas with other report elements to determine the function of that object. For example, if you have a data field that displays a datetime value, you can write a conditional formula to suppress the time portion if the time value is 12:00 midnight.

- **Record selection formulas.** Record selection formulas enable you to select only records meeting certain conditions. This is similar to a WHERE clause in a SQL statement and, like WHERE clauses, record selection formulas are optional.

- **Group selection formulas.** Group selection formulas enable you to select groups of records that meet certain conditions. This is similar to record selection formulas, but rather than acting on individual records, these formulas act on your report groups.

Formulas don't have to be complicated. With a simple formula, you can display a line of text in response to a value or condition on the report. For example, if the State field on a customer invoice report is "AZ," you could have the report print "Stores in Phoenix, Tucson, and Sedona." With more complex formulas, you can evaluate values and conditions of data and text, even other formulas. Formulas also make calculations, set variable values, format data, and more.

You can create dynamic text fields based on formulas that automatically update themselves. For example, you could create a formula to print a copyright notice. In the formula, you would use a function to print the current year (drawn from your computer's system date). Each year, the copyright notice would, essentially, update itself so you wouldn't have to revisit the report each year and make the change manually.

In conjunction with Seagate Crystal Reports Format Editor, you can use formulas to conditionally change the formatting of fields and static text. For example, in a report printing values in more than one currency, you could use a formula to format the number based on the type of currency. You could use a formula to print negative values in red. Or, you could write a formula that prints records in bold when they're less than one week old. If you find that you need to manipulate a field in your report, chances are you can do it with a formula.

Seagate Crystal Reports ships with a sample database called Xtreme. You can use this database, or a sample included with your own database software (such as the pubs database that comes with Microsoft SQL Server), to practice creating formulas. The tutorials included in this chapter use the Xtreme database.

Printing Calculated Values on a Report

When you need to calculate values and display them on a report, you can use a field formula very easily. Field formulas are inserted into the report as fields.

USING FORMULAS TO PRINT DYNAMIC TEXT

Report designers commonly use formulas to combine text and functions, as in:

"Copyright " + CHR(0169) + " " + ToText(CurrentDate,"yyyy") + " Acme Widget Company"

The formula above prints the following string:

Copyright © 1999 Acme Widget Company

Because the result of the formula is a string, the CurrentDate function must be converted to text, using the ToText() function. Since we only want to display the year, use the formatting string "yyyy" rather than something more familiar such as "mm/dd/yyyy". The resulting text, "1999," is then linked to the strings "Copyright ©" and "Acme Widget Company." At midnight on January 1, 2000, the string will display:

Copyright © 2000 Acme Widget Company

Using this formula to handle required changes to the text eliminates the need to edit the copyright string each year.

On the printed report, they cannot be distinguished from data or text fields. Use field formulas for performing calculations and analyses or printing dynamic text.

You can perform many types of calculations and analyses using field formulas. Field formulas can print numbers, text, Boolean values, currency values, dates, times, or datetime values. Any kind of field you need can be constructed with a field formula.

For example, suppose the Books Galore Publishing Company wants to write a report that shows royalty payments based on quantity of book sales for each author. The *titles* table contains the royalty percentage, and the *sales* table contains the quantity of books sold.

```
If {sales.qtysold} >= 10000
    Then {titles.royalty} * {sales.amount}
    Else 0.00
```

This formula prints the calculated royalty payment for authors whose books sold at least 10,000 copies, and prints 0.00 for all other authors. The formula would repeat for each author, and would perhaps be accompanied by a text field that identifies the author:

> Jones, Patricia: $2316.88
>
> Smith, Robert L.: $2667.34
>
> Doe, Chris: $0.00

The value beside each author's name is the result of the field formula shown in the above example.

Conditionally Altering Formatting and Other Report Characteristics

Using formulas and either the Format Editor (for fields and objects) or the Section Expert, you can specify how you want Seagate Crystal Reports to display or manipulate components of your report. Use conditional formulas with other report components to determine the function or appearance of that component. Conditional formulas can suppress a field, alter the format of the data in that field, or govern the appearance of the field such as font, size, and color—all based on a condition that you specify. Each report component can have no, one, or many conditional formulas attached to it.

For example, suppose you have sales from both the USA and England on a report. You want to display the correct currency symbol depending on the country in which the sale was made. For sales amounts where the country is USA, you want to display a dollar sign ($) and for sales amounts where the country is England, you'll want to display a pound sign (£).

To display the pound symbol (£), use the Seagate Crystal Reports function Chr() with the character value for the pound symbol (0163) within your formula. Use the Windows Character Map utility to find the character number for other characters not found on the keyboard.

Nearly anything that you want to alter based on the value of a field can be done with the combination of the Format Editor and Formula Editor.

Using Formulas in Record and Group Selection

Seagate Crystal Reports offers a powerful tool called the Select Expert, discussed in Chapter 4. Using the Select Expert and formulas, you can whittle your dataset down to your exact specifications.

Based on your selection or entry of items in lists and text boxes, the Select Expert constructs a record selection formula, which you can later edit if you so desire. Or, you can construct your own formulas for record or group selection without the use of the Select Expert, by using the Record Selection Formula Editor or the Group Selection Formula Editor.

The Record and Group Selection Formula Editors let you create formulas when the basic choices and options in the Select Expert don't meet the requirements of your report. For example, the Select Expert can only join conditions with "and." To join two conditions with "or," either edit the formula created by the Select Expert or build the formula yourself, as shown in Figure 6.1.

The Select Expert allows you to specify selection criteria for filtering records only. It does not work for group selection. To create group selection filters, you must construct formulas yourself with the Group Selection Formula Editor.

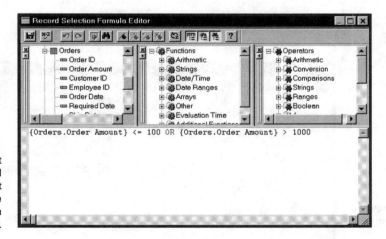

Figure 6.1

You can edit formulas created by the Select Expert in the Record Selection Formula Editor.

As powerful as the record selection formulas are, there are times when you'll want to limit not only the records included in the report, but the groups as well. The Group Selection Formula Editor lets you specify a formula to determine which groups to display (see Figure 6.2). Using group selection formulas, you can select sets of records based on a group summary, such as a subtotal, or on the group meeting a certain criteria. Say you want to show detail data only for customers living in the USA. You would add a group selection formula that identifies the country you want to filter.

You will notice when you use group selection formulas that the data appearing in the report matches the conditions of the formulas, yet the subtotals may include data that is outside the limits of the condition. This is because higher level groups are unaffected by the group selection formula.

For example, say your report groups on country first and region second. You want to show only data for the state of WA, so you create a group selection formula that looks like this:

```
GroupName {customer.region} = "WA"
```

When you view the report data, you see that detail data for all countries appear, but for the USA, only data for the state of WA appears. The subtotal for the USA will include data for all states, however. To avoid including totals for other states within the USA's subtotal, you would use a record selection formula to choose only records whose regions are "WA."

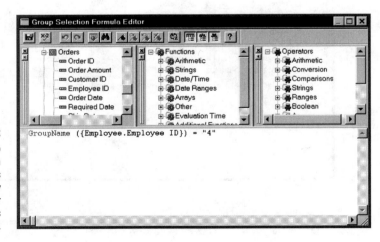

Figure 6.2

The Group Selection Formula Editor enables you to display data only for report groups you specify.

SUPPRESSING SECTIONS WITH CONDITIONAL FORMULAS

Sometimes you may want to use a conditional formula for an entire section, printing information in that section when the condition is met. For example, say you are using Seagate Crystal Reports to send letters to customers. If the customer's account is current, you want to print a coupon to use at Books Galore. If the customer's account is overdue, you want to print a reminder to mail payment today.

Your report could use two sections to differentiate the two types of responses. By setting conditional formulas on the suppress attributes for the two sections, you could suppress or print the coupon or the reminder, depending on the value of the customer account status field or current balance field.

To implement this, split the appropriate section (which may be the details, group header, or group footer section) into "a" and "b" sections by right-clicking the section and clicking Insert Section Below from the shortcut menu. Set up the "a" section to print a coupon and set up the "b" section to print a payment reminder.

Next, open the Section Expert for the "a" section by right-clicking the section and selecting Format Section (see Figure 6.3). Click the Conditional Formula button next to the Suppress option and enter a formula that will suppress the coupon section if the customer has an outstanding balance. For example, the formula might look like this:

{Customer.AccountBalance} > 0

Next, open the Section Expert for the "b" section and enter a formula to suppress the payment reminder section if the customer's account is paid in full, for example:

{Customer.AccountBalance} = 0

Now, if the customer's account balance is greater than 0, the coupon section ("a") won't print but the payment reminder section ("b") will; and, if the customer's account balance is 0, then the reverse will happen. You have now created a single report to accomplish two related purposes.

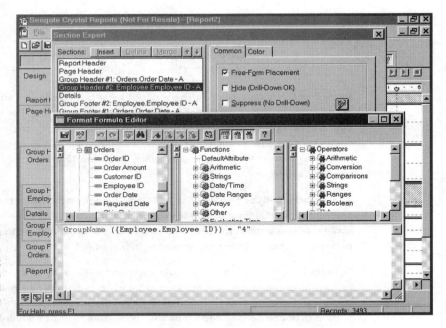

Figure 6.3

The Section
Expert dialog box
allows you to
enter conditional
formulas for the
report sections.

For more detailed information on selecting records and creating groups, refer to Chapter 4, "Selecting Records," and Chapter 5, "Standard Report Elements: Sorts, Groups, and Totals."

How Do I Write a Formula?

The procedure for writing formulas in Seagate Crystal Reports is quite simple. Writing formulas starts with opening the Formula Editor. The Formula Editor allows you to write, debug, and save your formulas. The following section introduces you to the Formula Editor, the rules for writing formulas, writing If-Then-Else statements, and using variables.

Using the Formula Editor

Seagate Crystal Reports includes a powerful Formula Editor to create fields that combine data, data and text, do calculations, format dates, and so on. The Formula Editor uses the Crystal formula language, which includes proprietary functions and commands to help you get the most out of your reports. You need to open the Formula Editor differently depending on the type of formula you are writing:

- **Formula fields**. Either click the Insert Fields button on the toolbar or click Insert, Formula Field. The Insert Fields dialog box opens with the Formula tab displayed. Either click New to start a new formula, or select an existing formula from the list and click Edit.

- **Conditional formulas**. Open either the Format Editor or Section Expert for the report object or section you want to conditionally modify. Click the Conditional Formula button beside the option for which you want to set a conditional formula.

- **Record Selection formulas**. On the Report menu, point to Edit Selection Formula, and then click Record.

- **Group Selection formulas**. On the Report menu, point to Edit Selection Formula, and then click Group.

Selecting Items from the Trees

The Formula Editor window contains three trees that can be very helpful when writing formulas: the Field tree, the Function tree, and the Operator tree (see Figure 6.4).

You can hide the trees by clicking the Field Tree, Function Tree, and Operator Tree buttons on the toolbar. The trees can also be resized by using the expand control to the left of each tree. You can easily add a field, function or operator to your formula by double-clicking the desired item in the tree.

On the left side of the window (see Figure 6.5), the Field tree displays the different kinds of fields currently defined for the report, such as database

Figure 6.4

The Formula Editor's Field tree, Function tree, and Operator tree make writing formulas more convenient.

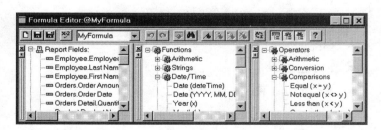

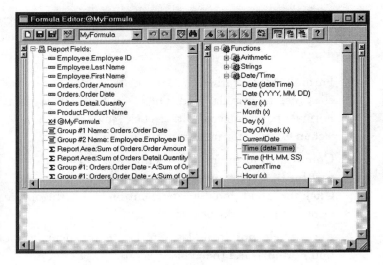

Figure 6.5

The Field tree shows the database fields, formulas, running totals and parameters defined in the report.

fields, parameters, formulas, running totals, summaries, and group names. The top of the Field tree lists those fields selected to appear on the report, beginning with database fields. The bottom of the tree reveals all of the tables used, so you can include a field in your formula that hasn't been placed directly on the report. Each field in the Field tree has an icon representing its type, such as a question mark (?) for parameters, an X+1 icon for formulas and a sum sign ( ) for r unning totals.

The Function tree displays the functions provided with Seagate Crystal Reports, grouped by function type (see Figure 6.6):

- Arithmetic
- Strings
- Date/Time
- Date Ranges
- Arrays
- Other
- Evaluation Time
- Additional Functions

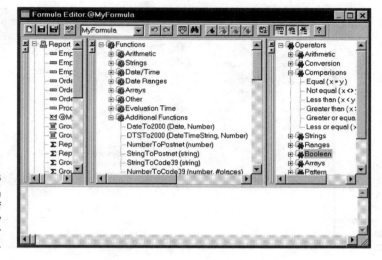

Figure 6.6

Use the Function tree to add one of SCR many functions to your formula.

Seagate Crystal Report online Help describes each function in detail. Search for the keywords "Functions Index."

The Operator tree displays the operators that can be used to define the formula, also grouped by type (see Figure 6.7):

- Arithmetic
- Conversions
- Comparisons
- Strings
- Ranges
- Boolean
- Arrays
- Pattern
- Other
- Scope
- Variable declarations

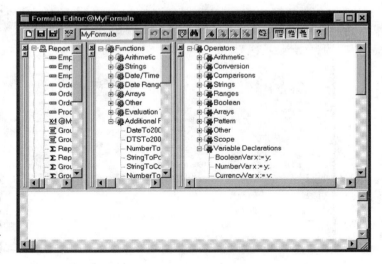

Figure 6.7

Double-click an item from the Operator tree to add it to your formula.

Again, Seagate Crystal Report online Help describes each operator in detail in the Operators Index.

The main difference between operators and functions is that functions generally return value or instruct SCR to evaluate data at a particular time, whereas operators are used on or between objects to compare them or change them in some way.

The Formula Text Box

Use the large text box at the bottom of the Formula Editor to write and edit your formula text. As you type or add items from the trees, the keywords and function names automatically appear in blue text and comments appear in green. You can change these colors by modifying the settings on the Editors tab of the Options dialog box (on the File menu, click Options).

The Formula Editor supports common Windows editing functions, such as Ctrl+C to copy and Ctrl+V to paste. You might want to use these functions to copy or move text from one formula to another, even from one report to another. To make your formulas more readable, follow some of these simple basic formatting guidelines:

- Type each keyword or command on a new line.

- Indent the text when a single command contains more than one keyword, such as with If-Then-Else statements.

- Capitalize (or type in all uppercase) commands and keywords to easily distinguish them from field names.

- Use double forward slashes to comment your formulas (//). When you or someone else returns to edit the formula months later, explanatory comments can be a real time-saver. Each comment line should begin with two slashes.

These tips are not requirements for writing formulas, merely suggestions. Refer to the next section, "Using the Correct Syntax," for information on rules for writing formulas.

Using the Correct Syntax

To write a formula, simply type it into the Formula Editor. The syntax of the formula depends on the functions you use; however, some general rules apply to all functions.

- For formulas with multiple statements, end each statement with a semicolon.

- Use curly braces {} around data fields.

- When referencing a formula within another, precede the formula name with an at sign (@).

- When using functions that take arguments, place parentheses around the arguments.

- Use double forward slashes (//) before comments.

- The Formula Editor is *not* case-sensitive.

- Database fields need to be addressed as *tablename.fieldname*. For example {Customer.Region}.

- Use square [] braces around array values and commas between each array value.

- To assign a value to a variable, use :=

- To check a value, use =

- You can't multiply 2 currency values together. (One must be a number).

- The plus sign (+) can link two strings.

- You can use double quotes "" or single quotes ' around strings. Remember to use the same type of quote marks to surround the string. ("Testing' is not valid.)

- When referencing a parameter field within a formula, precede the parameter field name with a question mark (?).

Formulas can be very simple, such as:

```
"This Report Designed by " + {File.Author}
```

The formula above outputs a string that displays:

```
This Report Designed by Destiny Mayer
```

Or they can be more complex, incorporating many different statements:

```
{@SalesGoal};
CurrencyVar cProjectedSalesAmt;
//get cProjectedSalesAmt from @SalesGoal formula
BooleanVar bGoal;
If cProjectedSalesAmt >= Sum (@BookPurchaseAmt, {stores.storeno})
  Then bGoal := true
   Else bGoal := false;
```

The formula above determines whether a store met its calculated sales goals. This chapter explains each of the elements used in this example (variables, If-Then-Else statements, comments, and references to other formulas).

Using Semicolons in Formulas

As mentioned, SCR requires semicolons to separate statements chained into a single formula. In a single formula, you may have variable declarations, If-Then-Else statements, variable assignments, and other kinds of statements. Each individual statement must be separated with a semicolon. Variable declarations are separate statements, usually inserted at the beginning of a formula (refer to "Using Variables in Formulas" later in this chapter for detailed information on using variables). To write a formula that simply declares a variable would not be terribly useful. You need to add other statements that make calculations and assign a value to the variable in order to make the formula useful. You accomplish this by using semicolons to add statements to a formula.

As an example, you might have two separate formulas that accomplish one task: to conditionally print one sentence or another on the report. The first formula calculates the value for a variable. The second formula then evaluates the variable and determines which line of text to print on the report. By using a semicolon at the end of the If-Then-Else statement, however, you can combine the two formulas into one.

```
//The first formula calculates the value for the variable cBonus;
CurrencyVar cBonus := 0;
If {Employee.State} = 'MS'
    Then If {Employee.Commissions} > 1000
        Then cBonus := 100
        Else cBonus := {Employee.Commissions} * .01
    Else If {Employee.State} = 'AR'
        Then If {Employee.Commissions} > 1000
            Then cBonus := 75
            Else cBonus := {Employee.Commissions} * .01;
//The second formula, which is now merged with the first, determines which
//sentence to print, depending on the calculated amount of cBonus.
If cBonus >= 100
    Then 'You earned ' + ToText(cBonus)
    Else 'Your bonus was ' + ToText(cBonus) + ': Try again next month'
```

The If-Then-Else Statement

Use If-Then-Else statements in your formulas when you want the report to take a certain action based on the true or false value of a condition, as in the following example:

```
If {Orders.ShipDate} < {Orders.PaymentReceivedDate}
    Then TRUE
    Else FALSE
```

If-Then-Else statements have three parts:

- **If.** The condition to be evaluated.
- **Then.** Specifies the action to take place if the condition is met.
- **Else.** Specifies the action to take place if the condition is not met.

The Else clause of the statement is optional. If you do not want to specify an action if the condition fails, simply omit the Else clause, as in the following:

```
If {Orders.OrderAmount} >= 100
    Then Discount = .10
```

Writing If-Then-Else Statements

Using the Xtreme sample database packaged with Seagate Crystal Reports, you can create a report using the following tables:

- Orders
- Employee
- Orders_Detail
- Product

1. Choose the table or tables you want to include in your report.

2. Next, place the following fields on the report:

   - Orders.OrderDate
   - Orders.OrderAmount
   - Employee.EmployeeID
   - Employee.LastName
   - Employee.FirstName
   - Orders_Detail.Quantity
   - Product.ProductName

3. Then, sort the report by:

   - Orders.OrderDate
   - Employee.EmployeeID

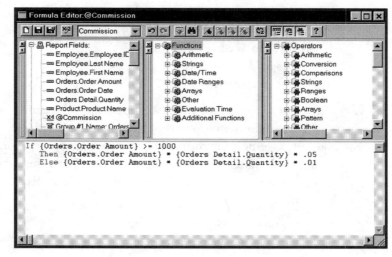

Figure 6.8

This If-Then-Else statement calculates a commission based on the customer's order amount.

4. Create totals for the following fields and place them in the Report Footer section:

   ▪ Orders.OrderAmount

   ▪ Orders_Detail.Quantity.

5. Now, add a formula to the report to calculate the employee's commission. Name it "Commission." In the text box in the Formula Editor, enter an If-Then-Else statement that evaluates the Orders.OrderAmount field as follows. If the value is $1,000 or more, then the commission is five percent of the amount of the order times the quantity; if the order amount is less than $1,000, then the commission is one percent of the amount of the order times the quantity (see Figure 6.8).

Nesting If-Then-Else Statements

You can nest an If-Then-Else statement within another in order to write more complex conditionals. One conditional can be part of the Then statement for another conditional. To write a multi-condition If-Then-Else formula, follow this syntax:

```
If  (first  condition)
   Then If (second condition)
      Then (second action)
       Else (second alternative)
    Else  (first  alternative)
```

If the first condition is not met, SCR performs the action in the last Else clause (the "first alternative") without even evaluating the second condition. For example, assume your company had a special incentive program for employees in certain states. To print a report showing bonuses for sales associates whose commission was over $1000 and who lived in Mississippi, you might use this formula.

```
If {Employee.State}= 'MS'
   Then If {Employee.Commissions} > 1000
      Then 100
      Else {Employee.Commissions} * .01
   Else 0
```

This formula would give a $100 bonus to employees in Mississippi who earned over $1000 in commissions, a one-percent bonus to employees in Mississippi who earned less than $1000 in commissions, and no bonus to employees outside of Mississippi.

A nested If-Then-Else statement can also function as the Else clause of another If-Then-Else statement, as in the following example:

```
If {Employee.State} = 'MS'
   Then If {Employee.Commissions} > 1000
      Then 100
      Else {Employee.Commissions} * .01
    Else If {Employee.State} = 'AR'
      Then If {Employee.Commissions} > 1000
         Then 75
         Else {Employee.Commissions} * .01
```

In this statement, the company gives incentive bonuses to sales associates in Mississippi and Arkansas. In each state, sales associates with less than $1,000 in commissions receives a bonus of 10% of their commission. But, in Mississippi, associates with over $1,000 in commissions receive a $100 bonus; associates in Arkansas with over $1,000 in commissions receive a $75 bonus. Sales associates in all other states receive nothing.

WRITING NESTED IF-THEN-ELSE STATEMENTS

You can expand the If-Then-Else statement you created in "Writing If-Then-Else Statements" into a nested If-Then-Else by adding the following condition:

If the order amount is $5,000 or more, the commission is ten percent of the order amount times the quantity value (see Figure 6.9).

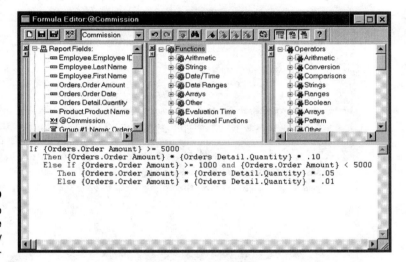

Figure 6.9

Add conditions to an If-Then-Else statement by nesting them.

Using If-Then-Else Statements in Conditional Formulas

Though you'll probably use If-Then-Else statements in many of your field formulas, you always use some form of this statement in your conditional formulas. However, the conditional formula may not appear to contain an If statement, because the If, Then, and Else keywords may be implied.

When assigning a conditional formula to a format option that can only be on (true) or off (false)—such as the suppress option—modify the syntax of the If statement to include only the condition. For example, let's say you have a report where you want to suppress a field if it contains a value less than 100. For the suppress option of that field, you would enter the following formula:

```
{TableName.FieldName} < 100
```

However, the formula implies an entire If-Then-Else statement:

```
If {TableName.FieldName} < 100
   Then <Suppress the Field>
   Else <Don't Suppress the Field>
```

For options that have a choice of several values, make the If, Then and Else clauses explicit in the conditional formula. For example, suppose you want to set a conditional formula on the decimals option of an Amount field. For countries whose currency is not divided into tenths or hundredths, you want

WRITING CONDITIONAL FORMULAS

Insert the Commission formula you wrote in the previous tutorial into the report beside the Order Amount field. Using the Format Editor, set the Font Color attribute with a conditional formula to print the commission amount in Green if it is $500 or more. Note that when you click the Conditional Formula button beside the font color, a special category of functions appears in the Function tree, called Colors. Use these functions to identify the color to use in your formula (see Figure 6.10).

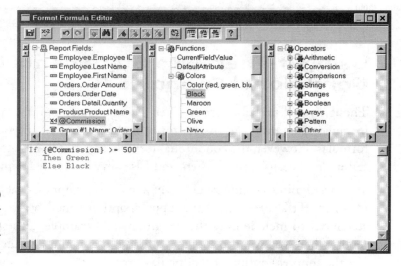

Figure 6.10

Use the Color functions to set a field's font color conditionally.

to show an integer. If the value of the currency type field is less than 10, you want the Amount field to display two decimal places; otherwise, you want to display an integer (no decimal places). You would assign a conditional formula similar to the following to set the decimals option for the Amount field.

```
If {Country.CurrencyType} < 10
    Then 2
    Else 0
```

Other properties of fields can be governed by formulas this way as well. For example, you could set the text color for the field based on the same condition.

```
If {Country.CurrencyType} < 10
    Then Green
    Else Black
```

This formula (written on the field's font property) prints the selected field in green if the currency type was less than 10.

 Some parameters, such as font style, cannot be set with a conditional formula, and do not have a Conditional Formula button beside it.

Datatype Consistency: Problems and Solutions

SCR has a particular requirement for If-Then-Else statements: The Then and Else clauses must use the same datatype, such as string or number. For example, SCR would generate an error against the following formula because the Then clause assigns a numeric value to the variable and the Else clause assigns a string value.

```
If {OrderAmount} > 100
    Then Discount := .10
    Else Discount := "none"
```

Even without using a variable, which must be declared as a particular datatype, the formula would still generate an error.

```
If {OrderAmount} > 100
    Then .10
    Else "none"
```

Though you may solve this problem by simply assigning the value 0 (zero) in the Else clause, this may not be a satisfactory solution for your report. A creative report designer could probably come up with many different ways to work around the datatype consistency requirement when they want to conditionally print values of differing datatypes. To help you start thinking creatively, the following two examples show you ways to work around SCR's datatype consistency requirement. The following example is correct:

```
NumberVar Discount;
If {Orders.OrderAmount} >= 100
    Then Discount := .10
    Else Discount := 0
```

Both the Then and the Else clauses assign a numeric value to the variable Discount. If the Else statement did not reference a number, Seagate Crystal Reports would generate an error. The two clauses can reference *different* variables or values, but they must have the same datatype.

```
NumberVar Discount;
NumberVar EmployeeNo;
If {Orders.OrderAmount} >= 100
    Then Discount := .10
    Else EmployeeNo := {Employee.SalesClerkID}
```

Changing Datatypes with Crystal Functions

There may be times when you will want to display a field as a different data type. Seagate Crystal Reports includes several functions that allow you do to this with ease:

- **ToText()**. Converts numeric, currency, date or datetime values into text.

- **ToNumber()**. Converts text into a numeric value (for example, converts "100" into 100).

- **ToWords()**. Converts numeric values into words (for example, 1001 converts to "one thousand one")

Say, for example, you have a database field that stores numeric values as strings. If you want to perform any calculation on those numbers, you must first convert them to numeric values with the ToNumber() function.

Suppressing Datatypes that Don't Support Null

One complication in the use of the If-Then-Else statement concerns Time or DateTime values. Time and DateTime datatypes cannot be null. This means you cannot construct an If-Then-Else statement that evaluates a field, uses a datetime or time value in the Then clause, and a null in the Else clause. For example, assuming that the {employee.hiredate} field has a datetime datatype, the following formula would generate an error.

```
If {employee.id} <= 100
   Then {employee.hiredate}
     Else  null
```

Even though SCR won't accept this formula, you can still get the intended result. Instead of creating a formula, place the datetime field directly on the report. Then, for the suppress option of the field, enter a conditional formula that contains this code:

```
{employee.id} > 100
```

Now the field prints only for employees whose ID is between 1 and 100.

Stacking Formulas and Fields

Sometimes you'll have a situation where you want to print only one of several values depending on a particular condition. For example, you might want to display a numeric value if a condition exists otherwise print text, such as "no entry" or "zero." But entering the formula like the following example generates an error.

```
If {Sales.Amount} <> 0
   Then {Sales.Amount}
     Else  "Zero"
```

Because the datatypes used in the Then clause and the Else clause differ, SCR cannot process this formula.

Stacking formulas and fields enables you to accomplish the desired objective. *Stacking* refers to the placement of one field on top of another field and setting the properties for them such that they are mutually exclusive. This can be done by enabling the Suppress If Zero property on one field and using a formula for the other that prints the desired string if the value is zero.

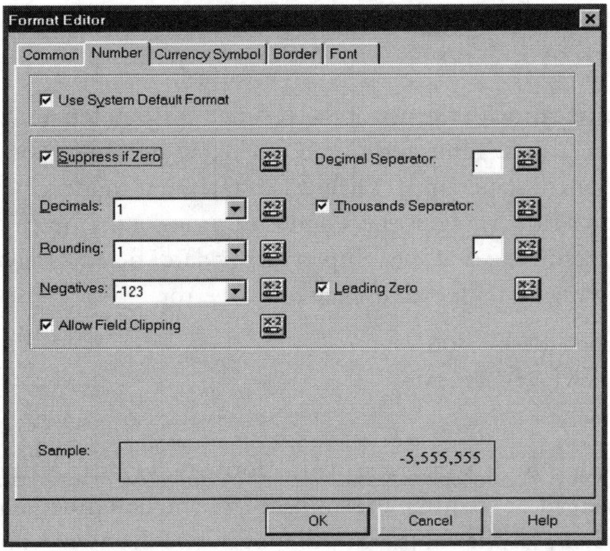

Figure 6.11

Select the Suppress If Zero check box to keep a field from printing when it contains a zero value.

1. Place the field you want to print on the report and select the Suppress If Zero check box (see Figure 6.11).

2. Create a new formula that prints the desired text string when the field contains a zero value, something like the following:

```
If {Sales.Amount} = 0
    Then "Zero"
    Else ""
```

3. In the report, place the formula field directly on top of the first field. If the original field value is zero, SCR suppresses the field and the formula prints the text "Zero." If the field is not zero, SCR displays the field value and the formula prints the text in the Else clause, which is an empty string ("").

This technique works well for fields you want to replace with text if the value is zero. In a similar manner, use the Suppress option with a conditional formula when you want to print text based on a value other than zero. For example, say you want to create a report that calculates and prints a value for salespeople who have earned a commission by generating over $1,000 in total sales, but prints a text message for salespeople who have not sold enough to

Figure 6.12

Placing a conditional formula on the suppress property of a text field prints the field only when the condition has not been met.

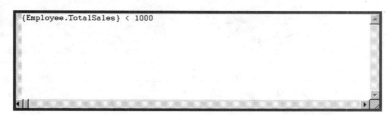

earn a commission. To accomplish this, you would create a formula to calculate the commission, but suppress it if TotalSales fall below $1,000. And, you would create a second formula that prints a message when TotalSales fall below $1,000 or otherwise prints an empty string.

To further illustrate, first create a formula, such as the following, to calculate the commission.

```
CurrencyVar Commission := {Employee.TotalSales} * .1
```

1. Place the formula field on the report, and then add the following formula to the field's suppress property.

   ```
   {Employee.TotalSales} < 1000
   ```

2. Create a text field that displays a message for salespeople who didn't earn a commission and set a conditional formula on the suppress property, as shown in Figure 6.12.

3. Place this text field directly on top of the formula field. Now, when TotalSales equals $1,000 or more, the formula prints the calculated commission and the text field is suppressed. But, when TotalSales falls below $1,000, the formula is suppressed and the text field prints the text message. The resulting report might look something like Figure 6.13.

Using Variables in Formulas

Variables are extremely useful in writing more complex formulas. They can reduce the number of lines of formula code you have to write. Once you declare and initialize a variable, you can access the value for that variable in other formulas. For example, you may have one formula that calculates a bonus level based on employee performance, and another that determines what dollar value

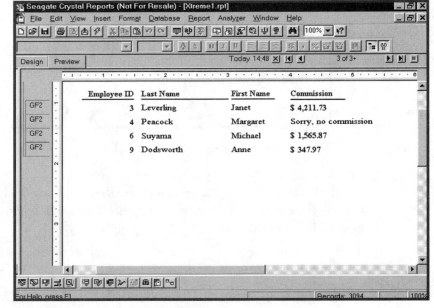

Figure 6.13
Stacking fields lets you print fields of different types depending on conditions you specify.

to add to the employee's paycheck for a given month. The variable that calculates the bonus level can be used to make the second calculation.

Declaring a Variable

Before you can use a variable in a formula, you must declare it. By declaring a variable, you specify the name of the variable, and the type of data the variable will contain. Two or more formulas can share a variable, but each formula must declare it. In this way, one formula can set the value of a variable and another formula can evaluate the variable and act on it. Naming a variable has three simple rules:

1. The variable name can be up to 254 characters.

2. Variable names are case *insensitive* (MyVar is the same as myvar).

3. A variable cannot have the same name as an operator or built-in function.

The datatypes that can be stored in variables include:

- String
- Number

FUNCTIONS FOR FORMATTING TEXT

Sometimes a field in a database has extra spaces that you want removed. Two functions provided with Seagate Crystal Reports make it easy to trim off extra spaces before and after a field.

For example, say in your database the Customers.CustomerID field has been defined as a char(10) field. Even if there are only 6 characters in the CustomerID, the field uses 10 character positions; the database application automatically fills in the remaining positions with spaces.

Now, say you need to print a list of customers with their ID numbers, but you want to avoid unnecessary spaces. Instead of printing a report that looks like this:

104468	Marguerite	Jones
104469	Tina	Parker
104470	Scott	Smith

You could use a formula to link the strings and trim off spaces:

Trim({customer.id}) + " " + Trim({customer.firstname}) + " " + Trim({customer.lastname})

This example prints:

104468 Marguerite Jones

104469 Tina Parker

104470 Scott Smith

- Currency
- Boolean
- Date
- Time
- Datetime

The method for declaring a variable is essentially the same regardless of the variable's datatype. The basic variable declaration consists of two words, the variable type and the variable name, as in the following examples:

```
CurrencyVar cBonus;
StringVar sEmployeeName;
BooleanVar bEarnedBonus;
```

Many report designers name their variables such that the first letter of the variable name represents the datatype of the variable, such as "n" for number variables or "c" for currency variables. By doing this you can tell by the variable's name what datatype it contains.

It is also a good idea to use complete words for your variable names rather than possibly confusing abbreviations. For example, the variable name "dBdate" could mean BusinessDate or BeginDate.

Assigning a Value to a Variable

After declaring a variable, you can assign or change its value. To assign a value to a variable, enter the variable name, a colon and equal sign, followed by the value. A few examples follow:

```
cRaise := 1000;
cCurrentSalary := {employee.salary};
cNewSalary := cRaise + cCurrentSalary;
```

Be sure to use both the colon and equal sign to assign a value to a variable. Using only the equal sign will *not* assign the value to the variable. It will tell the Crystal formula language to test the variable against the value and see if they are the same, producing a boolean statement.

Initializing a Variable

If you want to assign a value to a variable immediately in your formula, you can combine the declaration and assignment statements. Assigning a value to a variable at the beginning of a formula is especially useful in the event that conditions in the formula do not otherwise assign or reset the value. Ideally, you want to make sure that all variables have some value assigned to them, even if you do not end up using them. Initializing a variable is a good habit to get into.

To set the value of a variable when you declare it, type the variable declaration as described previously, the colon-equals assignment operator (:=), then the initial value of your variable. For example:

Table 6.1 Default Values for Variables	
VARIABLE TYPE	DEFAULT VALUE
NumberVar	0
CurrencyVar	0
BooleanVar	False (No,0)
DateVar	date (0,0,0)
StringVar	empty string (" ")
DateTimeVar	No default
TimeVar	No default

```
StringVar sEmployeeName :={Employee.FirstName} + ' ' + {Employee.LastName};
BooleanVar bEarnedBonus := {Employee.Commission} > 1000;
```

If you do not explicitly assign a value to a variable, Seagate Crystal Reports automatically sets the default value, as shown in Table 6.1.

Conditionally Assigning Values to Variables

You can use the If-Then-Else statement to determine what value a variable should have. For example, the following formula determines what bonus a sales associate has earned.

```
CurrencyVar cBonus;
If {Employee.State} = 'MS'
   Then If {Employee.Commissions} > 1000
      Then cBonus := 100
      Else cBonus := {Employee.Commissions} * .01
   Else If {Employee.State} = 'AR'
      Then If {Employee.Commissions} > 1000
         Then cBonus := 75
         Else cBonus := {Employee.Commissions} * .01
```

You can then place the formula on the report to print the variable value, or you can reference the variable cBonus in another formula.

Using Variables in Other Formulas

You can assign a value to a variable in one formula, then reference that variable (with its assigned value) in another formula. When you do this, the second formula must make explicit reference to the first in order to have access to the variable and its assigned value. To assign a value to a variable which can then be referenced in another formula, type the name of the formula in which the variable's value was assigned within curly braces ({}). This is Seagate Crystal Report's method of "passing a value" from one formula to another.

You can also share variable between formulas by using a scope identifier when you declare the variable. Scope identifiers tell SCR whether the variable should be available to formulas throughout the report, in subreports or just within the formula that is using it. Scopes include:

- **Global**. Allows variables to be used within any other formula or function in the report.
- **Shared**. Allows variables to be used within a subreport.
- **Local**. Restricts variables to use within the formula that defines them.

Another way to force SCR to evaluate your formulas in a specific order is to use the Evaluation Time functions. They allow you to specify when the formula is to be evaluated. In particular, you can use the EvaluateAfter() function to specify which formula you want SCR to evaluate before the current formula. In the example below, Formula A, which calculates the value of cBonus, is always evaluated first.

```
EvaluateAfter(@FormulaA)
CurrencyVar cBonus;
If cBonus > 100
    Then "You did it!"
    Else "Sorry, try again."
```

To further illustrate, the formula @SetBonusValue contains the following code:

```
CurrencyVar cBonus;
If {Employee.State} = 'MS'
    Then If {Employee.Commissions} > 1000
        Then cBonus := 100
        Else cBonus := {Employee.Commissions} * .01
    Else If {Employee.State} = 'AR'
```

```
        Then If {Employee.Commissions} > 1000
            Then cBonus := 75
            Else cBonus := {Employee.Commissions} * .01
```

Another formula, @PrintBonusStatement, needs to use the value assigned to the variable cBonus.

```
CurrencyVar cBonus;
If cBonus >= 100
    Then 'You're a winner!'
    Else 'Try again next month'
```

If you attempt to reference the cBonus variable in @PrintBonusStatement before the @SetBonusValue has been evaluated, the value of cBonus will be 0 (the SCR default for currency datatypes). Make sure that the @SetBonusValue is placed in a section above the @PrintBonusStatement. Or, use an Evaluation Time function in the @PrintBonusStatement formula. For more information on Evaluation Time functions, please see SCR online Help.

Using an Array in a Formula

Arrays are variables that can hold several values (elements) at a time. Use arrays when you want to predefine a list of values to use later when evaluating data or another variable's value. You declare and assign values to an array variable like single value variables, with three exceptions:

1. The word "array" follows the variable declaration.

2. Square brackets after the assignment operator identify the values (elements) stored in the array. A comma separates each element.

3. The array can contain up to 100 elements.

Use the keyword "in" to evaluate a field or variable value as it relates to elements in the array variable, such as in an If-Then-Else statement.

```
CurrencyVar cBonus;
NumberVar array nMonthsForBonuses := [1,4,7,10];
If Month(CurrentDate) in nMonthsForBonuses
    Then cBonus := ({Sales.Commissions} * .10)
    Else cBonus := 0
```

To extract one or more specific values from an array, follow the array—or the array variable—with a subscript. A subscript is either a single number or a range (in the format "x to y") within square brackets, illustrated in the following examples:

```
[1,2,3,5,7,11,13,17,19,23,29,31][3]
nPrimeNumbers [1 to 3]
```

The above examples contain arrays of prime numbers, one as an explicit array and the other as an array variable. The first example would return 3, the value in the third position in the array. The second example returns the values 1, 2, and 3, which are the first through third elements in the array.

Say, for example, the ABC Widget Company wants to promote its new SuperWidget to all customers who bought products from ABC Widget Company last year. Depending on which products the customer bought, ABC Widget Company wants to offer a variable discount on the new SuperWidget.

```
CurrencyVar cDiscount = 0;
CurrencyVar Array Level1 := [101,102,105,110,120,127,133];
CurrencyVar Array Level2 := [115,118,122,125,129,130];
CurrencyVar Array Level3 := [131,132,135];
If {orders.productid} in Level1
    Then cDiscount := .10
      Else If {orders.productid} in Level2
        Then cDiscount := .15
          Else If {orders.productid} in Level3
            Then cDiscount := .20;
```

Using a Range in a Formula

A range is like an array in that they both contain more than one value, but ranges fall between a minimum and maximum value whereas arrays are distinct, specified values. For example, say you have a report that sorts data by employee pay grade and you want a list of employees within a certain salary range. You could ask users to select a pay grade number (via a parameter, discussed in Chapter 8) and then use their selection to determine which employees get a raise with a formula:

```
BooleanVar bRaise := false;
NumberVar range PayGradeToRaise := 1 to 10;
If ?SelectedPayGrade in PayGradeToRaise
    Then bRaise := true
     Else bRaise := false
```

If the user enters a pay grade in the range of PayGradeToRaise, that is, between one and ten (inclusive), the formula evaluates to true. To declare a range variable, keep in mind the following rules:

- The word "range" follows the variable declaration operator.
- The name of the range variable follows the word "range."
- The word "to" separates the minimum and maximum values of the range.

In Seagate Crystal Reports, ranges have two main uses:

- To specify a range of values from a list of all possible values.
- To specify a range of characters from a string.

Use the word "in" to evaluate a field or variable value as it relates to the range variable, such as in an If-Then-Else statement.

```
NumberVar range Grade_A_Range := 90 to 100;
BooleanVar bEvaluateBonusQuestion := false;
If StudentTestScore in Grade_A_Range
    Then EvaluateBonusQuestion := true
     Else EvaluateBonusQuestion := false
```

When you want to specify a range of values from a list of all possible values, first consider the entire list of values, then determine which ranges you want to test for. For example, suppose your Human Resources department wants a report that lists the salary ranges for the various pay grade levels starting from the lowest salary and going to the highest. Then, suppose that the lowest salary is $10,000 per year and it is pay grade 1. The highest salary might be $100,000 per year, at pay grade 20. To list the salaries and the pay grades in which they fall, you might use ranges such as:

```
CurrencyVar Range Grade1 := 10,000 to 14,200;
CurrencyVar Range Grade2 := 14,201 to 18,400;
CurrencyVar Range Grade3 := 18,401 to 22,600;
```

```
CurrencyVar Range Grade4 := 22,601 to 26,800;
```

In a formula that uses these ranges, you can determine whether employees have reached the salary cap for their position, or whether a raise will move them into the next pay grade.

When you want to specify a range of characters from a string, first identify the entire string, then use a subscript to identify the substring. For example, say you want a report that identifies the area of town to which your pizza restaurant delivers the most pizza. You can determine the area of the city from which the customer called based on the telephone exchange (the first three digits of the customer's telephone number). Using a range, you can get the exchange from the customer's phone number, and then you might want to use an array to match the exchange against lists to find out from what city the customer's order originated.

```
StringVar Range sExchange := {customer.telephone}[1 to 3];
StringVar Array sPhoenix := [217,304,470,650,863,954,955,956]
StringVar Array sMesa := [366,496,517,545,827,832,833,834]
StringVar Array sScottsdale := [301,368,424,675,765,808,840,860]
If sExchange in sPhoenix
    Then "P"
    Else If sExchange in sMesa
      Then "M"
       Else If sExchange in sScottsdale
          Then "S"
          Else "Other"
```

Order of Precedence in Formulas

When Seagate Crystal Reports encounters an equation in a formula, it performs the operations based on a set order of precedence. SCR evaluates all multiplication and division operations first (in the order they appear), followed by addition and subtraction operations (also in the order they appear).

```
x + y * z
```

In this example, SCR multiplies y and z together first, and then adds x to the product.

Say you have a report in which you want to calculate the total sale amount including sales tax.

```
CurrencyVar cTotalSale := 0;
CurrencyVar cCalculatedSalesTax := 0;
CCalculatedSalesTax := {sales.amount} * {order.qty} * {state.taxrate}
cTotalSale := cCalculatedSalesTax + {sales.amount} * {order.qty}
```

This formula first multiplies the sales amount by the order quantity, then multiplies the product by the sales tax rate for the state. Next, it multiplies the sales amount by the order quantity, and to the product adds the calculated sales tax amount.

If you need to change the order of precedence within your formula, you can put parentheses around items to move them up in the order of precedence.

```
(x + y) * z
```

In this example, SCR performs the addition operation first, and then multiplies the sum by value z.

Formulas themselves also have an order of precedence that must be taken into consideration if one formula relies on a calculation or evaluation performed in another formula. The placement of the formulas within the report determine the order in which SCR evaluates them. SCR evaluates s formula in the Report Header before a formula in the Group 1 Header, and so on. In addition, by referencing Formula A within the definition of Formula B, you can guarantee that SCR will evaluate the referenced formula, Formula A, before Formula B, regardless of where you place them on the report.

For example, you might have a formula that evaluates the commission amount for each sales associate and stores it in a currency variable called cCommission. Another function evaluates the cCommission amount and prints a line of text depending on its value. By referencing the first formula within the second, you guarantee that SCR sets the value of cCommission properly and the correct text appears.

Summary

This chapter focused on the power of formulas and how they work. You learned the difference between a conditional formula and a formula field, how to construct a formula—including syntax rules—and how to use formulas in reports. You also learned about If-Then-Else constructs and variables.

With formulas, you can make your reports more powerful by evaluating conditions and data, by performing calculations and taking action on the results, and by altering the elements on the reports to suit the needs of your report and its data.

CHAPTER **7**

Formatting
Your Report

- Basic Report
  Formatting

- Formatting Fields

- Absolute vs.
  Conditional
  Formatting

- Formatting
  Sections

- Adding Graphics
  to Your Report

Seagate Crystal Reports provides many formatting options. You have the ability to control page attributes, which affect the printed copy of a report. You can also control field and object formatting for all fields you insert into a report. The options available depend on the type of field being formatted. For example, a text object has standard options, a number field has decimal place and other number specific options, and a date field has separator and date formatting options. Formatting fields on a report will be covered in this chapter, along with how to customize the default formatting settings to meet your specific needs.

As you know from Chapter 6, SCR gives you the ability to create conditional formulas wherever you see the Conditional Formula button. In this chapter, you will learn another way of performing conditional formatting using the Highlighting Expert. You will also explore how to format entire sections of a report—giving you flexibility with the standard sections and the ability to add more sections to a report.

Basic Report Formatting

To control the page layout options for a report, use the Printer Options command. To toggle between portrait and landscape orientation, click File, Printer Setup. From the resulting dialog box you can also select a different size of paper, such as legal, if your printer has the ability to print that size.

 If you share a report with others or use it on a computer not connected to a printer capable of any expanded size, letter size is the best choice.

Set the margins through File, Page Setup. Doing so opens a dialog box where you can specify margins. Using the system default allows this report to print correctly on any machine because it automatically uses that machine's system default.

SCR provides many options for controlling how your Design and Preview tabs look, along with settings for retrieving data and null values. Most of this information is scattered about this book as notes and tips where the information is pertinent. This chapter contains information on setting global options for field and object formatting.

Formatting Fields

When inserting fields on a report you may find that the fields do not always have the exact format you need. SCR uses the default format specified on the Fields and Fonts tabs in the Options dialog box (accessed via File, Options). You can, however, format that field right on your report. You can format one or many fields at a time by selecting either just one field or more than one field, and then applying formatting options.

 You can set and change the default formatting options to meet your needs. The section "Setting Default Formatting Properties" later in this chapter covers setting defaults.

Formatting Options for Every Field Type

The options available to format a field depend on the type of field you are formatting. You can change the field type using the Formula Editor. For example, you might have a string field that you want to format as a number. Using the function ToNumber() in the Formula Editor, you can change the string field to a number field, and then you can format the field as a number.

You must have the field you want to format selected. This way, SCR provides the correct formatting options based on the field's data type. Remember, you can select more than one field to format at a time. If the fields have different datatypes, SCR makes available only the common formatting options for the group. To change a field's format:

1. With one or more fields selected, click Format, Format Field. The Format Editor opens, as shown in Figure 7.1. You can also right-click the field you want to format and select Format Field from the shortcut menu.

 If you have selected more than one field to format, the menu command reads Format Objects instead of Format Field.

2. Three tabs in the Format Editor are available for all fields: Common, Border, and Font. Click from tab to tab to set formatting options for the fields selected. As you select formatting options for the selected fields

Figure 7.1
Use the Format
Editor to change
the format of
any field.

from any of the tabs, the Sample area at the bottom of the Format Editor shows you the formatting options in use.

Next to most options throughout the Format Editor, the Conditional Formula button indicates that you can write a formula to set a formatting option based on the value of the field or other conditions in the report. For more information on conditional formatting refer to Chapter 6 and to the section "Absolute vs. Conditional Formatting" later in this chapter.

3. Click OK at any time to apply to formatting options you selected and close the Format Editor.

General Field Attributes: The Common Tab

The Common tab of the Format Editor provides basic formatting options for any field (see Figure 7.2):

- **Suppress.** Use this option to suppress a field from printing on a report. You may want to sort based on a field, but not have that field print on your report. Or sometimes in formulas you need a field for part of a variable, but you do not want that value to print on your report.

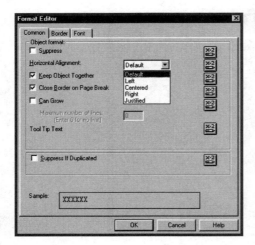

Figure 7.2

The Common tab is one of the three tabs available in the Format Editor dialog box.

- **Horizontal Alignment.** Open the list next to this option to view the alignment choices. Horizontal Alignment aligns whatever object you have selected within its field.

- **Can Grow.** This option is similar to text wrapping. By default no database fields automatically wrap or grow. This way you can be assured of the formatting and placement of fields on a report. Select the Can Grow check box to allow a field to grow vertically if need be. Use this option for fields in your database where comments or text may have been entered and you need to accommodate for any length of field. The field grows down vertically only; it does not grow horizontally. You need to manually size your field horizontally.

- **Tool Tip Text.** Click the Conditional Formula button to open the Formula Editor and write the text you would like to have appear in a text bubble when users rest their mouse pointer over a particular field. The formula is simply the text you want to show, enclosed in either single or double quotes. A sample formula would be "Report title for Movie Report" or "Gross movie sales per category." View the tool tip on the Design and/or Preview tab by resting the pointer over the field with the Tool Tip Text formula. If you do not see the tool tip text, go to File, Options and select the check boxes named Show Tool Tips in Design and Show Tool Tips in Preview.

- **Suppress If Duplicated.** This option suppresses a field if it contains the same value more than once consecutively. For example, you might have a report that prints a record for each order a customer placed in the past month. If the customer placed more than one order, you don't want to repeat the customer name on each record. Using the Suppress If Duplicated option, the customer name would be listed only once, on the line with the first order.

- **Keep Object Together.** This option is selected by default. When selected, this option prevents any page breaks within the section.

- **Close Border on Page Break.** This option does exactly as the name implies. It closes any border on the bottom of a page and reopens it at the top of the next page.

Borders and Background: The Border Tab

The Border tab provides options for adding and formatting a border and the background for a field (see Figure 7.3):

- **Tight Horizontal.** If you want to have a border around just the data in a field, not the entire field, select this check box. It narrows a field to accommodate just the width of the data within the field.

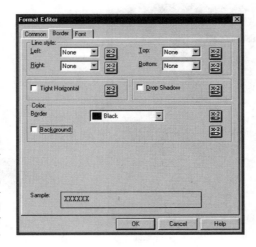

Figure 7.3
Use the Border tab to create a border, drop shadow, or background shading for a field.

- **Drop Shadow.** Select this check box to create a drop shadow around the selected field.

- **Color.** From the Border list, select the color for a border or drop shadow. If you want the field to have a background color, select the Background check box and select a background color. The border and background color cover the entire field area, as shown in the sample at the bottom of the Format Editor.

- **Border Tabs.** Each border line has its own set of line options. Use the drop-down list for each border line to select the type of line you want to use. You must make these selections one at a time.

Setting Text Style and Color: The Font Tab

The Font tab provides options for formatting the text style of the selected fields. Font, style, size, and color are some of the options available (see Figure 7.4). SCR also offers a Formatting toolbar that contains the font formatting options. If it's not available in your application window, you can turn it on using View, Toolbars.

Figure 7.4
Use the Font tab of the Format Editor to set the font for the field selected.

THE ARGUMENT FOR USING STANDARD FONTS

The Font list presents a comprehensive list of all the fonts available on your computer; however, not all fonts are necessarily available for use on your reports. If you select a non-Windows standard font, SCR may not support it. When you preview the report, SCR reverts to the default font selected for the field type on the Fonts tab of the Options dialog box if you select a non-supported font. SCR supports most standard fonts for database fields, while many of the fancy or symbol fonts are available for text objects only. Test the font you select by previewing your report. Fonts that change the basic spacing of letters or fields are not available.

Special Formatting Options

The Format Editor opened from any field contains the Common, Border, and Font tabs. String fields have only these three tabs, where other field types have additional tabs that provide formatting options for the particular field type. When you open the Format Editor, the dialog box holds all tabs related to the datatype of the field you have selected.

Date, Time, and Date/Time Fields

When formatting a Date, Time, or Date/Time field on a report, one to three additional tabs become available in the Format Editor.

Date Tab

The Date tab becomes available with either date or date/time field types (see Figure 7.5). This tab contains many options, and you should definitely experiment with them and watch as the sample at the bottom of the dialog box changes.

- **Date Type**. This option gives you the ability to select a pre-set formatting type. You do not need to set any custom options if you use one of the options here.

- **Format, Order, and Day of Week**. These areas of the dialog box give you the options to format the date to read exactly as you want. Any options you set show in the Sample box on the bottom of the dialog box.

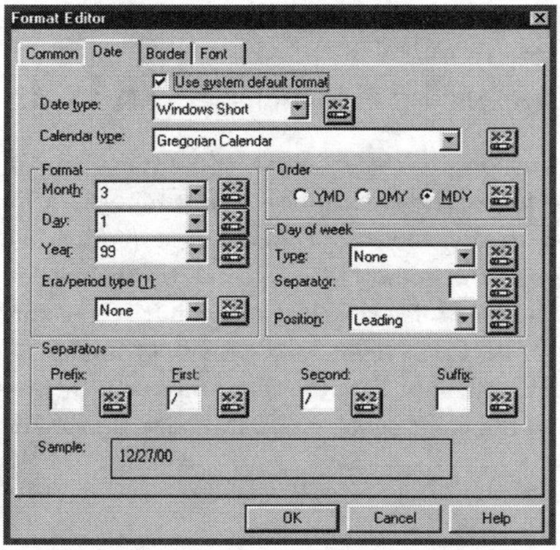

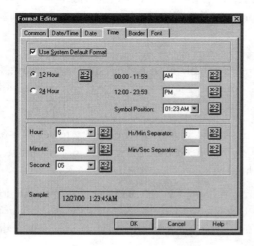

Figure 7.5

The Date tab provides many options for formatting a date or date/time field.

- **Separators.** This box allows you to set the separator between each different element of the date. Also, there is a separator box in the Day of Week section. You can enter a space (using the spacebar) in this field.

Time Tab

When formatting a Time field on a report, a Time tab appears in the Format Editor with the other tabs (see Figure 7.6). The options are:

Figure 7.6

Use the Time tab to format time fields on a report.

- **12 Hour and 24 Hour.** You can control whether to print the time using a 12-hour clock (usually with AM/PM added) or using a 24-hour "military" clock.

- **Symbol Position.** Set where you want the AM/PM to print if you use the 12-hour clock.

- **Hour, Minute, and Second.** Change the format of each component of a time field, including separators, as appropriate.

- **Use System Default.** This option forces SCR to use the data formats from either the International dialog box (Windows 3.x) or the Regional Settings dialog box (Windows 95/98), accessed via the Windows Control Panel. This option is on by default unless you change the option globally under File, Options, or manually change any of the tabs listed above.

Date/Time Tab

When formatting Date/Time fields, both the Date and Time tabs appear on the Format Editor. Additionally, a Date/Time tab offers a few supplementary options (see Figure 7.7). You can choose whether to print the date first or the time first, and whether to use a separator symbol between the two.

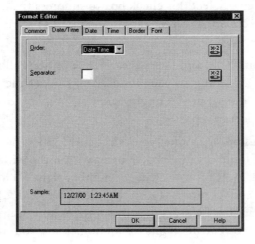

Figure 7.7
The Date/Time tab provides options for the format of Date/Time fields on your report.

Figure 7.8

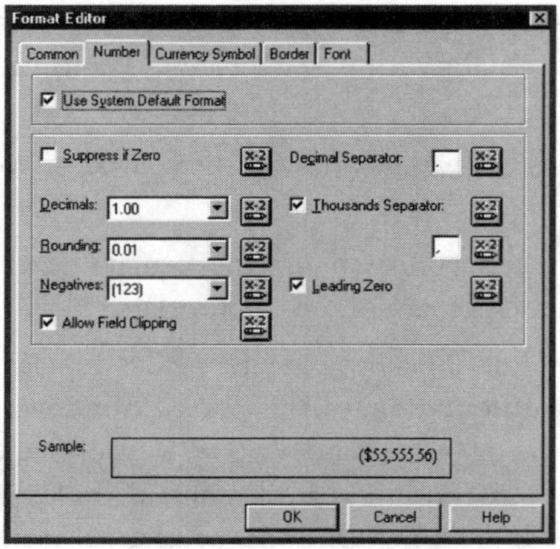

On the Number tab, you can choose to use the system default, or set up a custom format for numbers in the selected field.

Currency and Number Fields

Both the Number and Currency Symbol tabs appear in the Format Editor whether you selected a number field or a currency field to format.

Number Tab

The Number tab gives you options for formatting numbers on a report (see Figure 7.8). Many options help you customize the way numbers look on a report regardless of how they exist in your database:

- **Suppress If Zero.** Select this check box to suppress the field if it equals zero. The field still exists on the report and figures into any calculations, but does not print a zero.

- **Decimals, Rounding, and Negatives.** These options allow you to format numbers according to your needs. You can set the global default under File, Options, but you might find that number formatting needs differ from report to report.

- **Allow Field Clipping.** When you select Field Clipping, SCR cuts off extra digits of numbers too long to print within the width of the field. When cleared, SCR prints a string of number signs (#) to let you know that the number does not fit within the size of the field. Clear this check box for your number fields, especially subtotals and summaries. Otherwise, SCR may be cutting digits off a number and you won't realize it.

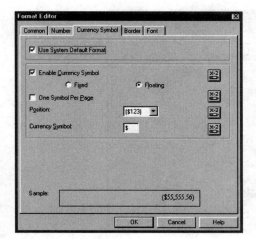

Figure 7.9

Use the Currency
Symbol tab
to format a
currency symbol
if you want to
include one with
the number.

- **Decimal and Thousands Separators.** Both of these separators can be set to whatever character you want, including a blank space.
- **Leading Zero.** Selecting this option prints a leading zero for any values under one, as in 0.45 instead of .45.

Currency Symbol Tab

The Currency Symbol tab gives you the option to print a currency symbol if appropriate, as well as choose the currency symbol and where to place it in relation to the number (see Figure 7.9).

- **Enable Currency Symbol.** If you select this check box, a currency symbol prints on your report. You can specify exactly where to print the symbol.
- **Position and Currency Symbol.** These two options allow you to set the position and type of symbol you want to use. Change the options and watch the sample to see exactly how the symbol will print on a report.

Boolean Fields

The Boolean tab gives you formatting options for Boolean fields (see Figure 7.10). SCR makes the Boolean tab available for both Boolean fields from your database and Boolean formulas that you write using the Formula Editor.

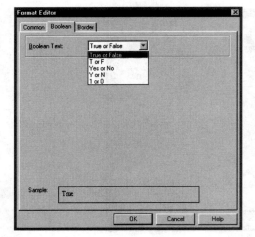

Figure 7.10

The Boolean tab sets formatting options for all Boolean fields used on a report.

Setting Default Formatting Properties

SCR gives you the ability to set the system defaults for all of the above formatting options. SCR installs with the defaults already set, but you can change the defaults to suit your needs at any time. To change the default formatting options:

1. Click File, Options and go to the Fields tab. This tab has buttons for each field type (see Figure 7.11).

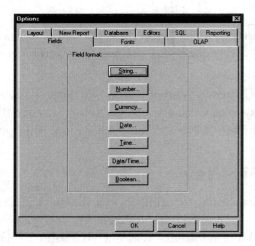

Figure 7.11

Click the button for each field type to set default formatting options.

2. Click the button of the field type you want to format, and then set the default formatting options. The field type determines the available tabs.

3. The String, Number, Currency, Date, Time, Date/Time, and Boolean fields all use the tabs shown in the previous section, "Special Formatting Options."

 When you change the default formatting settings, they apply to any new fields you add to the report, but do not retroactively reformat fields that already appear on the report. During a proper Windows shutdown, SCR saves any changes you make in the Options dialog box.

Absolute vs. Conditional Formatting

Absolute formatting refers to formatting that applies to a field or object each and every time it prints. So far, this chapter has discussed setting absolute formatting. *Conditional formatting* applies only if a condition is met. In Seagate Crystal Reports, conditional formatting takes precedence over absolute formatting.

Accounting provides a common example for using a conditional formula. For example, say a value in a currency field is less than or equal to zero, and you want the amount printed in red. You'd open the Formula Editor, click the Conditional Formula button next to the Color field on the Font tab, and enter the following formula.

```
If {amount} <= 0
   Then Red
```

The formula does not require an Else clause. When the condition does not apply, SCR automatically applies the default formatting.

There are countless examples of conditional formulas and when they could be useful in your reporting. Chapter 6, "The Power of Formulas," described the steps for creating a conditional formula. To help you start thinking creatively about what you could do with conditional formulas, the next section offers a few examples.

Conditional Formula Examples and Tips

In Table 7.1, you'll find examples of a few different conditional formulas that change certain formatting options for fields. These are sample formulas. Use your creativity to tell SCR exactly what you want it to do, so that your report data looks exactly the way you want it to.

Conditional Formatting with the Highlighting Expert

New in version 7, Seagate Crystal Reports offers the Highlighting Expert. This handy tool gives you the means to conditionally format font colors, borders, and background colors for number and currency fields without writing any formulas. You may find it easier to use the Expert because you can create

Table 7.1 Examples of Formatting with Conditional Formulas

GOAL	FORMAT ATTRIBUTE	FORMULA
All values zero or less print in red	Format Editor, Font tab, Color	If {table.field} £ 0 Then red Else black
Change the background color of any field whose payment has not been made and is 45 or more days past due	Format Editor, Border tab, Background Color	If CurrentDate - {Orders.Ship Date} > 45 and {Orders.Payment Received} = False Then yellow Else nocolor
Display field in red if less than average. The formula calculates the average of a group then compares the value of the field to the calculated average	Format Editor, Font tab, Color	If {table.field1} < Average ({table,field2}, {table.field3}) Then red Else black

NEW FUNCTIONS TO USE IN CONDITIONAL FORMULAS

Version 7 of Seagate Crystal Reports offers two new functions especially useful with conditional formulas, CurrentFieldValue and DefaultFieldValue.

Use the CurrentFieldValue function in place of a database field name, variable name, or calculation in a formula. The conditional formula then applies to the current value of the field without having to recalculate the value. Though this function can be used in most any conditional formula, it is especially useful when conditionally formatting cross-tab fields, which are basically summary calculations. For example, instead of the formula "If @Sum({amount}, {customer}) < 1000 Then red", you could simplify the formula with this new function: "If CurrentFieldValue < 1000 Then Red".

DefaultFieldValue allows you to set an absolute formatting option, and then use that default in the conditional formula. For example, you may want to format a field to have a green font color if a condition is met, and a blue font color otherwise. Change the font color on the Font tab of the Format Editor to blue, and then behind the Conditional Formula button your formula would be "If {table.field} > 20000 Then Green Else DefaultAttribute".

simple or complex conditional formatting, and you can see all font, border, and background conditions at once.

 The Highlighting Expert is only available with number and currency fields.

 You can use the Highlighting Expert for fields in cross-tabs, as well as individual fields on the Design tab of a report.

Once you open the Highlighting Expert, you'll see that the information and criteria you set in the Item Editor side of the Highlighting Expert dialog box show in the Item List (see Figure 7.12). The formatting options you set in the Item Editor show in the sample at the bottom of the Item Editor. To use the Highlighting Expert:

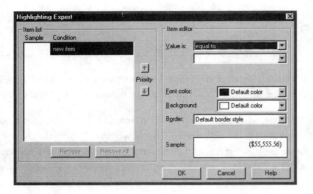

Figure 7.12

Use the Highlighting Expert to conditionally format number and currency fields.

1. Select the number or currency field for which you want to apply conditional formatting. Click Format, Highlighting Expert or right-click the field and click Highlighting Expert from the shortcut menu. The Highlighting Expert opens (refer to Figure 7.12).

2. In the Item Editor area, select a condition from the Value Is list. Type or select a value from the other drop-down lists.

Once you set criteria for formatting in the Value Is box, that value appears in the Item List as a condition. This way you can see all conditions you have set for the selected field.

3. Once you have a condition set, select the formatting options you want to use: Font color, Background, or Border (see Figure 7.13). These formatting options apply when the condition you entered has been met. For example, you might select font color and change it to red.

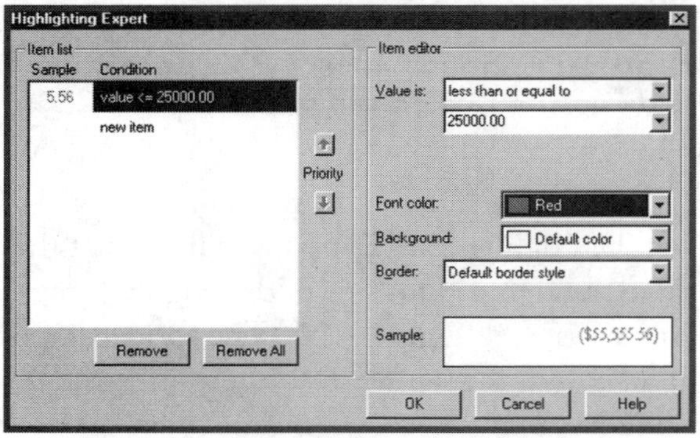

Figure 7.13

Set as many conditions as you want for a field. The Highlighting Expert lists each condition in the Item List.

4. Click "new item" in the Item List to start a new formatting criteria. If your first criteria worked with the font, you can set a second criteria to work with the background color.

5. Click OK to close the Expert and save the conditions you set. Go back to the Highlighting Expert at any time to add or delete conditional formatting.

Formatting Sections

Just as SCR gives you many ways to format fields, you can also format entire sections of a report. By formatting sections, you can force a page break after each group or hide the Details section of a report to create a summary report. Due to the nature of sections, formatting them differs from formatting fields. You do not set the font or style of a section; rather, you control how the sections act within your report. You will find that being able to manipulate and format sections greatly enhances your ability to create reports that look and act just as you need them to.

The Section Expert provides many absolute formatting options along with buttons for writing conditional formulas. The next section describes steps to open and use the Section Expert. Then the following sections describe in detail some of the options available to you using this Expert. To open and use the Section Expert:

1. Open the Section Expert by clicking Format, Section, or by clicking the Format Section toolbar button. The Expert can also be opened from any of the section area shortcut menus.

2. From the Sections list, select the section you want to format (see Figure 7.14).

3. Use any formatting options from either the Common or Color tabs. Note that along with check boxes to turn options on or off, you can write conditional formulas using the Conditional Formula buttons.

4. Use the Insert, Delete, and Merge Buttons to insert additional sections on your report, delete sections you added, or merge sections together.

5. Click OK to close the Section Expert and save any changes or formatting that you set.

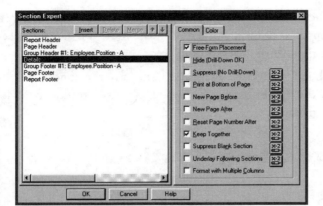

Figure 7.14

Use the many options available in the Section Expert to format the sections of your report.

Setting Page Breaks

Due to the sectional nature of Seagate Crystal Reports, you can set page breaks between sections. Select the New Page Before or New Page After check boxes on the Section Expert to set page breaks. For example, to have each group start on a new page, open the Section Expert for the Group Footer and select the New Page After check box. If you had summary information for the entire report in the Report Footer area and wanted that section to print alone on the last page of a report, you would select the Report Footer section and select the New Page Before check box.

To keep grand totals in the Report Footer from being stranded on the last page of a report, instead of selecting the New Page After check box for the Group Footer section, click the Conditional Formula button and write the formula "OnLastRecord = false." This creates a page break for every group that does *not* contain the last record. If the OnLastRecord command is true for the group SCR ignores the New Page After command.

Underlaying Sections

Seagate Crystal Reports gives you the ability to underlay sections of a report. Underlaying a section under another allows you to have different information side by side on a report. You can underlay existing sections, or extra sections can be added to facilitate underlaying while maintaining organization and space for information you do not want to be underlaid. For example,

ADDING, MERGING, AND DELETING SECTIONS

The Section Expert includes functionality to add, merge, and delete sections on a report. You can only delete sections you have added. The five main sections cannot be removed, as explained in Chapter 1. You can add and delete sections to meet formatting needs, some of which this chapter describes.

When you delete a section off a report, all information within that section also deletes. By merging two sections, SCR adds the fields in the lower section to the section above and only the section itself is deleted, not the information within it.

it looks great to have a Report Header or Group Header section containing a graph underlay the Details section so that the values being graphed print next to the graph. To make one section underlay following sections:

You will learn about inserting a graph in Chapter 9, "Adding Graphs and Maps for Better Data Analysis."

1. Using the Section Expert, add a second Group Header section by clicking the Insert button with the current Group Header section selected. You now have a Group Header 1a and 1b (see Figure 7.15) and the new Group Header 1b section appears in the Design tab.

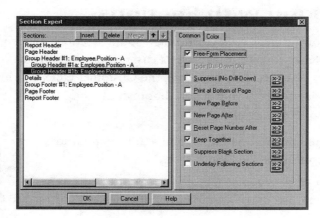

Figure 7.15
Create additional sections on a report using the Section Expert.

2. Add the information you want to underlay to the Group Header 1a area in the Design tab, and move any group headings to Group Header 1b. You may need to move some fields to achieve this.

3. Use the Section Expert to underlay Group Header 1a. Click OK.

4. Preview your report. Both sections display in the Design tab, but in the Preview tab Group Header 1a underlays Group Header 1b.

Suppressing Sections

The ability to suppress sections allows you to use Seagate Crystal Reports to run perfectly formatted invoices and letters, and any other type of report where you may have information missing but do not want blank spaces. You might also want to use the suppress option with a conditional formula to suppress a section only if a condition is met. Using the Section Expert, you can also select the Suppress Blank Section check box to prevent the section from printing if it is blank.

To suppress a section, select the Suppress check box in the Section Expert. This suppresses the section so that it doesn't print on your report. You can set a conditional formula here as well by clicking the Conditional Formatting button.

To suppress a blank section, select the Suppress If Blank check box in the Section Expert. This suppresses the entire section if it contains blank fields (fields with no data).

Working with Sections

The following steps walk you through adding sections to a report for use as a form letter or invoice. First, start a custom report using the Xtreme sample database. You need only one table, the Customer table, for this exercise. Do not add any fields to your report, but instead go right to the Section Expert once the Design tab opens.

1. Using the Section Expert add four Group Header sections, so that your report looks like Figure 7.16.

2. Go to the Design tab of your report, and insert the following fields: Add Customer Name to Group Header 1a; Address 1 to Group Header

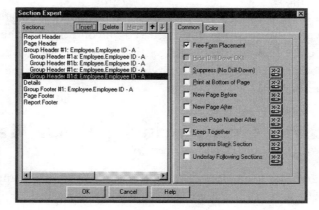

Figure 7.16

Add extra sections to give you individual formatting options for each section.

1b; Address 2 to Group Header 1c; and City, Region, and Postal Code to Group Header 1d.

3. Using the Section Expert, click the Suppress Blank Section check box for the Group Header 1b and Group Header 1c sections that you want suppressed (see Figure 7.17).

4. Click OK to close the Section Expert. Now when you preview your report, both one-line and two-line addresses print with no inconsistencies in spacing.

These few sections have provided a couple of examples of the flexibility and options available to you when using the Section Expert. Like with the field

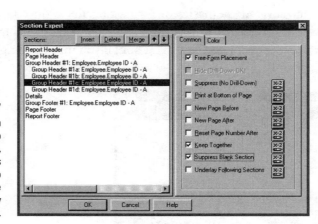

Figure 7.17

With the section you want to format selected, click Suppress Blank Section to suppress the section only if blank.

Format Editor, you can use the Conditional Formula buttons to write formulas that control formatting options based on conditions in the report. Using options in the Format Editor and Section Expert, as well as conditional formulas, you can give your reports style while also making them more useful and easier to read.

Adding Graphics to Your Report

Adding graphics to a report is straightforward. You can add any .BMP, .JPG, .PCX, .TGA, or .TIF graphic file to a report. To insert a graphic:

1. Click the Insert Picture toolbar button or click Insert, Picture to open the Open dialog box. Either double-click the picture you want to insert or select it and click Open (see Figure 7.18). The Open dialog box closes and "attaches" the picture to your mouse pointer.

2. Drop the picture on your report by clicking where you want to place it. Resize the picture using the resizing handles.

3. To format the graphic, right-click to open a shortcut menu. Options in the shortcut menu allow you to resize, add a border, and manipulate that border. You can also move the graphic anywhere you want on your report.

Summary

This chapter covered the basics of formatting fields on a report using the Format Editor. You learned how to look at the default settings and how to reset them to meet your exact needs. Though you may be tempted to change

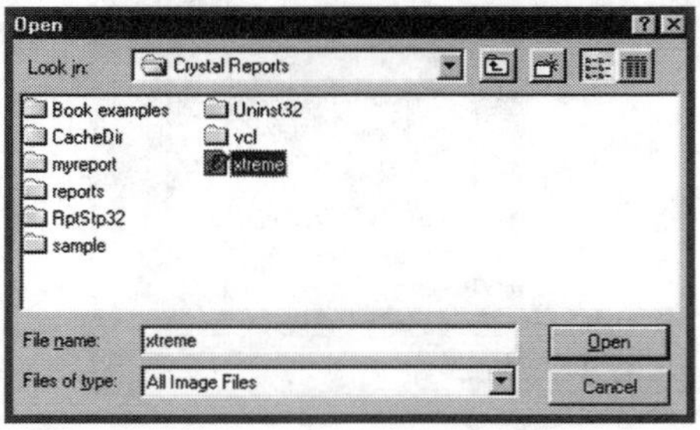

Figure 7.18
Navigate through your network to select a graphic file to add to your report.

the default settings, sometimes it is easier to adjust each report if you will be creating several different types of reports. Remember that you can use an existing report as a template for new reports, carrying forward all the formatting from the template.

You also found out how conditional formatting and the Highlighting Expert provide options for customizing reports and making information stand out. Conditional formulas can be used in many ways and places in Seagate Crystal Reports, many more than the few examples here. Be creative!

Lastly, you discovered how to format sections using the Section Expert and use conditional formulas to control formatting options that apply to entire sections.

PART III

Advanced
Reporting Topics

CHAPTER 8

Creating Advanced Reports

- Creating Subreports

- Creating Cross-Tabulation Reports

- Creating Drill-Down Reports

- Using Parameters

- Using the Select Expert with Parameters

In this chapter, you'll learn about advanced reporting tools such as subreports, cross-tab reports, drill down reports, and report parameters. You'll also discover how and why to use these report types, how to pass values from primary reports to subreports, how to capture user-provided values, and how to use those values to enhance reports and filter data.

Creating Subreports

A *subreport* is a report inside another report. Subreports have most of the characteristics of a primary (main) report. Subreports exist wholly within a primary report and usually do not exist as a separate file for viewing outside the primary report. You can, however, use existing reports as subreports. For example, you can insert a detail level report as a subreport into a summary level report. Remember these rules as you build your subreports:

- Subreports are inserted as objects inside a primary report.
- Subreports can be placed in any report section and the entire subreport prints in that section.
- Subreports cannot contain other subreports.

Why Use a Subreport?

You may want to use a subreport when you need to present a different view of your data within the same report. An expense report is a good example of such a subreport. In the main report, you might list each vendor with the invoice date, the expense category, a comment and the total amount due. A subreport could contain details such as the items purchased, the purchase date, and amount of the purchase.

Alternatively, you could use a subreport to show the same expense data broken down by project or department. In this report, you can view expenses from two perspectives: from a category perspective, and from a departmental perspective.

You can also use subreports to combine related reports into one report. For example, say you manage a mail-order bookstore. A report listing the books purchased in a given month can be combined with a report showing other books purchased by the same customers. In this way, you could establish a recommended reading list, based on the author or book subject, to help sell more books. Customers who bought "The Life and Times of Destiny Mayer" might also enjoy reading "My First Tooth" by Destiny Mayer or other auto-biographies.

Though a subreport can't exist independently—meaning, outside the primary report—it is an independent object within a report just like a database field, graphic object, or formula. For clarification, the term *subreport* is used in this chapter. It refers to the subreport object within a primary report; it does not refer to both the subreport *and* the primary report containing the subreport.

To create a subreport, you can either insert an existing report into a primary report, thus making it a subreport, or create a new subreport from within the primary report.

Inserting Existing Subreports into Primary Reports

If you have a report you want to include as part of another report, you can insert it as a subreport into a primary report. When you do this, the inserted report becomes a subreport object and no longer has any relation to the original and separate .RPT file. Within the subreport, you can make changes that do not affect the existing report file, so you can completely customize a subreport to meet your needs and the original report file remains intact. To insert an existing report as a subreport:

1. Create or open a primary report. Then, with the primary report open, choose Insert, Subreport, from the main menu, or click the Insert Subreport button on the supplementary toolbar.

2. Select Choose a Report, and then click Browse to select the report you want to insert as a subreport (see Figure 8.1).

3. You may need to link the subreport to the primary report. If so, see the steps in the section "Linking a Subreport." Otherwise, click OK.

4. Drop the subreport onto the primary report, just like placing any other kind of field or object, and format it as desired.

In the Design tab, the subreport appears as a movable, sizable object in the section in which you placed it. Another tab appears in the Crystal Report Designer to show the design of the subreport. The subreport's name appears

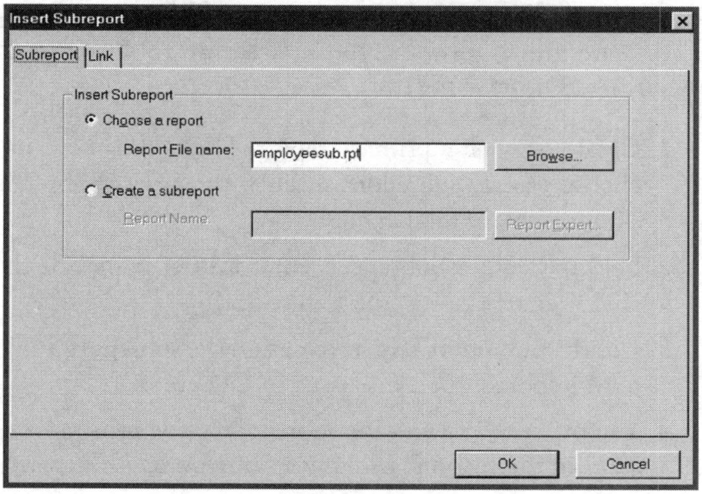

Figure 8.1

Use the Insert
Subreport dialog
box to insert an
existing report as
a subreport.

on the tab. You can restructure the subreport by clicking the subreport's De-sign tab and making the desired modifications. You can also double-click the subreport object, select it and click Edit, Subreport from the main menu, or right-click the subreport and click Edit Subreport from the shortcut menu. Remember that changes you make to the subreport no longer affect the origi-nal .RPT file and any changes you make to the original .RPT file do not affect the subreport. They become two separate entities.

> **You can save the subreport back out to a separate .RPT file by select-ing the subreport in the Design tab (or clicking the subreport's Design tab) and choosing File, Save Subreport As.**

Creating a Subreport within the Primary Report

While working on a report you may see the need for a subreport that does not yet exist. You can create a new subreport from within the primary report. The subreport you create typically exists solely within the primary report, but you can save it to a separate, independent file if you want. To create a new subreport within a primary report:

You can create both the primary report and the subreport at the same time with the Subreport Expert. Refer to Chapter 2 for details on using the Report Experts.

1. Create or open a primary report. Then with the primary report open, choose Insert, Subreport, or click the Insert Subreport button on the supplementary toolbar.

2. Select Create a Subreport, enter a brief name for the subreport, and click Report Expert (see Figure 8.2).

3. Use the Subreport Expert to design the subreport. It's just like the Standard Report Expert discussed in Chapter 2.

4. You may need to link the subreport to the primary report. If so, see the steps in the section "Linking a Subreport." Otherwise, click OK.

5. Drop the subreport onto the primary report and format it as desired.

In the Design tab, the subreport appears as a subreport object in the group or section in which you placed it. Just as when you insert an existing report as a subreport, another tab appears in the Crystal Report Designer to show the design of the subreport. You can edit the subreport as needed in the subreport's Design tab.

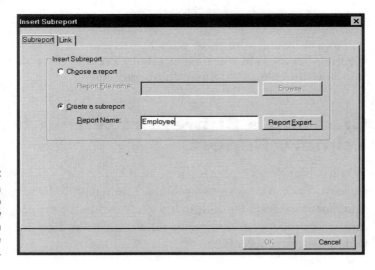

Figure 8.2
Choose Create a Subreport to create a new subreport from within the primary report.

Linking a Subreport to the Primary Report

Once you have designed the primary report and subreports, you may want to select a field or fields to link them together. This enables the report to show specific data in the subreport as it corresponds to a record in the primary report.

Whether you need to link the subreport to the primary report depends on the type of data shown in the subreport. For example, on a bill of materials report you might want to print the sub-components that make up each main component on the BOM. Since you've already used the Details section of the primary report to print the components, you can use a subreport to print the sub-components. But, you would need to link the sub-components to each component record based on a common field (or set of fields), such as Component ID. This way, you could then place the subreport in a Details b section and have the sub-component records print directly below the primary report's detail records.

On the other hand, when you combine two reports, such as in the earlier example of the mail-order bookstore, you would not necessarily need to link the data between the two reports. The list of books purchased by customers who bought the books shown on the primary report stands on its own perfectly well. You can place it at the end of the report (in the Report Footer section), and it will print data for all customers.

 Unlinked subreports have data unrelated to the primary report data. Subreports do not require a link to the primary report, but if the data in the subreport depends on a specific record in the main report, you'll probably want to link them.

To link a subreport and primary report:

1. If you're in the process of inserting a subreport, click the Links tab of the Insert Subreport dialog box. Otherwise, right-click the subreport object in the primary report and click Change Subreport Links on the shortcut menu. The Subreport Links dialog box appears (see Figure 8.3).

2. In the Available Fields list, select the field or fields in the primary report that you want to link to the subreport.

3. Click the right arrow button to copy the fields to the Field(s) to Link to list. The dialog box reveals two lists at the bottom (see Figure 8.4).

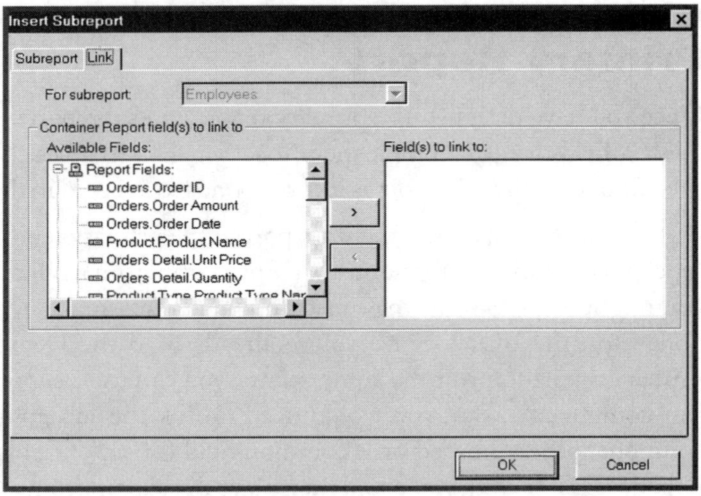

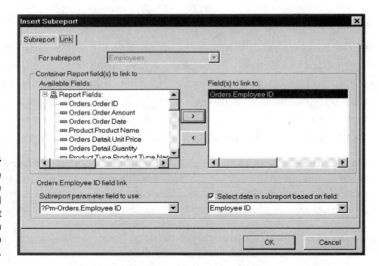

Figure 8.3

The Subreport Links dialog box or Link tab of the Insert Subreport dialog box lets you specify the fields that link the subreport to the primary report.

Figure 8.4

Specifying the links between the subreport and primary report instructs SCR in how to match up the two reports.

The list on the left shows the parameters that SCR automatically created in the subreport, corresponding to the fields in the primary report you selected to link the two reports together. When you run the report, Seagate Crystal Reports passes values from the primary report to the related parameter field in the subreport. The parameter name begins with "?Pm" followed by the name of the table and field passed from the primary report. The list on the right shows the fields in the subreport that you can match up with the selected fields on the primary report.

4. Select a field in the Field(s) to Link to list. Then, in the Subreport Parameter Field to Use list, select the parameter field in the subreport that you want to receive data from the selected field in the primary report.

5. If the subreport has a field that directly corresponds to a field you selected in Step 4, check the Select Data in Subreport Based on Field check box and select the field in the drop-down list below it. This is like a mini Select Expert, filtering records in the subreport based on the value of the field you specify. If the subreport does not have a field that directly corresponds to the field selected in Step 4, you can instruct the subreport to give you all records. To do this, clear the Select Data in Subreport Based on Field check box.

 You can examine the data in the subreport alone by clicking the subreport's Design tab and clicking the Refresh button (or pressing F5 on the keyboard). A parameter window opens to ask for a value for the parameters in the report.

Creating Cross-Tabulation Reports

Use cross-tabulation (cross-tab) reports to display large quantities of data summarized into a column and row format. This format makes the reports easy to read and allows readers to compare data between records instantly.

The cross-tab function automatically splits pages at the end of the appropriate column, and row headings can be repeated on each new page. Very large reports can span many pages and still be easily read and interpreted (see Figure 8.5).

When you create a cross-tab report, you actually place a cross-tab object into a regular report. You can place as many cross-tab objects as you want into a report or subreport.

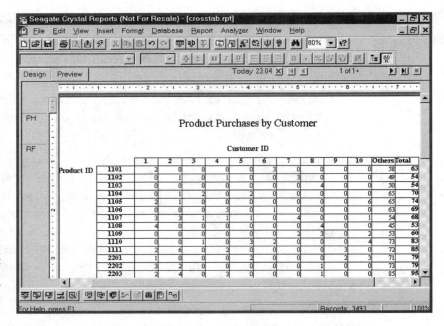

Figure 8.5
A cross-tab report
shows you data in
a column-row
format, much like
a spreadsheet.

Adding a Cross-Tab to a Report

When you add a cross-tab object to a report, you select three or more fields and arrange them in the following order: column headings, row headings, and summarized data. To create a cross-tab report:

You can also use the Cross-Tab Report Expert to create a report with a cross-tab from scratch. Refer to Chapter 2 for more information on using the Report Experts.

1. Create or open a report. With the report open, select Insert, Cross-Tab from the main menu, or click the Insert Cross-Tab button on the supplementary toolbar. The Cross-Tab dialog box appears. Refer to the next section, "Identifying Cross-Tab Fields," for details on completing this dialog box.

2. When you finish setting up the fields and options for the cross-tab, click OK. A rectangle attached to the pointer identifies the new cross-tab object.

3. Click in the section in which you would like the cross-tab to appear. You can reposition the cross-tab within the report by dragging and dropping the cross-tab object in the Design tab.

If you create a report that has a cross-tab but no detail information, drag the cross-tab to the Report Footer rather than leaving it in the Report Header. The Page Header information then appears above the cross-tab information.

Identifying Cross-Tab Fields

When you use the Cross-Tab dialog box, you specify the fields to use for the columns, rows, and summary data. The cross-tab object requires at least one field in the summary data list box; the columns and rows do not require fields (see Figure 8.6). To specify fields to put into the cross-tab object:

1a. To insert a field into a column, click the desired field in the Fields list, and then click the Add Column button. Alternatively, you can drag and drop a field name from the Fields list to the Columns list.

OR

1b. To insert a field into a row, click the desired field in the Fields list, and then click the Add Row button. Alternatively, you can drag and drop a field name from the Fields list to the Rows list.

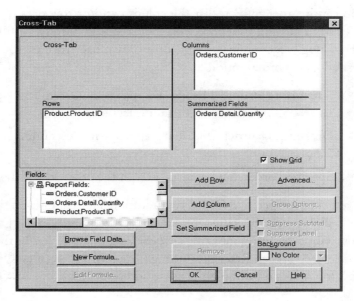

Figure 8.6
Use the Cross-Tab dialog box to identify columns, rows, and summarized fields in the cross-tab.

2. Summarized fields appear at the row/column intersections and total at the end of each row and at the bottom of each column. Select the fields to summarize from the Fields list and click Set Summarized Field. The cross-tab object sums numeric and currency values and counts all other fields.

3. You can place formulas as column, row, or summarized fields. Formulas that already exist in the report appear in the Fields list. Or, you can create a new formula by clicking New Formula. Refer to Chapter 6 for information on writing formulas.

4. To change the background colors for a column or row, first select the row or column from the Rows or Columns lists. Then, choose a color from the Background list.

5. To set the grouping order for a column or row, select the desired row or column from the Rows or Columns lists and click Group Options. The Cross-Tab Group Options dialog box appears. See the section "Selecting Group Order" for more instructions.

6. To further configure the cross-tab grid, click Advanced. See the section "Selecting Advanced Cross-Tab Options" for more instructions.

Selecting Group Order

You can instruct SCR to list the column and/or row data in the order you want by indicating your choice on the Cross-Tab Group Options dialog box. The dialog box contains a single drop-down list in which you can select the desired group order option:

- **Ascending order**. The data appears in ascending order (such as 1,2,3,4,5…). This is the default selection.

- **Descending order**. The data appears in descending order (such as …5,4,3,2,1).

- **Specified order**. The data appears in the order in which you specify.

If you choose Specified Order, two additional tabs appear on the Group Options dialog box: Specified Order and Others. Specifying group order for cross-tabs is basically the same as specifying group order for the main report, as discussed earlier. Refer to "Putting Groups into Specified Order" in Chapter 5 for details on completing these additional tabs.

note You do not need to select every data value if you want to see only a portion of the data in the cross-tab. You can select only those values that will appear in the column or row.

Selecting Advanced Cross-Tab Options

The Advanced Cross-Tab Options dialog box lets you further configure the cross-tab grid. You set most of the options by selecting or clearing check boxes, as described (see Figure 8.7).

- **Show Cell Margins.** Select this check box to have SCR automatically pad the grid cells with spaces, both vertically and horizontally. If you clear the check box, SCR removes all extra spaces so that the data takes up as little room within the cell as possible. The cells will then appear smaller and more condensed.

- **Suppress Empty Rows.** Select this check box to have SCR hide any rows that do not contain data.

- **Suppress Empty Columns.** Select this check box to have SCR hide any columns that do not contain data.

- **Keep Columns Together.** Select this check box to have SCR keep columns together on each page when they would otherwise split across pages.

Figure 8.7
The Advanced Cross-Tab Options dialog box lets you customize your cross-tab objects.

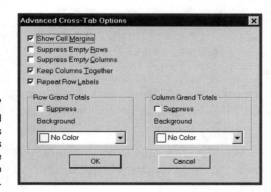

- **Repeat Row Labels.** Select this check box to have SCR print row labels on each page when the cross-tab prints across more than one page horizontally.

Formatting Cross-Tab Reports

With Seagate Crystal Reports 7, you can add color and font formatting to your cross-tab reports. Here are some tips and suggestions for formatting cross-tab objects:

 If you want to put a cross-tab in a section of the report that also has a formula, database field, or text object in it, insert a new section below the existing section and place the cross-tab in the new section. This avoids spacing problems as the cross-tab grows.

- To add color to the column that displays the subtotal for each row, click a field in the column area of the grid, and then select the desired color from the Background list on the Cross-Tab dialog box or Report Expert. If you want to choose the same color for all columns, you need to set the color of each column individually.

- To add color to the rows (including the summary field data), click a field in the row area of the grid, then select the desired color from the Background list on the Cross-Tab dialog box or Report Expert. If you want to choose the same color for all rows, you need to set the color of each row individually.

- To add color to the column totals, click the Advanced button. In the Column Grand Totals area, select the desired color from the Background list.

- To add color to the row grand totals, click the Advanced button. In the Row Grand Totals area, select the desired color from the Background list.

- To suppress the column grand totals, click the Advanced button. In the Column Grand Totals area, select the Suppress check box. The totals at the bottom of each column do not appear.

- To suppress the row totals, click the Advanced button. In the Row Grand Totals area, select the Suppress check box. The totals at the end of each row do not appear.

Creating Drill Down Reports

With Seagate Crystal Reports you can drill down on group or summary information from the Preview tab of the Crystal Report Designer, or from other interfaces in which users view reports, such as the runtime report viewer or Seagate Info's Info Analyzer. When you position the pointer over any summary value, the program displays a drill down pointer that looks like a magnifying glass. If you double-click the summary item, a new tab opens up to display the details behind that summary value. For example, if the drill down pointer becomes active over a publisher field, you can double-click to see all the titles published by the selected publisher. A drill down report can be set up with multiple levels. For example, the first level might show total royalties earned by each publisher, the next level might show total royalties earned by each author, and another level might show total royalties earned by each title. To create a drill down report:

1. Create or open a report. With the report open, hide (do not suppress!) the Details section and all other group sections except the Group Header 1 and Group Footer 1 sections.

2. Refresh or run the report and click the Preview tab.

Now, when you position the pointer over one of the group header or footer items, the drill down pointer (magnifying glass) appears. Double-click the header or footer item to expand it in its own tab, showing the items in the next group level, if there is one, or the detail data (see Figure 8.8). You can drill down on each header or footer item in this manner until you reach the report detail. When there are no more groups on which you can drill down, the pointer no longer changes to the drill down pointer.

If you drill down on the Group Footer section, the group expands to display the next group level or detail data as well as the subtotal lines for that group. If you drill down on the Group Header section, the subtotal lines do not appear.

Using Parameters

Parameters allow report users to input a value that affects the report output in some way. You, the report designer, determine the parameter's datatype and

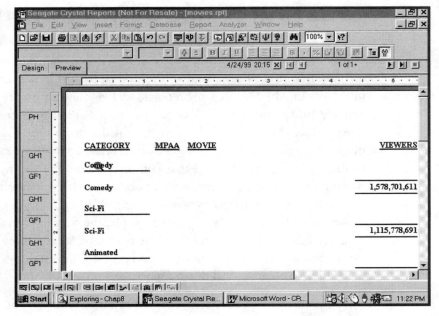

Figure 8.8
The drill down pointer positioned over a Group Header or Footer lets you expand that group to view its components.

its affect on the report. Most commonly, report designers add parameters to a report as a way to allow users to dynamically change the selection criteria for the report. For example, an HR report that prints employee personal and salary information might contain a parameter for department. When users run the report, SCR prompts them to enter a department, then uses that entry to filter the report data to include only employees from the selected department. A report can have more than one parameter, allowing users to define multiple selection criteria.

The first time a user runs a report with parameters, SCR prompts for the values for each parameter. Each time a user subsequently refreshes the report, SCR asks whether to use the current parameter values or prompt for new ones.

Creating Parameters

A *parameter* is a special variable that holds a value entered by the user. The value type for a parameter can be a string, number, date, date/time, Boolean, or currency, and each report can have more than one parameter. SCR prompts

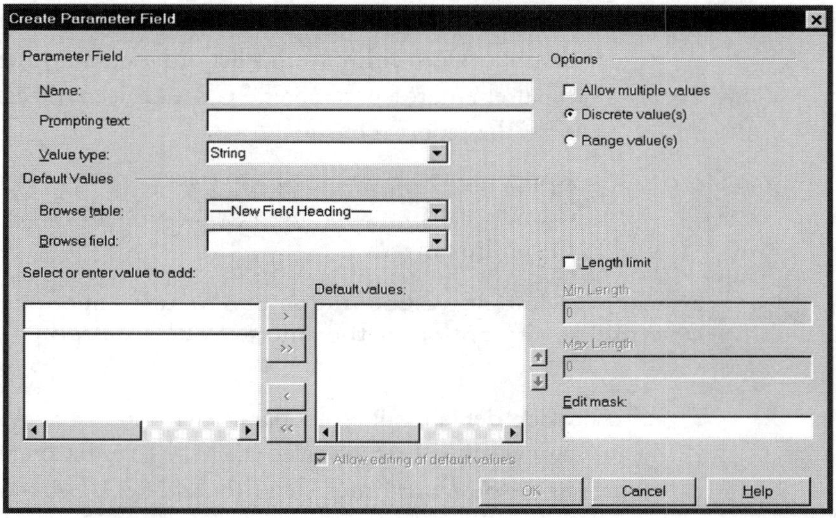

Figure 8.9

The Create Parameter Field dialog box allows you to create a new parameter to hold values entered by users.

users for the parameter values according to your specifications, using text you supply for the prompt, and accepting only the correct datatype for the values. To create a parameter:

1. Click the Insert Fields button on the toolbar or choose Insert, Parameter Field from the main menu. The Insert Fields dialog box appears.

2. Click the Parameter tab, then click New. The Create Parameter Field dialog box appears, as shown in Figure 8.9.

3. In the Name field, type a name for the parameter.

4. In the Prompting Text field, type the text you want users to see in the prompting Parameter Value dialog box. This text should give users enough information about the parameter to know what value to provide.

5. Indicate the datatype for the parameter in the Value Type field. The datatype can be string, number, currency, date, date/time, time, or Boolean. SCR makes sure that users enter values of the correct datatype.

6. Indicate the options that you would like to use:

   - **Allow multiple values.** If you want users to add values to a list box and select one or more choices from those values, select this check box.

- **Discrete values.** This option allows users to select one or more distinct values either from a list or typed in by the user. Each time the user enters a parameter, SCR adds it to the list for use the next time the report refreshes.

- **Range values.** Allows users to select a range of values. Users indicate the starting and ending values for the range, and SCR uses the entire range.

 The Allow Multiple Values option can be used in conjunction with the Discrete Values option or the Range Values option.

7. To provide default values for parameters, you can select a field from a table or you can enter the values yourself. To enter them yourself, enter a value in the Select or Enter Value To Add field. Use the right arrow button to move the value you typed into the list of Default Values. The items in the Default Values list appear in a list from which users can select.

8. To give users the option to edit the default values, select the Allow Editing of Default Values check box.

9. For parameters with a string value type, you can also apply an edit mask.

   Edit masks allow you to regulate the character input as users type. To use an edit mask, enter a mask character in the Edit Mask box for each character you want users to provide. When you select a mask character, SCR allows only characters of that type to be entered into the corresponding string position. Some mask characters allow data entry but do not require it; others require a character of the correct type for each mask character specified (see Figure 8.10). Mask characters include:

   - **A.** Requires alphanumeric characters
   - **a.** Accepts alphanumeric characters (not required)
   - **0.** Requires digits
   - **9.** Accepts digits (not required)
   - **#.** Accepts a digit, space, or plus/minus sign
   - **L.** Requires a letter from A to Z
   - **?.** Accepts a letter from A to Z (not required)
   - **&.** Requires any character or space

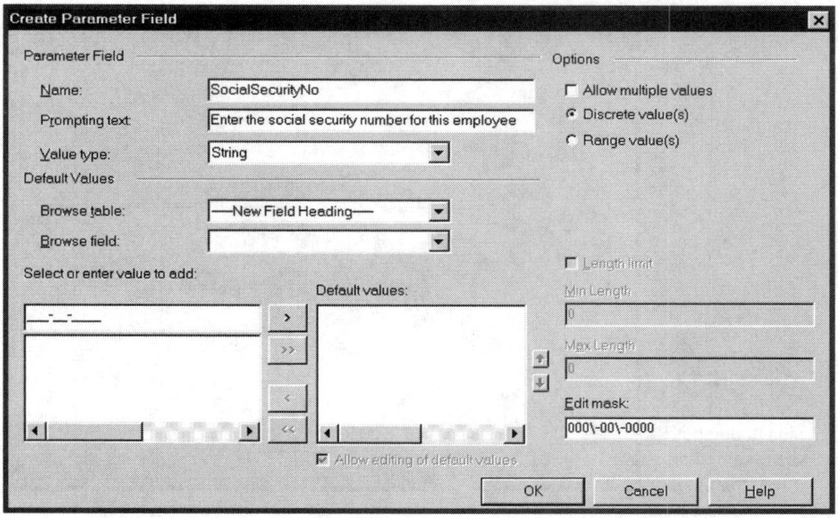

Figure 8.10

The Edit Mask field lets you specify the characters that can be accepted into a string field.

- **C.** Accepts any character or space (not required)
- **<, >.** Converts inputted characters to lowercase (<) or upper case (>)
- **\.** Inserts the next character as a literal (for example, 000\-00\-0000 would insert dashes between each set of digits in the social security number string)
- **"password".** Accepts a password for use in conditional formulas. When users type a value into the parameter text box, only asterisks (*) appear.

In order for SCR to prompt users for the parameters, each parameter must be used in the report either by inserting it directly onto the report (even if hidden) or by using it in a formula, usually a selection formula. When users open or refresh the report, they see the Parameter Value dialog box, as shown in Figure 8.11.

If the value entered by a user does not match the value type selected for the parameter, SCR presents an error message asking for a value of the correct type. For date and date/time values, the dialog box displays a calendar from which users can select a date. Once a user enters a value, you can have the report use it to filter records with the Select Expert, or use it in a formula you design.

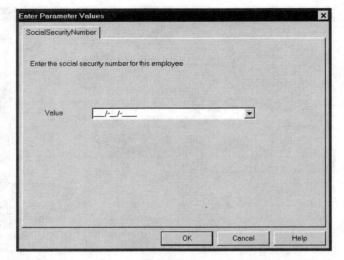

Figure 8.11
The Parameter
Value dialog box
as presented to
the user.

Using the Select Expert with Parameters

When you have parameters defined in your report, you can use the Select Expert to filter records based on the user's input. The Select Expert lets you specify how the data should relate to the value that the user provides. In doing this, you select a field or formula, and then specify its relationship to the parameter value. To use the Select Expert to filter records based on a parameter:

1. Click the Select Expert button on the toolbar or choose Report, Select Expert from the main menu. The Choose Field dialog box appears. This dialog box appears only the first time you use the Select Expert.

2. Select the field you want the parameter to filter. For example, if you want to show records for only the state selected by a user, choose the state field.

3. When you click OK on the Choose Field dialog box, the Select Expert appears (see Figure 8.12).

4. For the field selected, construct the appropriate conditional statement using the drop-down lists. Instead of selecting a specific value on which to filter, select the appropriate parameter name (preceded by a question mark (?)) from the drop-down list.

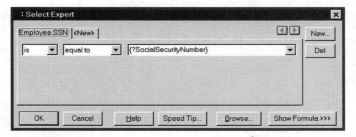

Figure 8.12

The Select Expert
dialog box allows
you to filter
records based on
a parameter.

5. Click OK to accept the selection criteria.

6. If the Preview tab is active, Seagate Crystal Reports refreshes the report automatically and asks you to select a value for the parameter. SCR applies the filter when you click OK on the Enter Parameter Values dialog box.

Summary

This chapter covered advanced reporting features such as subreports, drill down reports, cross-tab reports, and parameters. You learned what subreports are and why they are useful, and how cross-tab and drill down reports are created and used. In addition, you learned about report parameters and how to use them, and how to use the Select Expert with parameters to filter records based on user-provided values.

Using these advanced features of Seagate Crystal Reports, you have added to your arsenal of tools for creating custom reports that exactly meet your needs and the needs of those who will use them.

CHAPTER 9

Adding Graphs and Maps for Better Data Analysis

Using charts and maps in your reports can help users understand data by providing a visual representation. Charts are graphs such as pie charts, bar graphs, line graphs, and so on. Maps are geographical maps showing how data is distributed across a region.

If your report compares the sales of different bookstores in a particular city, for example, it might be helpful to see in a visual representation which store generates the most sales. While a report showing only the numbers is no less accurate, a graph can have a stronger impact on the user.

In this chapter, you will learn how to create charts and maps with the Chart Expert and Map Expert, and how to customize them with the Analyzer.

Integrating Charts and Maps in Reports

You can add a chart or map to a report with the Chart and Map Experts. Once you've created the charts and maps, you can adjust them with the Analyzer or the Expert.

Using the Chart Expert

The Chart Expert guides you through creating a chart to be placed on your report. With the Chart Expert, you can add any of the following types:

- Bar
- Line
- Area
- Pie
- Doughnut
- 3D Riser
- 3D Surface
- XY Scatter
- Radar
- Stock

Most of these chart types can be displayed one of several ways. The chart type format buttons on the Chart Expert allow you to select the format for the graph type you choose. A description of each format appears in the text box below the buttons.

The type of chart you should select depends on the data to be analyzed and how many fields you want to compare. For example, if you want to see what percentage of the total number of awards were won by science fiction films, you could use a pie chart. You could see how big a "pie slice" each film category got for number of awards won. If you want to see how many film categories won awards and how many received nominations, you might use a stacked bar chart. This would show each film category and the number of awards for both nominations and wins. To use the Chart Expert:

1. Click the Insert Chart button on the toolbar or select <u>I</u>nsert, <u>C</u>hart from the main menu. The Chart Expert appears with five tabs: Type, Data, Axes, Options, and Text (see Figure 9.1). The regular Report Experts also have a Chart tab that contains these five sub-tabs.

2. On the Type tab, look for the type of chart or graph you want to include in the report. You can use a Crystal Chart or a Custom Chart. The Chart Type list displays the available Crystal Charts.

You may also use a custom chart design using the Seagate Charts program. To design your own custom chart, select the Custom Chart option, and then click the Chart Editor button to open Seagate Charts. See "Enhancing Charts with Seagate Chart" later in this chapter for more information.

Figure 9.1
The Chart Expert guides you through creating a graph for your report.

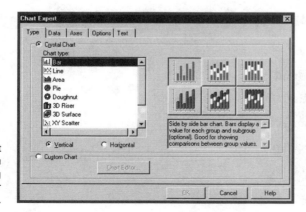

3. Select the chart type you want to use. Most of the chart types have two or more format options to choose from. As you highlight each chart type, the format options appear on buttons to the right of the Chart Type list. Click the desired format type button, according to its description directly below the group of buttons.

Selecting Data Options on the Data Tab

The Data tab lets you select the placement of the graph within the report, the layout of the graph, and the data for the graph points (see Figure 9.2). To select the data options:

1. Choose a layout option first; what you choose here determines your placement and data options. In the Layout area, select whether the points plotted for the chart should be for group data or detail data.

   - To plot points on group data, click the Group button. In the On Change Of box, indicate the group field you want to use as a condition for plotting. In the Show box, indicate the summary field values you want to plot in the graph.

   - To plot points on detail data, click the Detail button. Indicate the group field you want to use as a condition for plotting values by selecting a field from the Available Fields list, and then clicking the right arrow button beside the On Change Of box. Next, indicate the field values you want to plot in the graph.

Figure 9.2

The Chart Expert Data tab lets you select the fields and groups on which to base the chart.

2. In the Placement area, select where you want the chart to appear on your report. You can place the graph or chart in the Report Header or the Report Footer by choosing the Once Per Report option. Or, you can indicate that you want the chart to appear every time a particular group changes. If you place the chart on change of a group, the chart appears in the header or footer of that group, as you direct.

Selecting Axis Options on the Axes Tab

The Axes tab lets you select options affecting the chart's axes. You can set options for the gridlines, data values, and number of divisions. The options on the Axes tab apply only to those chart types that have x and y coordinates, such as bar charts, line charts, and area charts (see Figure 9.3). Pie and doughnut charts do not use the Axes tab. To set axis options:

1. In the Show Gridlines area, indicate which, if any, gridlines you want to display in the graph. You can display the major and/or minor guidelines for the x axis (group values) and the y axis (data values). You can also set the y2 axis (data2 values) for cross-tab or OLAP charts.

2. In the Data Values area, indicate whether you want to include only certain data ranges as minimums and maximums. Select Auto Range to use the default ranges.

3. In the Number of Divisions area, indicate whether you want SCR to set the number of divisions for the chart, or whether you want to set the

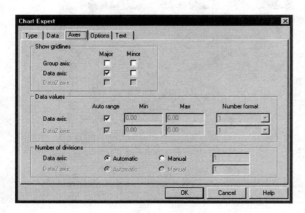

Figure 9.3

The Chart Expert Axes tab lets you define the appearance of gridlines and divisions, and to set minimum and maximum values.

number manually. The divisions represent the number of x-axis lines between the lowest value on the chart and the highest. If you choose the Manual option, indicate the number of divisions to set.

Selecting General Options on the Options Tab

On the Options tab you can select general chart options such as color or black and white, legend options, and labels for the data points (see Figure 9.4). To select general options for a chart:

1. In the Chart Color area, indicate whether you want the chart to appear in color or in black and white.

2. In the Data Points area, indicate whether you would like 1) no label to appear for each data point, 2) the field name as the label, or 3) the value as the label. If you select Value, you have the option of formatting it by choosing the desired format style in the Number Format list.

3. In the Customize Settings area, select options as described below:

   - **Pie Size** (for pie charts). Determines the size of the pie chart. This option includes five sizes to choose from: minimum, small, average, large, and maximum.

   - **Detach Pie Slice** (for pie charts). If you want the largest or smallest pie slice detached from the rest of the pie, select this option.

Figure 9.4

The Chart Expert Options tab lets you set options for the general appearance of the chart.

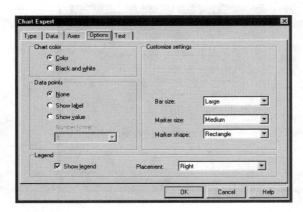

- **Bar Size** (for bar charts). This determines the width of bars on a bar chart. Choices include: minimum, small, average, large, and maximum.

- **Marker Size** (for line charts). This determines the size of markers on a line chart. The option also appears on other types of charts, but the marker size is most apparent on line charts where you see the markers more clearly.

- **Marker Shape** (for line and bar charts). This determines the shape of the marker in the chart. Available shapes include rectangle, circle, diamond, and triangle. For other chart types, the marker shape determines the shape of the markers in the legend.

4. In the Legend area, indicate whether a legend for the chart should appear, and where in relation to the chart itself. Choices include upper right corner, bottom center, top center, right, and left.

Selecting Text Options on the Text Tab

On the Text tab you enter the text that should appear on the chart itself. You can include a title and subtitle, labels for the x and y axes, and footnotes. You can also set font attributes for each of these items (see Figure 9.5).

1. In the Title field in the Titles Text area, type a title for the chart, if desired.

Figure 9.5

The Chart Expert Text tab lets you define the titles, subtitles, and other text that appears on the chart.

2. In the Subtitle field, type a subtitle for the chart, if desired.

3. In the Footnote field, type a footnote for the chart, if desired.

4. In the Group Title (x-Axis) field, type a title for the chart's x-axis, if desired.

5. In the Data Title (y-Axis) field, type a title for the chart's y-axis, if desired.

6. In the Data2 Title (y2-Axis) field, type a title for the chart's second y-axis, if desired. This option appears only when using a cross-tab or OLAP chart.

7. In the Format area, select the desired font attributes for each of the items listed in the Titles Text area.

8. When you finish with the Text tab and all previous pages, click the OK button. SCR draws the chart and places it as indicated in the report. To view the data in the chart, click the report's Preview tab.

Enhancing Charts with Seagate Charts

Seagate Charts allows you to fine-tune the appearance of the charts you use in your reports. You can select color gradations instead of solid colors, line styles and widths, and many other options that enhance the look and readability of your charts.

You can create a chart from scratch with the Chart Expert, or you can modify an existing chart. Modifying a chart is easy with Seagate Charts; you can create a chart using the Chart Expert, then open the Expert again and use Seagate Charts to customize it. To open Seagate Charts:

1. Open the Chart Expert by right-clicking an existing chart or, during initial chart creation, by clicking the Insert Chart button or Insert, Chart menu command.

2. On the Type tab, select the Custom Chart option and click the Chart Editor button. Seagate Charts opens (see Figure 9.6).

The Seagate Charts menu provides tools for creating and editing a chart. The toolbar on the left side of the window lets you draw objects and add text directly on the chart.

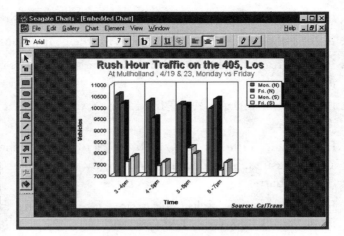

Figure 9.6

Seagate Charts is a powerful tool that lets you fine-tune your charts.

The Seagate Charts Menu

The main menu consists of eight menu selections: File, Edit, Gallery, Chart, Element, View, Window, and Help.

The File menu lets you save a chart, close the application and return to the Report Designer, and Apply a Template. The Exit and Close commands do essentially the same thing. If you want to use an existing chart to model a new chart, choose Apply a Template. The chart file you choose becomes a base template for your new chart.

The Edit menu lets you perform common Windows editing functions on the elements of your chart, such as cut, copy, paste, and undo.

The Gallery menu allows you to choose the chart type you want. All menu selections have a submenu that lists the possible choices for the currently selected type. A small graphic also appears on the submenu to depict the type of chart highlighted (see Figure 9.7).

The Chart menu gives you the axis and general options found in the Chart Expert's Axes and Options tabs. Most of the menu selections have a submenu that lists the possible choices for the currently selected chart option. A small graphic also appears on the submenu showing the implementation of the selected option (see Figure 9.8).

The Element menu lets you adjust the elements on the chart, such as the lines that define a bar graph or the alignment of the x- and y-axis titles

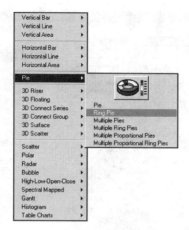

Figure 9.7
The Gallery menu shows you all of the chart types.

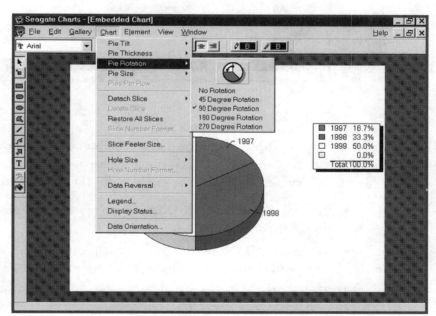

Figure 9.8
The Chart menu lets you select the chart options.

(see Figure 9.9). All of the menu selections have a submenu that lists the possible choices for the currently selected chart element. Depending on what elements of the graph you have selected, some submenu items may not be available.

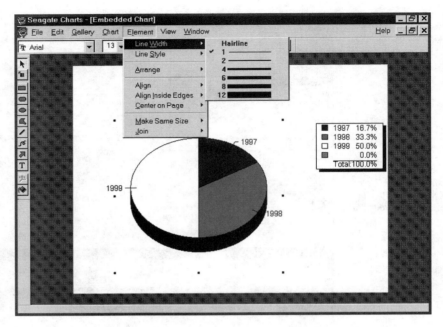

Figure 9.9
The Element
menu lets you
select options for
the chart
elements.

The View menu gives you palette options. By default, the Font, Tool and Color palettes are available. They appear in the toolbar areas of the window. The 3D View palette and the Fill Effect palette appear as floating dialog boxes, each with their own components. The items on the 3D View palette include:

- **3D Movement.** Click the red arrows to move the 3D chart in the direction of the arrow.

- **3D Zoom/3D Perspective/2D Pan.** Click the red arrow to zoom, pan or alter the perspective of the 3D chart in the direction of the arrow.

- **3D Box Proportions**. Click the red arrow to change the box proportions of the 3D chart in the direction of the arrow.

- **3D Rotation.** Click the red arrow to rotate the 3D chart in the direction of the arrow.

- **Undo.** Click to cancel all changes made since the last time the chart was redrawn.

- **Redraw.** To set the changes made with the 3D buttons and redraw the chart.

Figure 9.10

The Fill Effect
Palette.

The items on the Fill Effect palette include (see Figure 9.10):

- **Pattern**. Use the Pattern button to select the pattern for the fill. Choices appear in the list at the top of the dialog box.

- **Gradient**. Use the Gradient button to select a gradient fill (fading from one color to another across the surface of the chart element). Choices appear in the list at the top of the dialog box.

- **Texture**. Use the Texture button to select a texture to appear on the chart element. Choices appear in the list at the top of the dialog box.

- **Edit**. Click the Edit button to set specific effect options.

- **Apply**. Click the Apply button to apply the changes to the chart. Changes made to the data elements such as color and texture automatically reflect in the legend.

To suppress zero values on a line or bar chart, right-click the 0 value label on the y-axis and select Scale Range from the shortcut menu. In the Range Method area, clear the Automatic check box beside the From value and type 1 in the text box instead of 0. In the Range Display area, select the Don't Graph Out-of-range Values option.

To correct disjointed line charts at the 0 value point, right-click the line and select Curve and Fit Stat Lines from the shortcut menu. Select the Smooth check box.

Finally, if you need to format for black and white printed reports, patterns make a good choice instead of colors or textures. The charts look very nice, and you can choose from many different patterns.

Using the Map Expert

Maps help you analyze report data and identify trends based on geographical data. Once you create a map, you can drill down on the map regions, analyze the data, and format the appearance of the map. You can zoom in or out on an area of the map to see how the data is distributed over a smaller or larger area.

Maps are really only useful if you have geographical data in your report, such as countries, states, provinces, counties, or cities. Just identify the geographical field and the Map Expert draws the map and shows you how the data affects each region.

If you group on more than one geographical field, it is important that you select them in order from largest (country, at the top of the sort list) to smallest (city, at the bottom of the sort list).

When creating a map, remember that maps with a group layout must be based on a summarized field.

The Map Expert guides you through creating a map for your report. To use the Map Expert:

1. Click the Insert Map button on the toolbar or select Insert, Map from the main menu. The Map Expert appears (see Figure 9.11).

2. On the Data tab, indicate whether you want the map to appear in the Report Header or in the Report Footer. In the Layout area, select the layout of the map. If you have groups in your report, choose the group layout. If you don't have groups, or if you want to map on multiple values, select Detail. In the Data area, select the data on which to create the map.

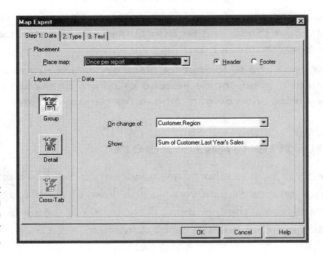

Figure 9.11

The Map Expert Data tab lets you select the information for the map.

- For group layouts, select the group on which to base the condition for the mapped data in the On Change Of list. Select the summary field on which to map from the Show list.

- For detail layouts, from the Available Fields list select the field on which to break down the data geographically and click the right arrow button beside the Geographic Field box. Select the group on which to base the condition for the mapped data and click the right arrow button beside the On Change Of list. Select the fields on which to map and click the right arrow button beside the Map Values box.

3. When you finish selecting the data elements for the map, click the Type tab.

Selecting the Map Type on the Type Tab

The Type tab lets you select the map type (see Figure 9.12). This determines how the data displays on the map, such as with colored map regions or with dots. Each map type has options specific to that type, as described in the following sections.

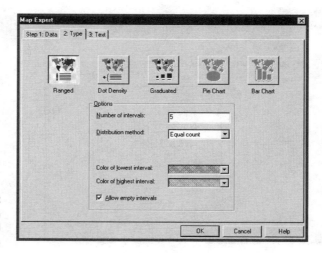

Figure 9.12

Options available for the Ranged map type.

Ranged Map

The Ranged map shows map regions shaded according to the distribution of the data.

- **Interval.** Select the number of color-coded intervals or ranges, such as county districts, countries in North America, or continents that you want to appear on the map.

- **Distribution Method.** Select the number of intervals selected above should be distributed across the map.

- **Color of Lowest Interval.** Select the color for the lowest interval in the range. Colors graduate from that selected for the lowest to that selected for the highest.

- **Color of Highest Interval.** Select the color for the highest interval in the range.

- **Allow Empty Intervals.** Select this check box if you want to show intervals that contain no data. If you clear this check box, only those intervals with data appear on the map.

Dot Density Map

The Dot Density map shows points on the map to indicate the data distribution. Choose whether you want the dots to appear small or large (see Figure 9.13).

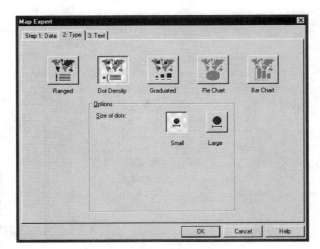

Figure 9.13
If you choose the Dot Density map type, you have only one option to set.

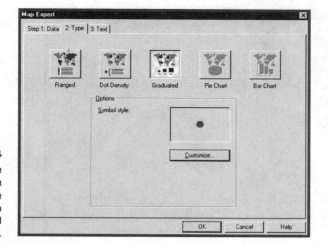

Figure 9.14
Click the Customize button to choose the type of symbol to use on Graduated map types.

Graduated Map

Graduated maps show a designated symbol in various sizes to indicate data distribution (see Figure 9.14). The symbol style determines the symbol that appears on the map to indicate the distribution of data. Click the Customize button to select the font style for the symbol, and other characteristics for displaying the desired symbol.

Pie Chart Map

Pie Chart maps display small pie charts on the maps to show distribution of data across the region (see Figure 9.15).

- **Size of Pies.** Use the slider to indicate the size of the pies to display under the map, ranging from small to large.

- **Proportional Sizing.** Select this check box if you want the sizing of the pies to be proportional to the amount of data they represent.

Bar Chart Map

Bar Chart maps display small bar charts on the maps to show distribution of data across the region. Use the slider to indicate the size of the bars to display under the map, ranging from small to large (see Figure 9.16).

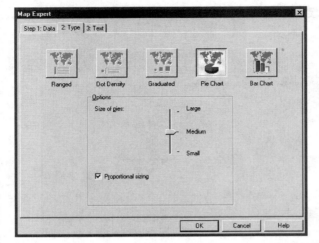

Figure 9.15

When you choose the Pie Chart map type, you determine the size of the pie charts.

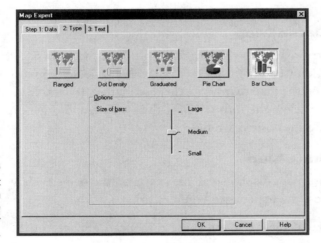

Figure 9.16

Like the Pie Chart map type, you can indicate the size of bars for the Bar Chart map type.

Selecting Text Options on the Text Tab

The Text tab lets you enter a title for the map and select legend options. To select the text options:

1. Type the desired title in the Map Title text box.

2. In the Legend area, indicate whether you want a full legend, compact legend or no legend. If you select full legend, you can select the legend title and subtitle options.

3. When you finishing setting map options, click OK.

Building Your Own Map

The following steps will guide you through creating a simple map that shows trends in customer purchases.

1. Using the Xtreme database that comes with Seagate Crystal Reports, build a standard report selecting the Customer table and the following data fields:

   - Country
   - Region
   - City
   - Last Year's Sales

2. Sort by Country, then by Region, then by City, and sum the Last Year's Sales for each group.

3. Optional: Use the Select Expert to get only records where the country = "USA".

4. Add a map to the report.

5. On the Data tab, select Group as the Layout option, Region and Footer for the Placement options, Customer City for the On Change Of field, and Sum of LastYearsSales for the Show field.

6. On the Type tab, select Ranged for the map type, 5 for the number of intervals and Equal Count for the distribution method. Select colors to use for the lowest and highest ranges.

7. On the Text tab, type a title for the map. Select Full Legend and Made by Map.

8. Click OK. SCR creates the map in the Region group footer.

Putting the Analyzer to Work

The Analyzer allows you to view and adjust maps and charts once they have been created. A map or chart opened with the Analyzer appears in its own window, allowing you to work on the map or chart apart from the main report. To open the Analyzer, right-click a map or chart and select Chart Analyzer from the shortcut menu, or select Analyzer, Launch Analyzer from the main menu.

Using the Map Analyzer

With the Map Analyzer, you can change many of the options you selected when you initially created the map. When a map appears in the Analyzer tab, you can use the menu to:

- Center the map.
- Zoom in and out, and pan the map.
- Change the map type.
- Reorganize the layers of report elements.
- Change the map title.
- Change the size of the map legend.

To center the map, right-click the map and choose Center Map from the shortcut menu, or select Analyze, Center from the main menu.

To zoom in, zoom out, or pan the map to the left or right, right-click the map and select Zoom In, Zoom Out, or Pan from the shortcut menu, or choose Analyze, Zoom In, Zoom Out, or Pan from the main menu. Click the map to execute the selected operation. When you finish adjusting the view or positioning of the map, right-click and choose None to change the pointer back to a regular pointer (or choose Analyze, None from the main menu).

Choosing the Map Type

Map types are different methods of showing the data distribution on a map. Refer to the section "Selecting the Map Type on the Type Tab" for descriptions of the map types.

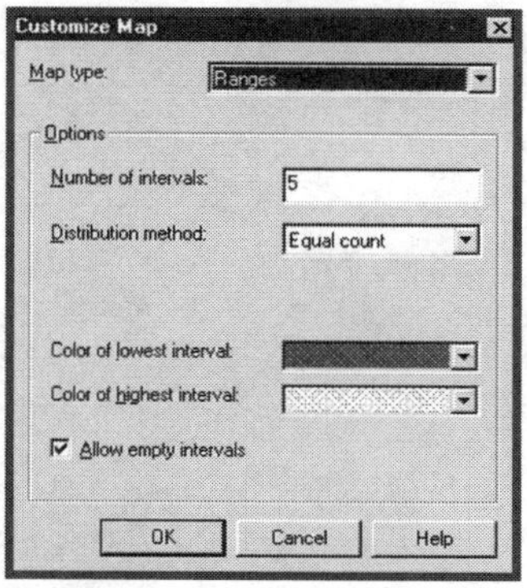

Figure 9.17

The Customize Map dialog box lets you fine-tune your report maps.

1. To change the map type, right-click the map and choose Change Map Type from the shortcut menu, or choose Analyze, Change Map Type from the main menu. The Customize Map dialog box appears (see Figure 9.17).

2. In the Map Type list, select the desired map type. You can also select the options for that map type on this dialog box.

3. When you finish, click the OK button.

Organizing Map Layers

When you create a map, Seagate Crystal Reports automatically constructs five map layers, each of which show the map regions at a particular detail level. You can change the order of the layers so that as you zoom in on the preview, you zoom to the next layer.

1. To reorganize the layers of the report, right-click the map and choose Change Layers from the shortcut menu, or choose Analyze, Change Layers from the main menu. The Layer Control dialog box appears (see Figure 9.18).

2. Click a layer name, and then use the Up and Down buttons to move the layers up or down in the hierarchy shown in the Layers list.

3. In the Properties area, select the Visible check box to indicate whether the selected layer displays. Each layer's visibility property can be turned on or off independently by selecting it in turn and selecting or clearing the Visible check box.

Figure 9.18

The Layer Control
dialog box lets
you rearrange
the layers for
the map.

4. To set Zoom layering properties, click the Display button. The Display Properties dialog box specific to the selected layer appears.

The Display Within Zoom Range check box allows you to determine whether to display the selected layer as you zoom closer, and at what point (in miles) the layer items appear and disappear within the viewable area.

Using the Chart Analyzer

With the Chart Analyzer, you can change many of the options you selected when you initially created the chart. When a chart appears in the Analyzer tab, you can use the menu to:

- Change the chart titles.
- Reverse series.
- Reverse groups.

To change the main chart title, right-click the chart and choose Change Title from the shortcut menu, or choose Analyze, Change Titles, Change Title from the main menu. The Change Label dialog box appears. Type the new title and click the OK button.

Figure 9.19

The Change Label
dialog box lets
you change the
labels that appear
on the chart.

To change the X-axis or Y-axis title, right-click the chart and select Change X-axis Title or Change Y-axis Title from the shortcut menu, or choose Analyze, Change Titles, Change X-axis Title (or Change Y-axis Title) from the main menu. The Change Label dialog box appears. Type the new title in the box and click the OK button.

To reverse the order of your data as it appears on the chart, and reverse the color scheme, right-click the chart and choose Reverse Series from the shortcut menu, or choose Analyze, Reverse Series from the main menu.

To reverse the group order along the X-axis, right-click the chart and choose Reverse Group from the shortcut menu, or choose Analyze, Reverse Group from the main menu.

Summary

In this chapter, you learned how to use the Chart and Map Experts along with the Analyzer tools to not only create charts and maps, but to fine-tune them. In addition, you learned how to use the Seagate Charts tool to adjust the look of the charts you create for your reports.

Advanced Database Concepts

This chapter describes some of the more advanced database topics, including the Structured Query Language (SQL) used to pull data from most databases for your reports. While you can create some reports without knowing SQL commands, there will be times when you'll want to refine the queries or write them yourself to get the data you need.

The SQL Designer is also discussed, and you'll learn how to use it to write and edit your own queries, how to create and use data dictionaries, and how to write reports based on stored procedures.

For reports using data sources that don't use SQL, like Microsoft Exchange and Outlook, the information in this chapter is generally not applicable. However, if you develop reports that either connect directly to a SQL data source or connect to any data source via an ODBC connection, you will find the information in this chapter quite useful.

Introduction to SQL

You can create reports with Seagate Crystal Reports without knowing a thing about Structured Query Language (SQL). However, most report designers find that some basic SQL knowledge comes in handy when creating record or group selection formulas and verifying that the Crystal Report Designer created a SQL query as you intended. Therefore, this section introduces you to a few of the mainstay concepts in the SQL language. If you are already familiar with SQL, skip ahead to "Benefits of Server-Side Processing."

Structured Query Language is a simple script language used to access data from databases. The American National Standards Institute (ANSI) standard for SQL includes a set of commands supported by all major databases. Many database manufacturers include their own version of SQL which supports the ANSI commands, as well as proprietary commands and functions.

SQL consists of a set of reserved words; that is, you cannot use these words to name a table, variable, or stored procedure. To do so would generate an error. Many of the reserved words are specific to creating and managing the database itself and should never be used in writing queries for reporting. This chapter discusses the two most common commands for returning datasets in SQL; for a more detailed discussion of the SQL language, consult a SQL reference book.

The Basic SELECT Statement

Only a handful of commands are typically used to return a set of data from a query, and of them the SELECT and WHERE commands are by far the most prevalent. The most powerful command in standard (ANSI/ISO) SQL is the SELECT statement. This statement allows you to view or select records from a specific table in the database. The syntax for the SELECT command is:

```
SELECT fieldname(s)
FROM tablename(s)
[WHERE search condition(s)]
```

All SELECT queries require the first two statements, SELECT and FROM. Basically, they tell the database what fields (columns) you want to see and what tables they come from. To select all fields from a table, use the asterisk (*) in place of the fieldnames, as follows:

```
SELECT * FROM authors
```

This example displays all of the data in the authors table. If you want only certain fields in the table, your query might look like this:

```
SELECT first_name, last_name FROM authors
```

This example displays the first name and last name for all authors in the authors table. When specifying fields to select, separate them with a comma. The last field listed should have no trailing comma.

 The use of uppercase for SQL commands is a common practice among database administrators and programmers. The SQL query language is not case-sensitive. The command "SELECT * FROM authors" gives the same results as "select * from authors".

Adding a WHERE Clause

More often than not, you'll want a dataset to match a particular set of criteria, such as transactions within a date range, books of a particular type, or names of customers in a single city or state. The WHERE clause allows you to specify the search conditions for the resulting dataset. Think of the WHERE clause in SQL as the equivalent of the Select Expert in Seagate Crystal Reports. The SELECT statement with a WHERE clause follows this syntax:

```
SELECT fieldname(s)
FROM tablename(s)
[WHERE <clause>]
```

The *<clause>* after the WHERE keyword specifies the relationship between fields or the condition that you want the data to meet. Usually the WHERE clause involves a comparison operator that designates how the data should relate to the statement. The operators permitted in the WHERE clause include:

=, >, <, >=, <=, <> (not equal)

Enclose strings and dates used in the WHERE clause in single or double quotes.

```
SELECT * FROM users WHERE state = "AZ"
```

This statement selects all fields from the users table for users who live in Arizona.

Multiple clauses can be strung together in the WHERE clause for more complex queries.

```
SELECT * FROM users
WHERE state = "AZ"
AND gender = "M"
AND position <> "management"
```

This statement selects all fields from the users table for male users who live in Arizona and who are not managers.

Benefits of Server-Side Processing

Server-side processing refers to those report processing functions performed on the database server. Mostly, those functions have to do with gathering the data from the query for use in the report. The benefits of server-side processing include:

- Less time connected to the server
- The client computer requires less memory to process the report
- Less time to transfer data from the server to the client.

When you turn server-side processing on, the client computer sends the SQL statements to the database server through ODBC, which then processes and returns the dataset. Seagate Crystal Reports relies on the server to process the SQL request, sort the data and return it so that the client computer can perform other duties. Keep in mind a few rules when considering whether to use server-side processing:

- You must sort and group your reports in order to use server-side processing. For simple lists and other types of reports that are not sorted and grouped, the server has very little processing to do, other than simply returning the dataset.

- You must choose a data source that supports SQL. Reports based on a non-SQL data source such as a query or data dictionary cannot use server-side processing.

To perform the sorting and grouping on the server, your report must:

- Have the Perform Grouping on Server option turned on.

- Use some form of grouping.

- Have the Details section hidden. The server processes only hidden sections.

- Have grouping on a database field. Formula fields are processed only on the client.

- Have all running totals based on summary fields.

- Not contain Average or Distinct Count summaries.

- Not contain Top N values. Use the Sort All option.

- Not contain specified order grouping.

If a report contains Date and Time fields, server-side processing works if you group on days or on seconds. Server-side processing does not work if you group on month, year, minutes, or hours.

When you drill down on a hidden section of a report that has server-side processing turned on, SCR automatically initiates a connection to the server. If the client cannot connect to the server, drilling down on data generates an error.

To turn on server-side processing, choose File, Options from the main menu, and then select the Perform Grouping On Server check box on the Database tab.

Using SQL Expressions Directly on a Report

SQL Expressions are special SQL statements that take advantage of some of the more powerful functions provided with your database, such as aggregate functions, date/time functions, or other database-specific functions. A SQL Expression is very similar in function to a Crystal formula. Once you create the SQL Expression, you can include it as a field on your report, reference it in formulas, and more. You can also sort or group data based on the results of a SQL Expression. SCR evaluates SQL Expressions on the server, making them fast and efficient. The two most common ways of forming a SQL Expression include the following:

FUNCTION(Table.fieldname)

Where FUNCTION is an aggregate function or other database function, use the FUNCTION as instructed by your database documentation.

Many databases provide special functions called aggregates that perform summary calculations on database fields. Examples of aggregate functions are SUM, COUNT, MIN, MAX, and AVG. How these functions are used depends on the specific database you are using; refer to your database documentation for instructions on using these and other functions.

Table.fieldname [arithmetic operator] Table.fieldname

You can also use SQL Expressions to perform arithmetic expressions on database fields, such as adding, subtracting, multiplying, and dividing fields of the same data type. The following examples work for Microsoft SQL Server databases.

SUM(sales.amount)
DATEPART(MM,titles.pubdate)
(sales.qty)   *   (titles.price)

To use the SQL Expression Editor:

1. Select Insert, SQL Expression Field from the main menu. The SQL Expression Name dialog box appears.

2. Type a name for the SQL expression into the Name field and click the OK button. The SQL Expression Editor appears (see Figure 10.1).

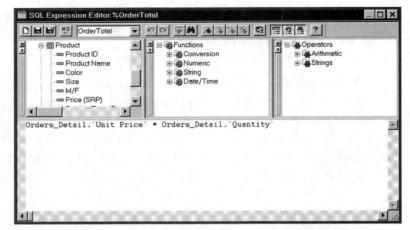

Figure 10.1
You can use SQL Expressions to access special database functions.

> 3. Type the SQL expression into the Editor, using the Field, Function, and Operator trees to add components to the expression.

Using the Crystal SQL Designer

Crystal SQL Designer is an application included with Seagate Crystal Reports that lets you build a SQL query outside of the Crystal Report Designer. When you build queries independently of reports, you can use them for multiple reports, such as in detail level and summary level reports. This way, you build a single query that can be reused. You can build a query using any of these three methods:

- By using the Seagate Query Expert
- By entering the SQL statement directly
- By starting from an existing Seagate query

The Crystal SQL Designer uses tabbed dialog boxes similar to the Report Experts. Start the Crystal SQL Designer from the Start, Programs, Seagate Crystal Reports menu. The Crystal SQL Designer window opens. The standard toolbar in the Crystal SQL Designer offers a quick way to execute the following menu functions:

▪ Start a New Query

 ▪ Open a Query

 ▪ Save a Query

 ▪ Edit a Query

 ▪ Execute a Query

To create a new query, you click the New Query button on the toolbar, or select File, New from the main menu. This opens the New Query dialog box, which allows you to select the options for creating your query (see Figure 10.2):

▪ If you want to use the Seagate Query Expert, see the section "Using the Seagate Query Expert."

▪ If you want to enter a SQL statement directly, see the section "Entering a SQL Statement Directly."

▪ If you want to start from an existing query, see the section "Starting from an Existing Query."

Figure 10.2
The New Query dialog box lets you specify how to create a new query.

Using the Seagate Query Expert

The Seagate Query Expert is a simple tool that uses a tabbed dialog box similar to the Report Experts. After clicking the Use Seagate Query Expert button on the New Query dialog box, the Create SQL Expert appears.

Tables Tab: Selecting the Data Source and Tables

The Tables tab lets you specify the name of your query and choose the data source and tables for your report (see Figure 10.3). To select the data source and tables to use in the query:

1. Type the name for your query in the Query Name box.

2. Choose the source for the data. To select a data dictionary, click the Dictionary button. To select a SQL or ODBC data source, click the SQL/ODBC button.

   - If you select SQL/ODBC, the Log On Server dialog box appears (see Figure 10.4). Go to Step 3.

   - If you select a data dictionary, the File Open dialog box appears. Select the dictionary file to use and skip to Step 5.

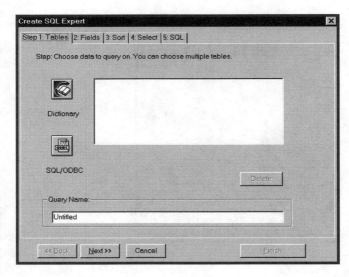

Figure 10.3

The Tables tab on the Create SQL Expert allows you to specify the tables to include in the report.

Figure 10.4

The Log On Server dialog box lets you select the ODBC data source where you can find your database tables.

3. In the Log On Server dialog box, select the name of the SQL or ODBC server you want to log on to and click OK. If the log on is successful, the Choose SQL Table dialog box appears (see Figure 10.5).

4. Select the tables you want to include in the query. Click the Add button to add each one to the list on the Create SQL Expert.

If you need to log on to another server to access additional tables, click the Log On Server button.

5. When you finish selecting tables, click Done. The Links tab appears automatically. If you selected a data dictionary in Step 1, there are no links to set up—click the Fields tab and skip to the section "Fields Tab: Selecting Fields."

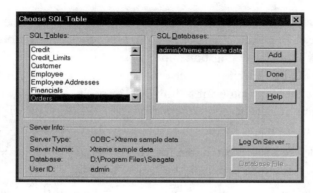

Figure 10.5

The Choose SQL Table dialog box lets you select the tables to include in your query.

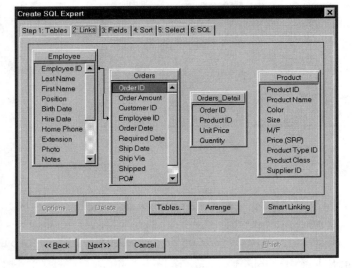

Figure 10.6

The Links tab on the Create SQL Expert allows you to specify the relationship between the tables by linking foreign keys.

Links Tab: Linking Tables

On the Links tab, you specify the relationships between the tables (see Figure 10.6). Its use is very similar to that in the Crystal Report Designer. To indicate foreign key relationships between tables:

1. Click the primary key field on one table and drag it to the corresponding foreign key field in another table. This establishes a foreign key link.

A table's primary key is one or more field with a unique index that differentiates records in that table. When one table has a field or fields that match the primary key field in another table, that field is referred to as a *foreign key*.

2. If you want to set the link options to take advantage of an index for the tables being linked or specify a join type, click the Options button. The Link Options dialog box appears (see Figure 10.7). Use the Index In Use field to specify an index to use other than the primary key. Next, enter the field you want to link on. To specify a join type other than the default, select the desired join type from the SQL Join Type area. Click OK to return to the main screen of the Links tab.

3. To delete a link created in error, click the line that identifies the link and press the Del key or click the Delete button.

4. Click the Tables button to view a description of the tables selected.

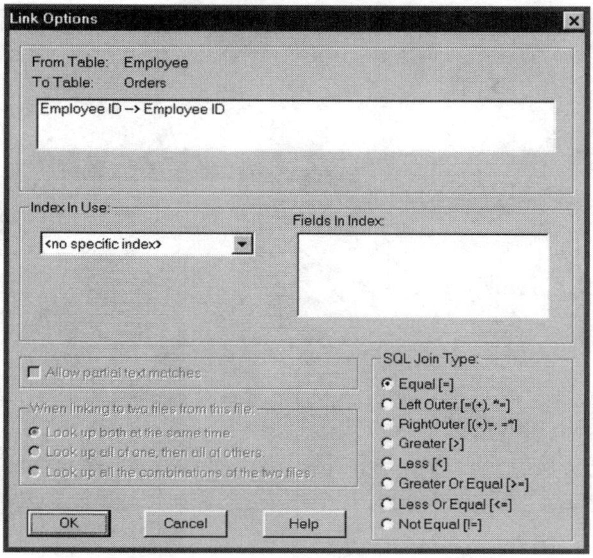

Figure 10.7
The Link Options
dialog box lets
you configure
how to link fields
between tables.

5. Click Arrange to arrange the tables so that their links are easier to follow.

6. Click Smart Linking to have SCR's Smart Linking tool "guess" the links between tables.

7. Continue creating links until you've identified all of the table relationships.

8. Click the <u>N</u>ext button, or click the Fields tab.

Fields Tab: Selecting Fields

The Fields tab lets you indicate the fields to include in the query. You can place table fields or SQL Expressions in the query using the Fields tab options (see Figure 10.8). To choose the fields to include in the query:

1. Select the fields to appear in the query's dataset from the Database Fields list and click the Add button to add them to the Query Fields list.

You can move the field names up and down in the list by clicking the up and down arrow buttons just above the Query Fields list. This is the equivalent of changing their order in the SELECT statement, and only serves to change the order in which they appear in the query results.

2. To browse through the data in the table for a particular field, select a field in the Database Fields list, and then click the <u>B</u>rowse button.

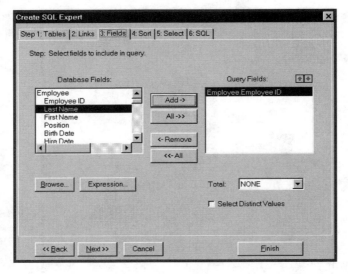

Figure 10.8

The Fields tab on the Create SQL Expert allows you to specify the fields you want to include in your report.

3. To add a SQL Expression for a particular field, select a field in the Database Fields list and click the Expression button. You are asked to enter a name for the expression. Type a new name to create a new SQL expression, or type an existing name to edit an expression. The SQL Expression dialog box appears (see Figure 10.9). You can double-click the field name in the Fields list to use it in your SQL statement.

4. To create a summary field, select a field in the Query Fields list, and then select the desired aggregate function in the Totals list. The aggregate types

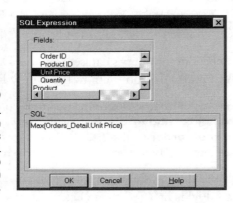

Figure 10.9

The SQL Expression dialog box lets you specify a SQL Expression to include in the query.

are SUM, COUNT, AVG, MIN, and MAX. These functions are performed for the entire group of records in the report.

5. Select the Select Distinct Values check box to construct the query to show only distinct values for *all* of the fields.

6. Click the Next button, or click the Sort tab at the top of the Create SQL Expert dialog box.

Sort Tab: Sorting and Grouping

The Sort tab lets you define groups for the query (see Figure 10.10). The fields you select here will be written to the query's GROUP BY clause. This can make the data more meaningful by providing groupings such as by date, by location, and so on. To indicate the fields on which you would like the query results grouped and sorted:

1. Select a field name in the Database Fields list and click Add to display the field name in the Group Fields list.

2. To specify the order for the data, select the desired choice from the Order list.

3. Click Next or the Select tab.

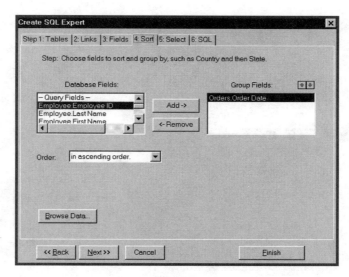

Figure 10.10

The Sort tab on the Create SQL Expert allows you to sort and group data.

Select Tab: Indicating the Select Conditions

The Select tab lets you narrow down the conditions for the dataset (see Figure 10.11). The field conditions you specify here will be written to the query's WHERE clause. This tab is very similar to the Select tab on the Standard Report Expert. Refer to Chapter 2 for detailed instructions on using this tab. To filter data on a particular field:

1. Select the field in the Database Fields list and click Add to display the field name in the Select Fields list.

2. Below the field name list boxes, select the operators and values to complete the filter. Refer to Chapter 2 for details on these operators and how they are used.

3. To see the data in the tables for the field selected, click Browse Data to open a dialog box listing all the values in that field.

4. Click the Next button or the SQL tab.

SQL Tab: Viewing the SQL Statement

The last tab on the SQL Expert lets you view the SQL query that the Expert created for you (see Figure 10.12). To view and run the SQL statement:

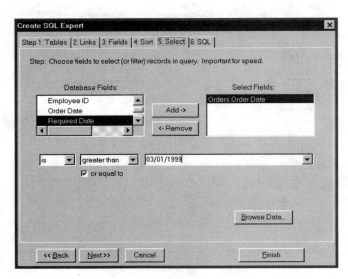

Figure 10.11

The Select tab on the Create SQL Expert allows you to create a WHERE clause.

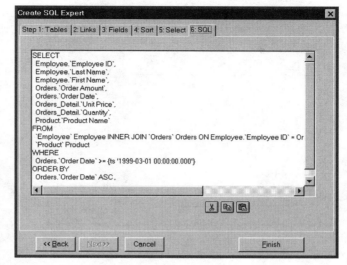

Figure 10.12

The SQL tab on the Create SQL Expert shows you the SQL statement the Expert created.

1. Make any necessary adjustments to the SQL statement as desired and click Finish to execute the query. A dialog box appears, asking if you want to process the query.

2. To save the query and its dataset, select File, Save As and provide a path and file name. Refer to the section "Creating Reports from Saved SQL Queries" later in this chapter for instructions on creating a report from a saved query.

 The Save Data with Query command on the File menu is checked by default. This option allows you to edit and work with your query in the SQL Designer without having to wait for the database to return a dataset. For large datasets, this option saves time during query design and edit.

Entering the SQL Statement Directly

Crystal SQL Designer also gives you the option of entering a SQL statement directly (see Figure 10.13). If you're comfortable writing SQL statements, you may prefer to use this option. Also, if a SQL statement has already been written and saved to a text file, you can import and use it to build your query. To type the SQL statement directly:

1. Click the Enter SQL Statement Directly button on the New Query dialog box. The Enter SQL Statement dialog box opens.

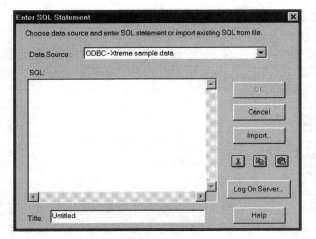

Figure 10.13

The Enter SQL Statement dialog box lets you type your SQL statement directly and store it for later use with a report.

2. Type the name of the query in the Title box at the bottom of the dialog box.

3. If you have logged on to more than one data source, you can select the data source to use for this query by choosing it from the Data Source list.

4. Type your query in the SQL box.

5. If the SQL query you want to use has been saved to a text file, you can import it by clicking the Import button. Select the path and file name to import and click OK. The query opens in the SQL box. You can edit the query as desired without affecting the original file.

6. Click the Log On Server button to select a different server for the query. Specify the ODBC data source to use and provide a logon name and password. The new data source appears in the Data Source list.

7. Click OK when you finish typing the query. Crystal SQL Designer displays a message asking if you want to process the query now. Click Yes to test and run the query.

8. To save the query and the dataset, select File, Save As and provide a path and file name. See "Creating Reports from Saved SQL Queries" later in this chapter for instructions on creating a report from a saved query.

The Save Data <u>w</u>ith Query option on the <u>F</u>ile menu is checked by default. Most times you will want to execute the query and update the data each time the report is run, so—once you've gotten your query just the way you want it—clear this option before saving the query a final time.

Starting from an Existing Query

If you have already written a query that is useful for one report but only needs a few changes in order to make it useful for another report, you can use that query to write another. This eliminates the need to rewrite the portion of the query that is useful in your new report.

When you start from an existing query, you use the same dialog box and tabs you used when you initially created that query. The steps that follow call attention to only those items that you may need to use differently. To base a new query on an existing query:

1. Click the Start from Existing Seagate Query button on the New Query dialog box. The File Open dialog box appears, listing existing queries in the default query path (see Figure 10.14).

2. Select the query file you want to use and click OK. The query opens in the SQL Designer window.

3. Click the Edit Query toolbar button, or click the <u>E</u>dit, <u>Q</u>uery menu command. The Create SQL Expert appears.

4. Enter a name for the new query in the Title text box.

Figure 10.14
The File Open dialog box lets you indicate the existing query you want to use as a template.

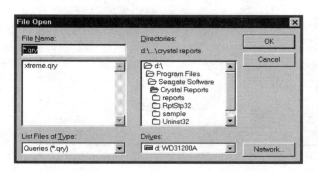

5. Edit the query text as required. Click OK when you finish. Refer to the section "Entering the SQL Statement Directly" for more detailed information on using this dialog box.

If you've previously saved data with a query, and you execute the revised query by clicking the Execute Query button or by selecting Edit, Refresh Data, the SQL Designer discards the saved data and runs the query against the database again.

Creating Reports from Saved SQL Queries

Once you have created a query with the Crystal SQL Designer, you can use it to create a report. The procedure for creating a report based on a query is nearly identical to that for creating a report based on a table, with the exception that you select Query on the Data tab of any Report Expert rather than SQL/ODBC or another type of data source.

1. From the main menu, click File, New, or click the New button on the toolbar.

2. Click the desired report type from the Report Gallery. The corresponding Report Expert appears.

3. Click the Query button on the Data page. The File Open dialog box appears.

4. Select the Seagate Crystal Reports Query file desired and click Open (see Figure 10.15).

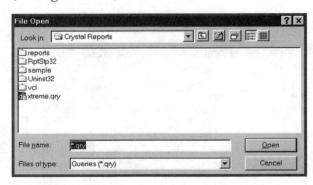

Figure 10.15

Select the query file to use for the new report

5. Click the Fields, Sort, Total, TopN, Graph, Select, and Style tabs in turn as needed to finish designing the report. Refer to Chapter 2 for more detailed instructions on using the Report Experts.

Using Dictionaries

A *Crystal Dictionary* is a customized, simplified view of data. Once created, a dictionary serves as a data source, eliminating the need to search through large and often cryptic databases.

Dictionaries allow the developer to design, organize, and create less complicated datasets that are friendlier and easier to understand. Databases can be massive and require extensive mapping directions to find just the tables and fields needed to build reports. Often the report writer does not understand the field and table names used in databases.

A dictionary can be created containing only the tables that the report writer needs. Through the dictionary, table and field names can be changed and help text added for more detailed descriptions and clearer understanding of the data needed for building reports.

A dictionary can also contain complicated manipulations of data without requiring the report writer to understand formula concepts or how to manipulate data. Formulas may be established in the dictionary and then used when creating reports.

The Benefits of Using Dictionaries

Dictionaries may be created for specific users, such as individual departments in a company. Such dictionaries would contain specific data that that department needs to develop reports. For instance, a Human Resources departmental dictionary may include employee tables containing salaries, job history, starting dates, job history, social security numbers, employee ID, and information needed only by the Human Resources department. The Sales department might require a departmental dictionary including account tables containing account names, product types, sales volume, and information vital to the Sales department.

When creating reports, each department would access the appropriate departmental dictionary to build the reports they need. By accessing the dictionaries rather than the tables themselves, the report writers do not have to spend time wading through the database.

Dictionaries provide not only a faster and easier report developing process, but they can restrict access to sensitive data by preventing unauthorized users from viewing data in tables to which they should not have access.

Creating Crystal Dictionaries

The Crystal Dictionaries application is a component of your Seagate Crystal Reports installation. You should close any other open programs before starting Crystal Dictionaries, including the Crystal Report Designer.

Upon opening Crystal Dictionaries, you have two main options: start a new dictionary or open an existing dictionary (see Figure 10.16).

It's a good idea to determine the tables and fields you will need in your dictionary before you begin building the dictionary. You'll also want to plan how you'll access that data. Do you want to access the data through a data file or

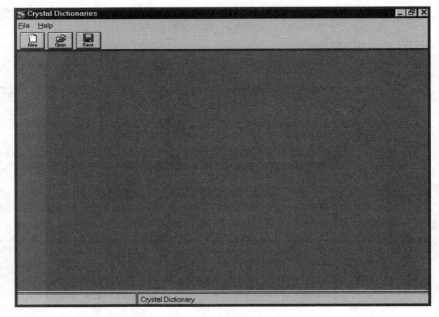

Figure 10.16

Use the toolbar buttons in the Crystal Dictionaries window to create, edit, and save data dictionaries.

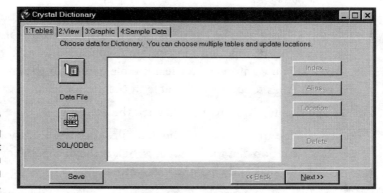

Figure 10.17

The Crystal Dictionary Expert guides you through creating a dictionary.

SQL/ODBC? You may not use data from different data sources in one dictionary. To create a new dictionary:

1. Click the New button. The Crystal Dictionary Expert appears (see Figure 10.17).

2a. To create a dictionary based on a data file, click the Data file button. Select the data file name in the Open dialog box and click Add. Repeat this process until you've selected all required data files. Click the Done button when you finish adding tables.

OR

2b. To create a dictionary based on an ODBC or SQL data source, click the SQL/ODBC button. Select the data source from which you will pull data, including the tables in the desired database. For detailed instructions on selecting a data source, logging in, and choosing tables, refer to Chapter 3.

After selecting a data source, the Index, Alias, Location and Delete buttons on the right side of the Expert become available.

3. To change the name or location of a table's index, click Index. The New Location dialog box appears. Select the new file name for the index and click the OK button.

This option applies only to databases that support external indices. If you select tables from a database that does not support external indices, the Index button is not available. For example, Paradox tables support external indices, whereas SQL Server tables do not.

4. To change the alias (name) of the table, click the Alias button. The Set Table Alias dialog box appears. The *alias* is the name for the table that appears in the report when you build your report based on the dictionary. If you want to create clearer table names for the end user, you can use an Alias to identify the table in the dictionary.

5. Type the new alias name and click the OK button.

6. To change the location of the data file, click the Location button. The New Location dialog box appears. Select the new path and file name for this table alias and click the OK button.

7. To delete tables shown on the Tables tab, select a table and click Delete.

Links Tab: Indicating Table Relationships

If you have selected more than one table, the Links tab appears (see Figure 10.18). Click the Links tab to specify the foreign key relationships between the tables you have selected.

Establish a foreign key relationship between the tables as needed. Refer to the discussion of the Visual Linking Expert in Chapter 3 for detailed information on how to do this.

Figure 10.18
The Links tab lets you specify the relationship between the tables.

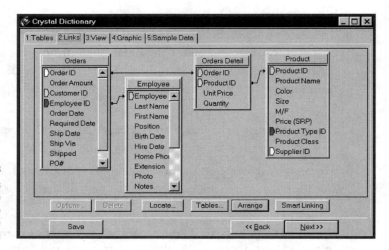

If you get an error while establishing the link, it is possible that the two fields cannot be linked. Remember that the two fields being linked must be of the same data type. For example, you cannot link a string field with an integer field.

To use Smart Linking to establish your foreign key relationships, click the Smart Linking button. Smart Linking finds fields in tables that have the same name and data type and draws the connecting lines between them. You may edit the links if necessary.

 Once linking is established in the dictionary, the links may not be altered when using that dictionary as a data source for a report.

View Tab: Specifying Field and Heading Aliases

When you select fields to appear in a dictionary, they do not retain their original database structure within the tables. That is, the dictionary user cannot tell which tables the field names came from or how the data was originally organized in the database. With the View tab, you can not only group fields into logical tables, but you have complete control over the field names, as well, through the use of aliases.

Using aliases gives you a lot of flexibility in the way your dictionary looks to the end user. If you want to keep the original database structure completely hidden, you can change the field names and group them under headings of your choosing. Or if the table and field names in the database are not intuitive, you can make it easier for dictionary users to select the fields they want by giving them more meaningful names.

The View tab also gives you the opportunity to add help text to the fields and headings in the dictionary. Adding help text can greatly assist the report writers in using the dictionary. Help text appears as a pop-up hint or "bubble help" when the user places the cursor over the field to which the help text was added. To select fields and headings:

1. Click the View tab. The tables selected on the Tables tab appear in the Tables & Fields from Database list on the left (see Figure 10.19).

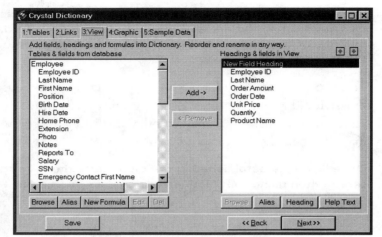

Figure 10.19

On the View tab you can select the database fields and their headings for your dictionary.

To show and hide the field names within a table or heading, double-click the table or heading name.

2. To include fields in the dictionary, select the desired fields in the Tables & Fields from Database list and click the Add button. Each field selected appears in the Headings & Fields in View list on the right. To remove a field from the Headings & Fields in View list, select the field and click the Remove button.

Hold the Shift or Ctrl keys while clicking fields in the Tables & Fields from Database list to add multiple fields to the Headings & Fields in View list at one time.

You can move fields from the Tables & Fields from Database list to the Headings & Fields in View list by dragging them, but to remove them from the Headings & Fields in View list, you must select them one at a time and click the Remove button.

3. To add a heading to the dictionary, click the Heading button. The Insert Field Heading dialog box appears. Using field headings helps you organize the fields in the dictionary. When you group fields under a field heading, the fields appear to the dictionary user as though they are in "tables." Type the desired name of the field heading.

4. You have the option of creating a formula to include in the dictionary. To create a formula, click the New Formula button. The Formula Name dialog box appears.

5. Type a name for the formula and click the OK button. The Formula Editor appears. Type the desired formula. (Refer to Chapter 6 for information on writing formulas.) Once you create the formula, it can be added to the dictionary just like any other field.

 You can browse the data in a field if you would like to see a sample of the data in the table. To browse the data, select a field and click the Browse button below it.

6. You can change the alias (name) of the headings and fields in your dictionary to make their use more clear. Setting a field or heading alias determines what will appear to the report designer or user as a field or "table." To change the name of a heading or a field, select it from the Headings & Fields in View list. Click the Alias button below the list. The Set Field Alias dialog box appears (see Figure 10.20). Type the new name and click the OK button.

 When you add the first field to the Headings & Fields in View list, a default heading is automatically inserted, called "New Field Heading." You can change it to something more meaningful with the Set Field Alias dialog box.

 You may want to order the data beneath headings for ease of use. For example, you might place all the customer fields under the heading CUSTOMER and all the fields for orders under a heading called ORDER INFORMATION. You can reposition fields by selecting the field you wish to move and using the arrow buttons above the Headings & Fields in View list.

Figure 10.20

You can change the names of the database fields and headings for your dictionary with the Alias button.

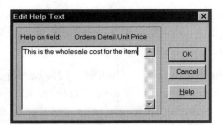

Figure 10.21

You can add help
text to a
dictionary field
or heading.

7. To add help text to a field or heading, select the field or heading and click the Help Text button. The Edit Help Text dialog box appears (see Figure 10.21). Type the help text into the field on the dialog box, and then click OK.

Graphic Tab: Adding Graphics to the Dictionary

The Graphic tab allows you to add to the dictionary pictures—such as company logos, watermarks, and so on—that the writer can add to reports (see Figure 10.22). The pictures must be created and stored in one of the following file formats:

- BMP (Windows or OS/2 Bitmap)
- .PCX (PC Paintbrush)
- .JPG (Joint Photographic Experts Group)
- TIF (Tagged Image File Format)
- .TGA (Truevision Targa)

To add one or more graphic images to the dictionary:

1. Click Add. The File Open dialog box appears. Select the path and file name for the image you want to add, and click OK. The file name appears in the graphics list. You can add as many image files as you like.

2. To remove a graphic image from the list after it has been added, select the file name and click Delete.

 Clicking the Delete button does not remove the file from the path from which it was selected; it only removes it from the data dictionary.

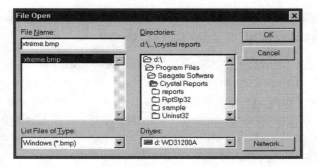

Figure 10.22

The Graphic tab allows you to include graphic images in the dictionary for easy access in creating the reports.

3. To change the path (location) for a file, select the desired file name and click the Location button. The Choose New Location dialog box appears. Select the correct path and click OK.

 If the graphics file changes and you want to update it, use the Choose New Location dialog to identify the updated file.

4. To choose an alias for the file that appears in the dictionary instead of the file name, select the desired file name and click Alias. The Set Graphic Alias dialog box appears. Type the alias name as desired and click the OK button (see Figure 10.23).

   This does not change the file name, only the name to which the file is referred within the dictionary. You can give the file a more descriptive alias instead of simply using the file name to identify the graphic image. Aliases can contain up to 80 characters, including spaces.

SCR does not limit the number of graphics you can use in the dictionary. The dictionary actually makes a copy of the image and stores the copy. If the image changes, you need to update the copy stored in the dictionary; it does not update automatically.

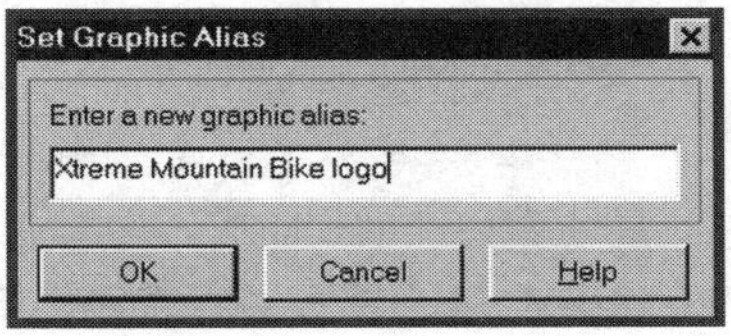

Figure 10.23

Using an alias for the graphic files can help dictionary users identify the images.

Sample Data Tab: Previewing the Dictionary's Result Set

The Sample Data tab allows you to collect and store a preview of the data for any or all of the fields you selected. This allows the dictionary users to view the preview data as well, giving them an example of the data that each field contains while creating reports from the dictionary. The report writer can create a report without connecting to the actual database. Keep in mind that the sample data is collected only for the purpose of identifying the data, not for final reporting.

The Sample Data tab is divided into two sections: Headings & Fields in View, and Browsed Data (see Figure 10.24). The Headings & Fields in View list contains the tables and fields placed in the dictionary. You may collect sample data for any of the fields it contains.

1. To collect sample data, select a field in the Headings & Fields in View list and click the Collect button. The sample data appears in the Browsed Data list.

2. To modify the sample data, select a value in the Browsed Data list and click the Edit button. The Edit Value dialog box appears (see Figure 10.25). Edit the field data as desired and click OK.

3. To remove an item from the sample data, select the value in the Browsed Data list and click Delete.

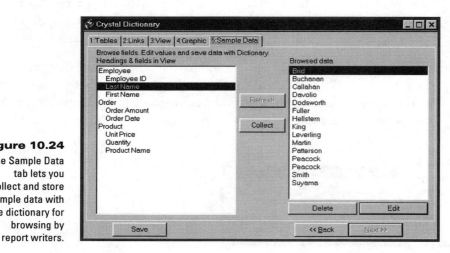

Figure 10.24

The Sample Data tab lets you collect and store sample data with the dictionary for browsing by report writers.

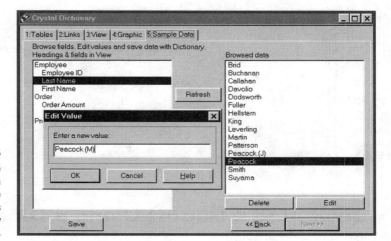

Figure 10.25

Modifying the sample data changes what the dictionary users see when they browse data.

 Editing or deleting the sample data does not change the data in the database, only the sample data the user sees in the dictionary. Reports based on the dictionary display the actual data, not the values shown in the sample data preview.

4. To update the sample data after the database itself has changed, click the Refresh button. The sample data updates to reflect what is currently in the database for the selected fields.

Saving the Dictionary

Once you have completed walking through the Crystal Dictionary Expert, be sure to save your work.

1. To save the dictionary when you finish, click the Save button on the toolbar, the Save button on the Expert, or click the File, Save As menu command. The File Save As dialog box appears.

2. Enter the path and file name where you want to save the dictionary, preserving the default extension .DC5. Click OK to save the dictionary (see Figure 10.26).

You have now completed the dictionary and can use it as a data source from which to build reports.

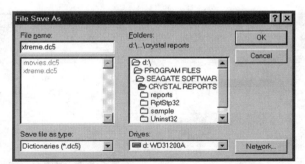

Figure 10.26

Save the
dictionary file
with the default
extension of .dc5.

Designing a Report Using a Dictionary

Once you have created a dictionary, you can create reports using the dictionary as a data source. Dictionaries are fast and efficient; using them eliminates the need for establishing database connections. Only a few rules apply to using dictionaries in a report:

- The data contained in the dictionary is the only data that may be accessed for report. No other databases may be added.

- If the report requires additional data, the dictionary must be edited to include that data.

- You can use only one dictionary in a report.

To build a report using a dictionary:

1. Open the Crystal Report Designer and start a new report using the Report Expert of your choice. For instructions on creating a new report using the Report Experts, refer to Chapter 2.

2. When choosing a data source for the report, click the Dictionary button. The File Open dialog box appears.

3. Navigate to the path and file name for the dictionary you want to use (see Figure 10.27). Click the Open button. All other options on the Data tab of the Report Expert become unavailable.

4. Click the <u>N</u>ext button or the Fields tab. Select the fields as desired. To browse the data, click the Browse Data button. The data browser dialog box appears displaying the data collected while the dictionary was

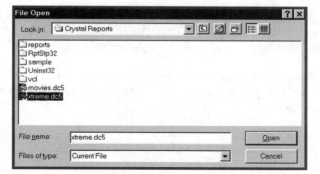

Figure 10.27

Select the file
name of the
dictionary to use
as a data source.

being designed. If no sample data was collected and saved, the dialog
box will be empty.

5. Continue building the report as described in Chapter 2.

Creating Reports from Stored Procedures

For very complex queries, it may be beneficial to have the query run on the
database server rather than on the client PC, then port the data into the
report. Doing so can speed up the time it takes to generate the data, especially
if the report is many pages long.

A *stored procedure* is a SQL query or series of queries executed upon a call to
the stored procedure name with the SQL EXEC command. The main difference between SQL statements in a saved file and a stored procedure is that
a stored procedure can take parameters (values you can pass into the procedure), it can use variables, and it can access database system functions.

The main advantage to using a stored procedure over a query is that the
dataset created with the query is saved with the query. Any new records
stored in the database after the query is created do not appear on the report.
A stored procedure runs when users refresh the report so the dataset is
always up-to-date.

To base a report on a stored procedure, first write the stored procedure and save it on the database server. Your stored procedure can use parameters, if you would like. You can specify the values to pass in later.

Not all SQL database types support stored procedures. Check the documentation for your database to determine whether this is an option for you.

To create a new report based on a stored procedure:

1. Start a new report, choosing SQL/ODBC as the data connection type. The Log On Server dialog box appears.

2. Select the SQL/ODBC data source for the desired database, and then click OK. If you use a database that supports views and stored procedures, the Allow Reporting On dialog box appears (see Figure 10.28).

3. Indicate the database objects to choose from (tables, views, procedures, or system tables) by checking the boxes beside the objects you want to list in the Choose SQL Table dialog box. Be sure to select the Procedures check box and then click the OK button. The Choose SQL Table dialog box appears.

4. Select the stored procedure as you would select a table name. It may appear in the list alphabetically under Proc(StoredProcedureName) or something similar.

5. Continue building the report as described in Chapter 2.

When you click the Design Report button, SCR creates the report. Each time you refresh the report data by clicking the Preview tab or Refresh button, SCR pulls data from the tables and fields you identified in the stored procedure's SELECT statement. If your stored procedure requires parameters the Stored

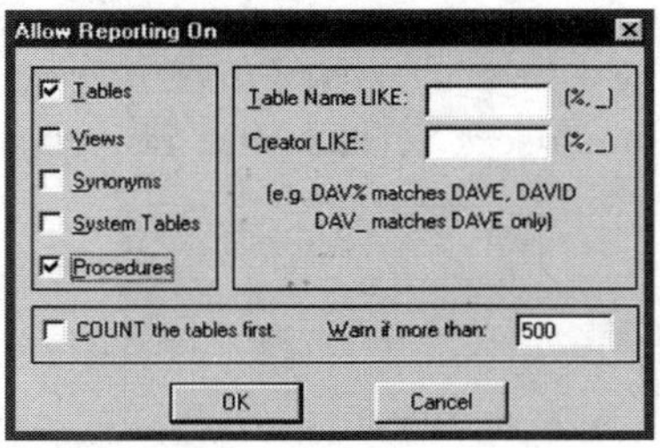

Figure 10.28

The Allow Reporting On dialog box lets you select the types of data objects upon which you can base your reports.

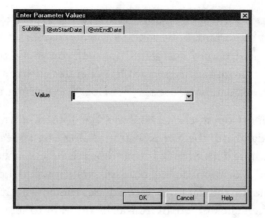

Figure 10.29

The Enter Parameter Values dialog box lets you fill in parameter values to design and debug your report.

Procedure Input Parameters dialog box appears, enabling you to enter values for each parameter (see Figure 10.29).

Verifying a Database

If a table, query, or stored procedure changes after designing a report, it is a good idea to have the Crystal Report Designer query the database to update its own internal references. For example, if a field in the database was changed from a varchar data type to a char data type, you may get an error when you try to run a report using that field. By running the Verify Database utility, however, you can put the report in sync with the updated database.

1. With the affected report open in the Crystal Report Designer, choose Database, Verify Database.

2. If the table, query, or stored procedure has been changed since the report was created or the last Verify Database operation, you are asked whether you want to update the report. If the report has the current data, a message box lets you know that the database is up to date.

Changing the Location of a Database

From time to time you might need to connect to a database on a server other than the one you used when you created the report. This might happen if you develop the report on a test database and move the report to a production database later. It is important, however, that the two databases have matching table names and field names and definitions. If you move the report to a database that differs from the original, SCR generates an error. To specify the location of a different database, use the Set Location command.

1. With the report open, click Database, Set Location. If your report is based on a database, the Set Location dialog box appears (see Figure 10.30). Continue with Step 2. If your report is based on a dictionary, the Choose New Location dialog box appears showing the current path and file name for the data file selected. Set the new path and file name as desired, then click Open. SCR asks if you want to set (propagate) the path for all the tables in the database to the newly selected path. You do not need to take any other action to change the location.

2. Select the table name for which you need to change the location from the Databases list.

3. Click the Set Location button.

   If you change the location of SQL/ODBC tables the Choose SQL Table dialog box appears showing the tables for the currently selected database. Click the Log On Server button to log on to another database. Once you've done so, you can select the table that matches the one you selected in Step 2. The new data source appears in the SQL Databases list. Select the new data source and identify the table in the SQL Tables list that corresponds to the original table. When you click

Figure 10.30

Use the Set Location dialog box to change the location of the report tables.

OK, SCR asks whether you want to set (propagate) the locations for the remaining tables using the newly selected data source. This makes it easy to change the location of all tables without having to set their locations individually.

If you change the location of a data file database, query or dictionary, the Choose New Location dialog box appears showing the current path and file name for the data file selected. Set the new path and file name as desired, then click Open. SCR asks if you want to set (propagate) the path for all the tables in the database to the newly selected path.

 If you use a SQL/ODBC data source, you may want to remove the server name from the location. This way, the report can be copied to multiple servers and databases without having to set the location each time it is copied. To do this, simply remove the server name from the table's location in the Table text box. Thus, for example, rather than having the authors table displayed as "pubs.dbo.authors," it appears as "dbo.authors".

4. To set the location of the tables to the same database the report is currently logged into, click the Same As Report button. The Same As Report button only becomes available when you choose a database file as the data source, and you have saved the report to a path other than that in which the database files are located.

5. To set the database field path to a Universal Naming Convention (UNC) format, click the Convert to UNC button. The UNC format is a "short cut" to a server, such as \\servername\path\filename. Refer to Windows documentation for more information on using the UNC format.

6. When you finish setting the location for all the tables, click the Done button.

Changing the Database Driver

Sometimes a situation arises in which you need to change the driver with which you connect to a particular database, such as when moving from an ODBC driver to a native driver. To convert to a different database driver:

1. Choose the Database, Convert Database Driver menu command. The Convert Database Driver dialog box appears (see Figure 10.31).

Figure 10.31

Use the Convert
Database Driver
dialog box to
change the driver
used to access
the database.

2. Select the Convert Database Driver on Next Refresh check box. You
cannot set the name of the driver unless you've selected this check box.

3. The current database driver being used is listed. To change the driver,
select the desired driver from the To list.

4. Click OK. SCR attempts to connect to the database using the selected
driver. Depending on the database driver through which the report connects, you may be asked for server or ODBC data source information
(see Figure 10.32).

caution

**Be very careful with the Convert Database Driver function (see Fig-
ure 10.33). If the driver you select is not compatible with the database
the report is based on, errors will occur. You should make a backup
copy of the report before using this command.**

Figure 10.32

You must log on to
the server and
database for the
new driver
connection.

Figure 10.33

SCR asks you for
permission to
update the table
data when it
changes
database drivers.

Summary

You can retrieve data from a database to use in a report in several ways:

- Let Seagate Crystal Reports build a SQL query for you
- Use the Crystal SQL Designer to type in your own SQL statements
- Base reports on a data dictionary
- Base reports on a stored procedure.

Once you define a report, you can also use SQL expressions directly in the report as though they were a field in the database tables. SCR evaluates these SQL expressions on the server, which speeds up their performance.

Through the Verify Database feature, you can query the database to update the fields in the report based on changes to tables or stored procedures. If you need to change the location of a database or table, you can use the Set Location option to designate a different database or server upon which to base the report.

Creating Ad Hoc Reports with Seagate Query

- The Components of Seagate Query

- Installing Seagate Query

- Creating a Report with the Crystal Query Client

- Sections of the Crystal Query Client

- Additional Crystal Query Client Functions and Settings

S eagate Query, a new component of Seagate Crystal Reports 7, allows the creation of reports without the Crystal Report Designer. It creates basic ad hoc reports that can, however, be opened in SCR for additional functions.

Seagate Query opens the door for IT departments to allow users to create simple ad hoc reports quickly without the need to install all of Seagate Crystal Reports. Seagate Query also works from a Web browser and is 100 percent Java so reports can be created from most platforms over the Web.

Only the 32-bit version of Seagate Crystal Reports Professional includes Seagate Query.

This chapter reviews the functionality of the Seagate Query tool so users can begin creating ad hoc reports quickly. For experienced Seagate Crystal Reports users, a comparison of the functionality of Seagate Query and the Crystal Report Designer is included. Seagate Query does not replace the Crystal Report Designer, but it does support many report writing basics for those who do not need all the functionality of Seagate Crystal Reports.

Seagate Query performs most report processing at the database server, sometimes referred to as the *back end*. This means you do not need database drivers on the client machine. The connection to the database occurs on the server, not the client. This makes report generation accessible to anyone in an organization with access to the Web.

The Components of Seagate Query

Two components make up Seagate Query. First is the Query Client, which can be installed on a Windows machine or installed in a Java-compatible Web browser. The Query Client has functionality similar to the Crystal Report Designer but does not include all of the features. The tool does save files in the .RPT format—the native Crystal Reports format—making them available for further editing in the Crystal Report Designer.

The second component is the Query Server, which connects to the database server. The Query Server accepts requests from the Query Client and processes the ad hoc report. The Query Server also allows you to configure and modify settings that can control the amount of work that the server does.

Installing the Seagate Query components is easy. Check to see whether you already have them installed by looking in your Seagate Crystal Reports program group. If you don't see the components you need, read the next sections to find out how to install and configure Seagate Query components. If installed, you may see either or both Query Client and Query Server items. Even if both components have been installed, you may want to read over the next section, "Installing Seagate Query," anyway to make sure that you've configured the Query Server correctly. By default, the installation adds some extra text to the file path that needs to be removed if you've installed both components on the same machine.

 Seagate Software has a white paper available with more in-depth information on installing Seagate Query. Search for the phrase "Installation and Configuration Guide" in the Knowledge Base area of Seagate Software's Web site (www.seagatesoftware.com).

Installing Seagate Query

Normally you install the Query Server on one machine—a server—and the Query Client on one or more other machines—user workstations. To get familiar with Seagate Query, you can install both components on one computer. Whether you install the Query Server and Query Client on one or more machines, it is strongly recommended that you install the Query Server on a Windows NT machine for the best performance and stability. From testing, it appears that the Query Server requires less memory and resources in Windows NT than in Windows 95/98. However, the Query Server does run in Windows 95/98.

 If you plan to install the Query Server and Query Client on different machines, make sure you have a Share Name defined on the server before starting the installation.

A *share name* refers to sharing a folder or drive on a machine. In the process of creating the shared folder, you provide a share name so that you know what the folder is called when you look at it over the network. You will need to enter the Share Name for the Seagate Software folder in Step 5 of the installation.

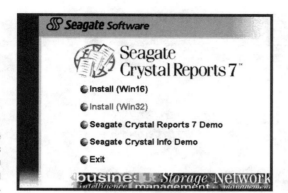

Figure 11.1

Start the Seagate
Crystal Reports
Setup from
the opening
dialog box.

To install Seagate Query, insert the Seagate Crystal Reports CD and wait for the opening dialog box to display (see Figure 11.1). If it doesn't display automatically, explore the CD and double-click Setup in the main directory.

1. Choose Install (Win 32). The Seagate Crystal Reports Setup program starts. The following steps are the specific options you'll need to consider when installing Seagate Query.

2. Walk through the installation process until you reach the dialog box titled "Installation Options."

3. Under Installation Mode, click Custom. In the Installation Directory box, enter the directory where you want to install the software, or click Browse to locate or set up the directory. Click Next.

4. When the Custom Installation Options dialog box appears, select either Query Client, Query Server, or both if you want to install both components on one machine. You may want to clear all other check boxes, unless you mean to install or reinstall additional components (see Figure 11.2).

5. The setup program asks if you want Query Server to start automatically when you turn the computer on or reboot. If you're installing on a Windows NT machine, the setup program asks if you want to add Query Server as an NT service. If you're installing on a Windows 95/98 machine, the setup program asks if you want to add Query Server to the

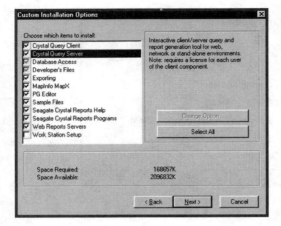

Figure 11.2

On the Custom Installation Options dialog box, determine which components of Seagate Query to install. Double-check that you have enough disk space to install the selected components.

Startup program group. It is recommended that you answer yes to either option.

6. The setup program copies the Seagate Query program files to your machine, and then opens the Crystal Query Server Options dialog box. By default, the setup program inserts "<Share Name>" into both the UNC Path boxes.

7. If you installed the Query Server and Query Client on the same machine, change the path to point to these files on your machine (see Figure 11.3). You do not need to share a folder or drive to make the Query Server work if you install both components on the same machine.

8. If the Query Server is on your server, change the "<Share Name>" to the name of the shared drive.

 Seagate Query Server commonly fails when the Share Name issue (in Step 5) has not been properly addressed. Having Seagate Query work successfully depends on properly setting up the UNC paths.

9. After setting the Crystal Query Server options you'll need to restart your machine; doing so allows these new files to be loaded in at startup so that they function properly.

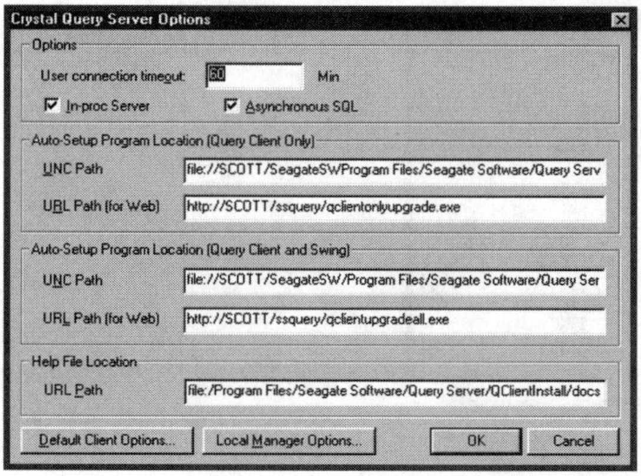

Figure 11.3

Change the path in the Crystal Query Server Options dialog box to make Crystal Query Server work correctly.

Starting the Crystal Query Server

After installing the software, you first need to start the Crystal Query Server so your Crystal Query Client has something to connect to. You can start the Crystal Query Server as an application or as a service (Windows NT only).

Starting the Query Server as a Service (Windows NT)

If you work on a Windows NT machine, you can simply go to Control Panel, Services, look for Crystal Query Server, and click Start (see Figure 11.4).

It is a good idea to also click the Startup button in the Services dialog box. In the subsequent Service dialog box, select This Account in the Log On As area, and then set up a logon name and password information. This allows

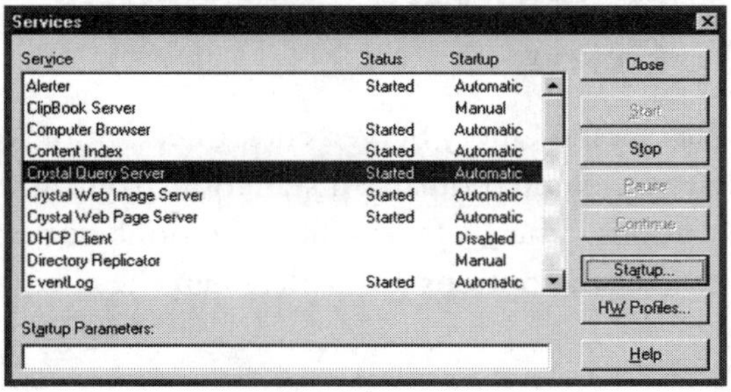

Figure 11.4

From the Control Panel, open the Services dialog box and select Crystal Query Server.

Figure 11.5
For Crystal Query
Server service,
select the options
Automatic and
This Account.

Crystal Query Server to run even when no one has specifically logged on to the machine (and it is locked or logged off). Choose a Domain Administrator logon and password in order to ensure that Windows NT grants the proper rights to the Crystal Query Server. If you use the System Account, this service only works when someone has specifically logged on to the server machine (see Figure 11.5).

Starting the Crystal Query Server as an Application

If you installed Crystal Query Server on a Windows 95/98 machine, or if you do not want to set up the Crystal Query Server as an NT service, simply select Crystal Query Server from the Seagate Crystal Reports program group to start the application. If you use Windows 95/98 and do not want the Crystal Query Server to start up automatically, you can delete the shortcut from the Startup group on the Start menu.

Setting Crystal Query Server Client Options

After you start the Crystal Query Server, click File, Options. Notice the same path settings that you entered during installation. You can choose two buttons to change options. The Default Client Options button opens a dialog box where you can set the options available when the client connects to this

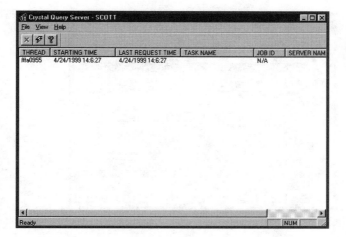

Figure 11.6
Crystal Query
Server running as
an application
displays threads
and jobs.

server (see Figure 11.7). An important setting is the maximum number of records to return in a browse field window; this setting helps reduce network traffic. The other settings select which sections to display by default in the Crystal Query Client. For now leave the settings at their defaults; you may want to come back later and change settings based on your specific needs.

The Local Manager Options button opens a dialog box that stores the paths that you set to allow the Crystal Query Server to work with existing Crystal Reports (see Figure 11.8). By default, you should see the \Seagate Software\Crystal Reports\reports folder. This keeps reports created with Seagate Query in the same directory as your Seagate Crystal Reports.

Figure 11.7
You set default
Crystal Query
Client options
from the Crystal
Query Server.

Figure 11.8

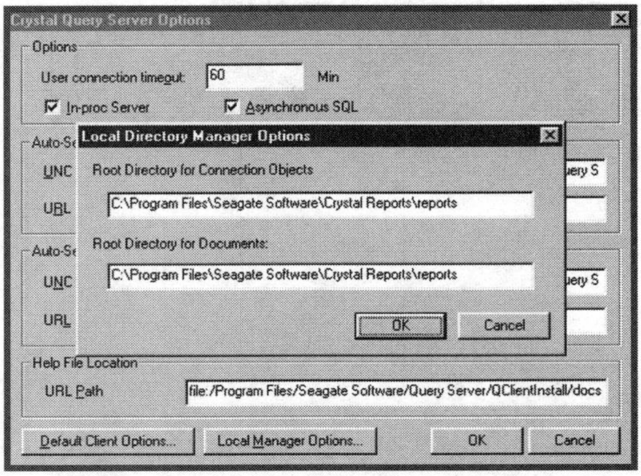

Use the Local Directory Manager options to set the location for report files.

Starting the Crystal Query Client

Seagate offers two different ways to work with the Crystal Query Client: in Windows or through a Web browser. The Windows version of the Crystal Query Client is faster because you install the program files locally on the machine. If you won't be working from a Windows platform or prefer the Web to build ad hoc reports, follow the instructions for the Web browser installation.

Installing the Crystal Query Client— Windows

Launch the Seagate Crystal Query Client from your program group. The Enter Query Server dialog box appears (see Figure 11.9).

1. Enter Localhost in the Enter Query Server dialog box if the Query Server is on the same machine as the Query Client; otherwise, enter the machine name or IP address of the Query Server machine.

Figure 11.9

Localhost (or an IP address of 127.0.0.1) refers to your local machine.

2. Once the Crystal Query Client connects, it checks to see if the Crystal Query Client files have already been installed on this workstation. If not, the program asks if you want to install the software.

3. Choose Yes, and then click Finish to begin the installation. Follow the on-screen prompts. Once setup completes, you'll need to restart your computer and then start the Crystal Query Client and connect to the Crystal Query Server.

Installing the Crystal Query Client— Web Browser

To install the software, connect to the Crystal Query Server via your Web browser by following these steps:

1. Connect to the Query Server via your Web browser at http://<server>/ ssquery (where <server> refers to your server's machine name). The Seagate Crystal Query page opens, as shown in Figure 11.10.

Figure 11.10
Install Seagate Crystal Query from the default Web page.

2. Choose from two options: If you use Internet Explorer, choose Use Crystal Query Microsoft Internet Explorer 4.0 (or later). This option uses the Microsoft Java Virtual Machine. If you use another browser, such as Netscape Navigator, choose Use Crystal Query with Sun Java Plug-in. This option supports machines that do not support Microsoft's Virtual Machine.

If you use the Sun Java Plug-in, it's important to note that the Seagate Query Client has been optimized for 1064x768 resolution. If you set your machine's resolution to a lower resolution, then Crystal Query Client cuts off the right edge.

3. After choosing the correct option the Crystal Query Client checks to see whether the files have already been installed. If not, a message box appears asking whether you want to install the application. Click Yes.

4. In the File Download dialog box, choose Open This File from Its Current Location, and then click OK (see Figure 11.11).

5. The program then prompts you to accept the digital certificate from the Crystal Query Client distributed by Seagate Software. Click Yes to proceed.

6. Click Finish to begin the installation. After installation, you'll need to close your browser and restart your computer for the Query Client to work properly.

When you install from a Web browser, you actually install software on the client machine. If you would like to remove the software later, go to Control Panel, Add/Remove Programs.

Figure 11.11
Open the file from the Crystal Query Server to begin installation.

Creating a Report with the Crystal Query Client

The screen shots and steps are the same in both the Web and Windows versions of the Crystal Query Client. After starting the Crystal Query Client, choose which action to take from the Welcome dialog box. You can create a new report or open an existing report. For now, click on New Report and get familiar with the interface of the Crystal Query Client (see Figure 11.12).

Two tabs appear: Query and Report. The Query tab resembles the Design tab in the Crystal Report Designer. On the Query tab you build the ad hoc report and place formulas, summaries, and fields on the report.

On the Report Tab you can view the report and the data. You interact with the report on this tab just like the Preview tab in the Crystal Report Designer. Also like the Preview tab, you have the ability to drill down, move fields, and hide sections. A key difference between the Crystal Report Designer and the Crystal Query is that not all functions are available in the menus. For example, you can only build charts from the Report tab or create summaries from right-clicking a field in the Query tab.

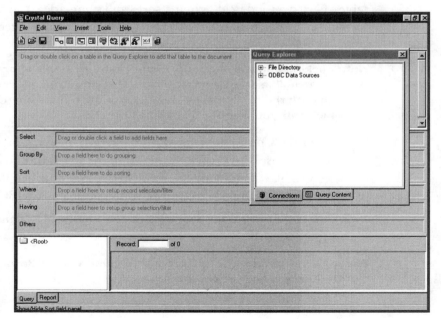

Figure 11.12

A new report in Crystal Query Client, showing all sections and the Query Explorer.

The Query Explorer floats on the desktop to the right of the screen and connects to the database through ODBC. The Query Content tab displays what is on the report. Use this tab when you need to access a specific field, formula, or parameter. The Query tab contains eight panels or panes, each of which represents a portion of the query:

- Linking
- Select
- Group By
- Sort
- Where
- Having
- Others
- Result Set

Designing a Basic Report

Building an ad hoc report in the Crystal Query Client parallels the report design process in the Crystal Report Designer. First, you select data and link tables. Next, you add fields, groups, sorts, and summaries. You can add charts, formulas, and parameters, too. To begin building an ad hoc report:

Like in the Crystal Report Designer, some options are available by right-clicking various sections. Experiment with this shortcut method. Note that unlike the Crystal Report Designer, not all commands appear on both the toolbars and menus, and the menus change depending on which tab you're on.

1. From the Connections tab of the Query Explorer, choose which data source to use. If you click the plus sign to the left of File Directory, you see ODBC Data Sources that you can use. If you click the plus sign to the left of ODBC Data Sources, you see available ODBC connections.

2. You can choose from two types of data sources: User and System (see Figure 11.13).

For information on the difference between User data sources and System data sources, see Appendix A.

Figure 11.13

Query Explorer with the Xtreme sample tables displayed.

3. Once you choose your data source, double-click the tables you want to work with, or drag and drop them into the top section of the Query Client—the Linking section. Make sure you get all the tables, so that you can close the Query Explorer and link the tables (see Figure 11.14).

 To reopen the Query Explorer later, choose Query Explorer from the View menu.

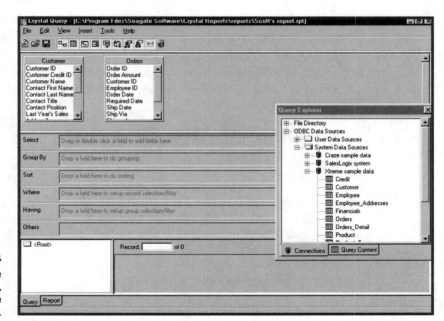

Figure 11.14

Tables in the linking pane, ready to be linked.

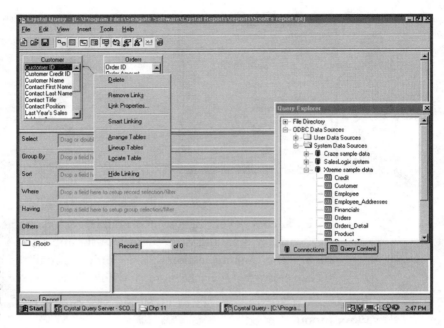

Figure 11.15

Right-click a link
to see the linking
options.

4. You can create links manually by dragging one field to another table, or you can use Smart Linking by choosing Smart Linking from the Edit menu. You can right-click the link to modify the type of link (see Figure 11.15) and drag and drop to arrange tables. Additionally, you can choose to hide the Linking section. Refer to Chapter 3 if you need a refresher on Smart Linking.

Sections of the Crystal Query Client

Now, you'll learn about the sections that make up the Crystal Query Client, and what you can do in each one. Each of the following sections builds the related section of a SQL query.

Select Section

The Select section contains fields from the tables that you want to appear or use on the report. Any fields that you double-click or drag to this section

MORE PRACTICE CREATING A SIMPLE REPORT

1. Choose the Xtreme data source in ODBC Data Sources, System.

2. Select the Customer and Orders tables by double-clicking them.

3. Create a link between the Customer and Orders tables using Customer ID.

4. Drag Customer Name, Region, and City from the Customer table to the Select section. Drag Order Date from the Orders table to the Select section.

5. Drag Country from the Customer table to the Where section.

6. Double-click the Country field and make the condition equal to USA (see Figure 11.16).

7. Click the View menu and choose Preview to bring back the records in the Results section.

8. Choose the Report tab to view your ad hoc report.

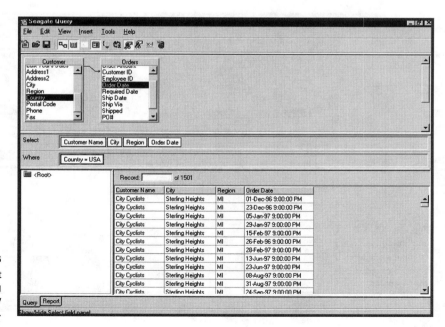

Figure 11.16

A simple report created using Crystal Query Client.

appear on the report. This is just like dragging a field to your report using the Design tab in the Crystal Report Designer.

 Notice that when you place a field in the Select section you do not always see the field. This is a programming issue. If you click the Refresh button or click the Report tab, you'll see the fields on the report.

Creating Summaries and Totals

You can create Summaries in your report by selecting the field to summarize in the Select section. Right-click a field and click Create Summary Field from the menu that appears (see Figure 11.17). You can also summarize a field for all groups by choosing the next option, Create Summary Field on All Groups.

You can change the summary function by double-clicking the summary field you created and selecting a different summary operation (see Figure 11.18). These summary fields show in the Select section as additional fields.

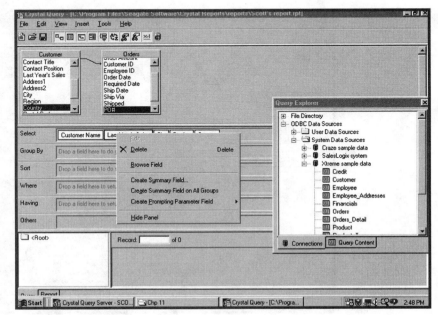

Figure 11.17

To create a summary field, right-click the field to summarize in the Select section.

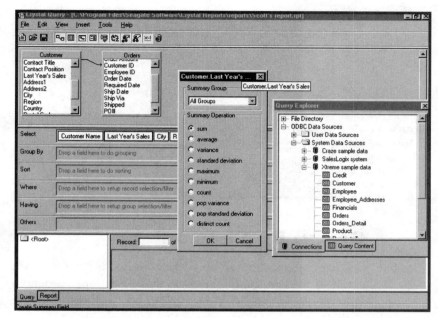

Figure 11.18
When you build a summary by right-clicking a numeric field, you get more summary options.

Adding Parameters for Interactive Reports

You can create a single value or multiple value Parameter field, much like when creating parameters in the Crystal Report Designer.

1. To create a Parameter field, choose Parameter from the Insert menu.

2. Fill in the name of the Parameter and what type of data it contains.

3. Set the browse field data by selecting the correct field from the folder at the bottom of the window.

 You can set what values show in the drop-down list by skipping the previous step and entering the values.

5. Choose Refresh from the View menu to set the value of the Parameter.

6. When you click the Report tab, you see the results based on the parameter value you entered. If you don't give a value for the parameter, your report includes all records.

Figure 11.19

Build specified
groups by
right-clicking a
field in the Group
By section.

Group By Section

Placing items in the Group By section builds groups on the report. For example, if you put the Region field in this section, the detail records hide and
only the group (Region) shows. You can still drill down on the group and
view the details. This function differs from that in Crystal Report Designer
because you can't stop the process from hiding the Details section automatically. However, you can show the details again by changing a format option.
(Changing format options will be discussed later in this chapter.)

The sections of the ad hoc report are the same as in the Crystal Report Designer. They include a Report Header, Page Footer, Group Header, Details,
Group Footer, Report Footer, and Page Footer. You can format these sections
just like in the Crystal Report Designer. Right-click the background in the
Report tab and choose Format Section. You'll see the same options, like New
Page After and Suppress Blank Section. Please refer to Chapter 7 for a review of these functions.

You can create more than one level of groups, like the Crystal Report Designer, by adding additional fields to this section. Right-click a field in the
Group section to open the Edit Specifying Group dialog box and set up specified or custom groups (see Figure 11.19). Refer to Chapter 5 for more
information on Specified Groups.

Sort Section

The Sort section allows you to change the way information sorts on your
report. As with the Crystal Report Designer, any groups on the report sort

Figure 11.20
Double-click a
field in the Sort
section to change
the sort options.

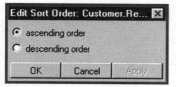

first. With the Sort function, you control the information inside each group (or the Detail section on the report). If the report does not include groups, then the Sort function takes precedence. To change the sort direction, double-click the field in the Sort section to open the Edit Sort Order dialog box and change from ascending order to descending order (see Figure 11.20).

Where Section

In the Crystal Report Designer you can change record selection using the Select Expert. In Crystal Query Client, the Where section allows you to determine record selection. Double-click or drag fields to the Where section, and then double-click the fields to open the Edit Field Range dialog box and set the conditions for the records you want pulled from your database (see Figure 11.21). You can choose the same options as in the Crystal Report Designer, including any value, equal to, or one of. (See Chapter 4 for more information on record selection.)

Since Seagate Crystal Reports 7 contains the first release of Seagate Query, you might encounter some problems while using the Crystal Query Client. Be patient if you get an error message or if something doesn't look right. By using your knowledge of the Crystal Report Designer, you will probably get Crystal Query Client to do what you want. Check Seagate Software's Web site to see if they've posted any patches to fix the problems that you encounter.

Figure 11.21
Right-click a field
in the Where
section to change
Record Selection.

Having Section

The Having section corresponds to group selection in the Crystal Report Designer. An example of group selection is the Top N function where a report, for example, might display the top 5 accounts by last year sales. Drag and drop fields to make up the HAVING clause of the SQL statement.

Others Section

The Others section typically contains parameters, formulas, and special fields that were added in the Crystal Report Designer. You can create fields that show in the Others section, but they won't show on the report unless they also appear in the Select section. Crystal Query Client ignores the fields it can't create (like Special Fields) when you refresh or preview the report.

You can add a parameter field, formula, or a SQL expression to your report from the Insert menu. The procedures duplicate those in the Crystal Report Designer, but the dialog boxes look slightly different.

Result Set

The Result Set appears at the bottom of the Query tab and displays the data in a tabular format. To the left, you can see the groups displayed as folders. To the right, the data and fields added in the Select section appear.

The Preview option in the View menu populates these two windows. To hide this information, right-click and choose Hide Result Set from the dialog box that appears.

Additional Crystal Query Client Functions and Settings

The Crystal Query Client allows for many functions in addition to the basic functions described above (for example, you can change settings to balance performance for your network). Many of the functions coincide with those found in the Crystal Report Designer; how you use them will sometimes differ.

Maximizing Performance

Crystal Query Client options allow you to balance performance on your network. To work with the options, go to the File menu and choose Options. The Edit Application Options dialog box opens, allowing you to set the maximum number of records to return to the client (see Figure 11.22). If the number of records to be returned does not surpass the Maximum setting, Seagate Query returns all records. However, if the number of records matching the query's selection criteria exceeds the Maximum setting, then Seagate Query only returns the maximum number of records specified.

Several related options can be set:

- **Batch Size.** Refers to the number of records that return at one time when refreshing the data in the Query tab.

- **Browse Size.** Allows the client to change the number of records returned when browsing data (so that you can see what type of data a field stores). By default this is set at 100 (as in Crystal Report Designer). If it takes a long time to return records, you can reduce the Browse Size to improve performance.

- **Perform Group By on Server.** Allows for processing to take place on the database server instead of returning the raw data over the network to the client. It's a good idea to leave this option selected so that processing occurs on the server when possible; this can greatly improve report and network performance.

Figure 11.22
You can set the maximum number of records to

Formatting the Report

Commands on the Edit menu allow you to change the Auto Report Format Style of the report. This function matches the Style Expert found in the Crystal Report Designer. Use it to quickly format a report into a predefined style.

The Visible Columns option allows you to hide a field on the report. You can include fields on the report and hide them so that they don't print. This is helpful, for example, if you need to sort on a field but don't want it to display on the report (like a zip code). On the Report tab, right-click a blank section of the report and select either Show All Sections or Show/Hide Sections from the menu that appears (see Figure 11.23).

You can also change the properties of the section. Right-click an item and a dialog box will open from which you can format the section. The list of format options is very similar to that in the Crystal Report Designer, but you also get the option to change the background color. If you don't like any of the colors available, click the ... symbol and the Color Chooser dialog box will open, from which you can choose the color you want (see Figure 11.24).

Figure 11.23

Right-click the background on the Report tab to display options.

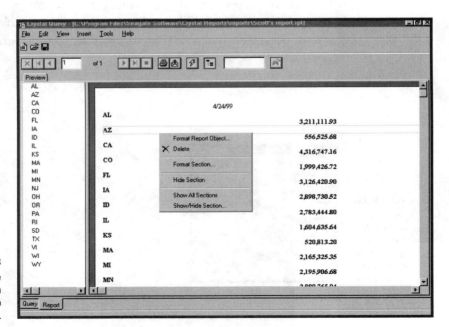

Figure 11.24
Choose different font and background colors from the color wheel.

To format a field, right-click it and choose Format Report Object from the menu that appears. The Format Report dialog box appears, allowing you to change the horizontal alignment (along with tight horizontal and drop shadow), border, and text color of the field (see Figure 11.25). Again, these options resemble those found in the Crystal Report Designer.

 Notice that you do not have the ability to change the format of date, time, date/time, numeric, and currency objects. Use a formula to get around this. For example, to print only the date from a datetime field, create a formula called @date and use the Date (datetime) function to eliminate the timestamp (see Figure 11.26).

You can move items around on the report, as in the Crystal Report Designer. There is one difference, though: If a field is not wide enough, Crystal Query Client still allows the field to print in its entirety. Therefore, you can't control where a field ends. Be careful when you place objects near one another, because they may overlap when you generate the report.

Figure 11.25
Click different sections and objects in the report and right-click to format the report object.

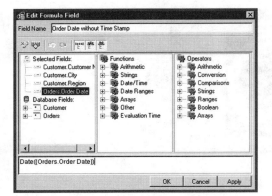

Figure 11.26
Use a formula to format datetime fields.

Viewing Sections and Other Display Options

The choices in the View menu allow you to toggle between the Query and Report tabs and show or hide sections of the Query tab. A quick overview of the menu commands include:

- **Show Long Fieldname.** Displays {table_name.field_name}.

- **Group Content.** Shows only the data for the selected group in the Result Set section.

- **Auto Refresh.** Allows the Crystal Query Server to automatically refresh the Result Set section at the time set in the Query Server.

You can also toggle the Query Explorer, Linking, and Result Set sections.

Searching in the Query Tab

The Search command allows you to search through the returned data for specific information. The Search tool differs from the one in the Crystal Report Designer.

The Search dialog box contains three tabs (see Figure 11.27). In the first, specify the search criteria. Drag and drop a field from the top section to the Expression box. Double-click the field in the Expression box and two drop-down lists appear, similar to those in the Select Expert. Complete the expression according to what you are searching for. You can have more than one field in your expression.

Figure 11.27

The Search tool differs from the one in the Crystal Report Designer.

In the second tab, Result Fields, indicate what you want to display in the third tab, Search Results. Select the field on the left that you want to display and click the right arrow button to add it. Choose as many fields as you want to display.

The Search Results tab displays the selected fields for the records that meet the search criteria in the first tab.

Searching in the Report Tab

From the Report tab, the Search tool is different and simpler to use. With the Report tab open, look for the place to enter data on the toolbar (to the right). Enter the data to search for and click the button to the right to search the report for instances of the data. The data must appear on the "level" of the report you're looking at for the tool to find the data. For instance, if you're looking at a summary report (no details showing) and search for an item in the Details section, you will not find the data. However, if you show the Details section and then search for the data, Crystal Query Client highlights the first occurrence.

Looking at the SQL Statement

The SQL Statement command on the Insert menu allows you to view the SQL statement that Crystal Query Client sends to the database server. Unlike the Crystal Report Designer, you cannot edit this statement.

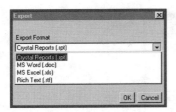

Figure 11.28

Export options
available from
the Crystal
Query Client.

Exporting to Other Programs

You can export your report from the Report tab. Choose from four types of files to export to: Crystal Reports (.RPT), Microsoft Word (.DOC), Microsoft Excel (.XLS), and Rich Text File (.RTF). You can also specify in which directory to save the exported file (see Figure 11.28).

Charting Your Data

Access the chart function from the Report tab by choosing Create Chart from the Tools menu. The Chart Expert dialog box opens (see Figure 11.29). The charting functions in the dialog box are same as in Seagate Crystal Reports.

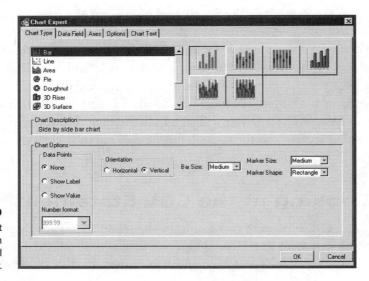

Figure 11.29

The Chart Expert
is the same as in
the Crystal
Report Designer.

Where to Find Help

Although Seagate does not include a book for Seagate Query with the software, they have provided online documentation that installs on your machine when the Crystal Query Server component installs.

If you're using the Web version of Crystal Query Client, direct your browser to c:\program files\seagate software\query server\qclientinstall\docs\default.htm. You'll also find an index of topics at c:\program files\seagate software\query server\qclientinstall\docs\index.htm.

 These paths are the default settings for the location of the files. If a different directory was selected during installation, the files will be located there.

The Help menu of the Windows version of Crystal Query Client only refers you to Seagate Software's Web site. The Help menu is limited because it offers no links to the files already installed on your machine.

Summary

This chapter provided an overview of what Seagate Query can do for you. With this tool, you can build ad hoc reports in Windows or in a Web browser.

You were walked through the installation of the Query Server and Query Client. In addition, you also learned that the Crystal Query Client is very similar to the Crystal Report Designer in that it has two tabs, Query and Report, that resemble the Design and Preview tabs.

12

OLAP
Reporting

This chapter introduces you to OLAP concepts and focuses on designing reports from an OLAP data source using the OLAP Report Expert in Seagate Crystal Reports. You must have knowledge of your specific OLAP data source in order to design reports for it.

An OLAP report looks similar to the cross-tab type report you have already seen. In some ways, OLAP describes the data source being used more than the style of the report.

What Is OLAP?

OLAP, short for Online Analytical Processing, is a technology for creating multidimensional structures for use in data analysis. The term *cubes*, or *hypercubes*, refer to these structures. They are referred to as cubes throughout this chapter.

OLAP technology allows people to design cubes of data; SCR provides the tool to design reports using those cubes as the data source. This multidimensional concept (OLAP) allows for more sophisticated and compound analysis of data. Multi-Dimensional Data (MDD) sources (cubes) have become more popular due to the analysis power of looking at data in three or more dimensions rather than in only two.

The only difference between a cube and a hypercube is that a hypercube has more than three dimensions. The OLAP industry uses both terms to generically describe OLAP structures. You can use SCR to design reports from both cubes and hypercubes. As mentioned earlier, both structures are referred to simply as cubes throughout this chapter.

Since Seagate Crystal Reports does not include a cube building tool, this book does not encompass that topic. However, Seagate Info uses Seagate Holos OLAP technology and includes a cube designer tool, which you can use to design actual cubes. (Go to Chapter 15 for an introduction to Seagate Info).

Seagate Crystal Reports helps you design reports based on existing cubes. These reports take advantage of the dimension and hierarchy structure of cubes. Think of OLAP reports as a smaller, more manageable subset of the cube data.

Finance, marketing, and modeling research and analysis companies (or areas of companies) commonly use cubes and OLAP because of the powerful analysis capabilities they offer. Cubes provide a large amount of data all at once, all in relation to other data, allowing deeper analysis.

How OLAP Differs from Relational Databases

Relational databases are two-dimensional, and tables are linked to have all of the fields from each table available for a report. OLAP uses a different structure. OLAP defines a data set in terms of *dimensions* and *hierarchies*. These dimensions and hierarchies display in a three or more dimensional grid structure. Picture something like a Rubik's cube (see Figure 12.1). The major entities, factors, or components of a data set represent the *dimensions*. If you typically work with key fields in relational databases, you can think of dimensions as being like a key field.

Each dimension contains data organized in hierarchies. *Hierarchies* have multiple levels representing the different levels of data in a dimension. A date dimension might have hierarchical levels such as year, quarter, and month. Each level of the hierarchy is referred to—in this case, year, quarter, and month—as *members* of the date dimension.

Figure 12.1

You can think of an OLAP cube like a Rubik's cube, where each side represents a different dimension of the data.

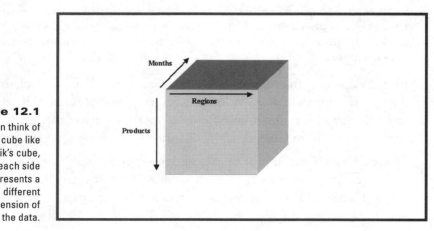

The relationships between levels can have many different names. Each OLAP tool uses specific names for the relationship among hierarchical levels. Some common names include levels, children, parents, or descendants. Generally, a downward connection from a parent to children is a one-to-many relationship, whereas an upward connection from children to parent is a many-to-one relationship.

To better understand the relationships within a dimension, look at the sample dimension in Figure 12.2, named Order Date. This date dimension is from a Seagate Holos cube. The following bullets explain the relationships in this date dimension:

- Any value in the dimension is called a member. The Year, Quarter, and Month (levels 0,1,and 2) are all members of the Order Date dimension.

- Generally, a member can have only one parent. Here, Year (level 0) is the parent of Quarter (level 1); Quarter has no other parent.

- A member with no parent is the root member. Year (level 0) would be the root member—it has no parent.

- A member with no children is a leaf, leaf node, or outermost branch member. Month (level 2) is an outermost branch member. It has no children.

Figure 12.2

The Date dimension has a hierarchical structure. Seagate Holos uses the word "Level" to describe the different hierarchical levels of data in the Order Date dimension.

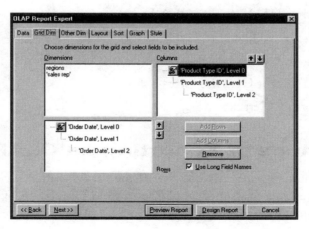

- All children of a parent are sometimes called descendants. Thus, all levels below Year (levels 1 and 2, Quarter and Month) would be considered descendants.

In the Order Date dimension shown in Figure 2.2, notice that Seagate Holos refers to the hierarchical levels of data as level 0, level 1, and level 2. As mentioned earlier, you must know your OLAP data source, or at least the particulars of the cube you use for a report. This now becomes evident because, to use this cube, you need to know that level 0 represents years, level 1 represents quarters, and level 2 represents months.

You do not need to know how to design cubes (assuming you can access cubes built by others), but you do need to understand their structure and the relationship between dimensions and hierarchies to design meaningful reports. If you feel comfortable designing reports based on relational databases, you can become accustomed to designing reports based on OLAP cubes.

OLAP Data Sources

You can use Seagate Crystal Reports to design a report from any of the following OLAP data sources:

- Hyperion Essbase
- DB2 OLAP Server
- Microsoft SQL Server OLAP Services
- Info OLAP Cube
- Seagate Holos
- OLEDB for OLAP Sources
- Informix Metacube

Methods of Reporting on OLAP Data

If your company currently uses any of the OLAP data sources listed above, you can design a Seagate Crystal Report from that source. SCR uses several different methods to design reports from OLAP data sources; your options are described below. The OLAP Report Expert used in this chapter employs the Grid Object Method.

Grid Object Method

You can use the Grid Object method to report from any of the mentioned data sources. A Grid Object resembles a cross-tab object, plotting data across rows and columns and organizing hierarchies that you specify into bands. Three or more dimensions can be included in a single grid object, and that object can be formatted and pivoted to meet your analysis needs. SCR's OLAP Report Expert uses this method.

Report Script Method

In addition to the Grid Object method, you can also use the Report Script method to report from Hyperion Essbase and DB2 OLAP Server data sources. If reporting from an Essbase data source, SCR presents a Essbase button on the Data tab of the Report Experts for you to use. You can also use the OLAP Report Expert.

 Seagate Crystal Reports works extremely well directly with Essbase data. The Report Experts contain an Essbase button on the Data tab that allows you to connect directly to an Essbase data source (no need for an ODBC connection). Many features available for reporting with Essbase make SCR an excellent choice when working with this type of data source.

 SCR's online Help contains a lot of useful information specific to Essbase features and creating reports using Essbase data. Search using the keyword "Essbase" for several Help topics. Specifically, search the keyword list for "Essbase: creating a report with," which leads to a step-by-step tutorial.

MetaCube Reporting

If reporting on a MetaCube, SCR makes a MetaCube button available on the Data tab of the Report Experts. See the Seagate Crystal Reports User's Guide for basic information to help you design a report from this type of data.

Creating OLAP Reports

The next section guides you through using the OLAP Report Expert. The steps are fairly generic because each data source differs slightly. Once you have an OLAP report or two designed based on your particular OLAP source, you will become familiar with the language and details of your specific data source and find these reports to be exceptionally useful.

 To use the OLAP Report Expert you need to have an OLAP data source. The screen shots in this section use an Info OLAP cube, created in Seagate Info.

Opening the OLAP Report Expert

First you must open the OLAP Report Expert. The Expert walks you though designing a report step-by-step, just like the other Report Experts described in Chapter 2.

In the Crystal Report Designer, click File, New or the New button to open the Report Gallery. Click the OLAP button to open the OLAP Report Expert with the Data tab displayed (see Figure 12.3).

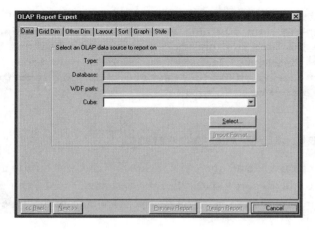

Figure 12.3

Start with the Data tab in the OLAP Report Expert. The Select button allows you to choose a data source type.

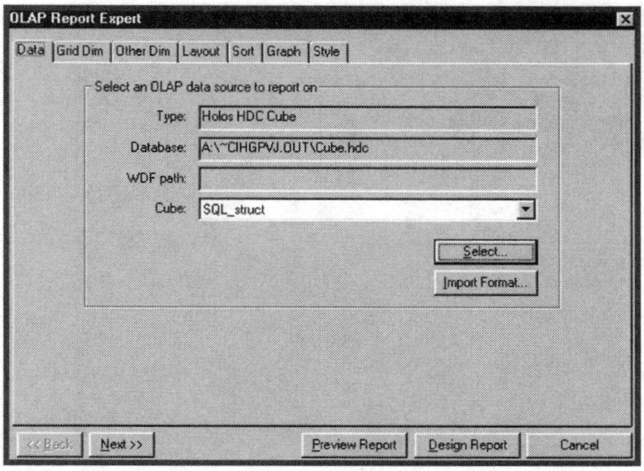

Figure 12.4

After setting the path to your data source, SCR fills in the appropriate fields on the Data tab.

Selecting Your Data Source on the Data Tab

The Data tab contains blank areas when you first open it. You specify your data source here, but unlike selecting a button on the Data tab of the Standard Report Expert, you need to maneuver through a few dialog boxes to select your data source. To select a data source for your OLAP Report:

1. Click Select to open the Choose OLAP Type dialog box. The options listed here may vary from network to network, depending on the data sources available to you.

2. Click the type of OLAP data source you want to base your report on. The Browse for Database dialog box opens next.

3. Enter a path, or click the Browse button and specify the path to your data source. Then click OK. Doing so brings you back to the Data tab with the appropriate fields filled in, as shown in Figure 12.4.

Setting the Main Dimensions on the Grid Dim Tab

The Grid Dim(ension) tab lists all the dimensions of your cube in the Dimensions list. This tab allows you to select which dimensions you want to

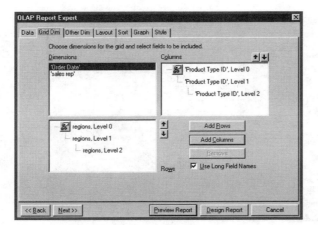

Figure 12.5

Select the row
and column
dimensions
for your report
from the
Dimensions list.

use for your report. Add the dimensions that you want for the rows and columns in your report by selecting the name of the dimension from the Dimension list and clicking the Add Rows or Add Columns buttons. Once you add the dimensions you want on your report, notice that the entire dimension, including all its hierarchical levels, moves to the Row or Column list (see Figure 12.5).

This tab looks and acts similar to the cross-tab dialog box described in Chapter 8. Similarly, the report created using this Expert has a cross-tab feel.

Working with Remaining Dimensions on the Other Dim Tab

The Other Dim(ension) tab lists the dimensions that you did not include in a row or column of the Grid Dim tab. These dimensions do not directly print on your report, but their data affects the data in the row and column dimensions. Use the boxes below the Other Dimensions list to control how this data affects your report (see Figure 12.6). For example, you could use a dimension here to narrow down the information on the report (similar to the effect of the Select Expert). Cubes generally have very large amounts of data. A Date dimension, for example, could have data for 10 years, but you may only want to look at data for the current year.

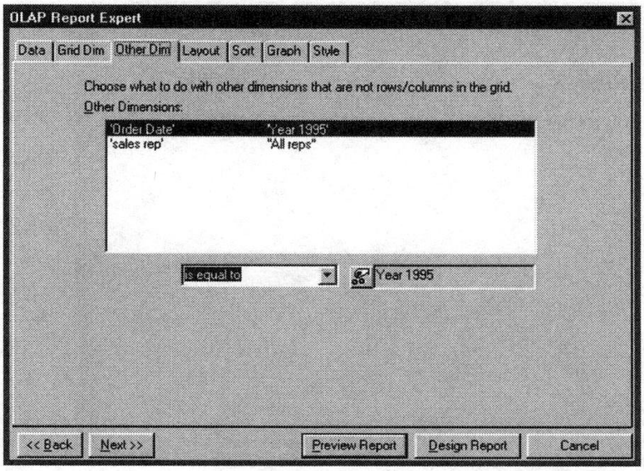

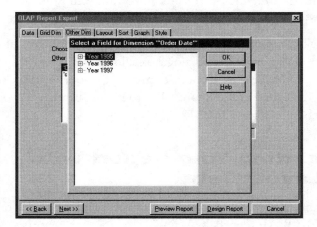

Figure 12.6
The Other Dim tab allows you to control how the dimensions *not* on your report affect the report.

To modify other dimensions using the Other Dim tab:

1. Double-click a dimension name. The Select a Field for Dimension dialog box opens (see Figure 12.7). This works somewhat like selection criteria, but due to the structure of OLAP cubes, it is not exactly the same.

2. Click the values in the selected dimension that you want to include on your report. Click OK.

Figure 12.7
Use the Select a Field for Dimension dialog box to select the data you want on your report.

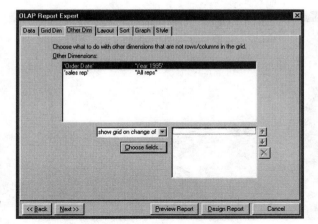

Figure 12.8

Group your data into individual grids using the *show grid on change of* option.

3. In addition to the data selection criteria you just set up, open the selection criteria list below the Other Dimensions list (see Figure 12.8). Use this list to set a type of selection criteria for your report.

Think of this list as a sort of a cross between grouping and selecting, rather than being exactly like the Select Expert. The *is equal to* option shows just one grid for whatever level you set the dimension equal to. The *show grid on change of* option shows one grid for each group or section, based on the level in the dimension hierarchy you set the criteria for. Once you complete an OLAP report, you should experiment with the different options here and see how your report looks and what data it includes.

4. Click Choose Fields to open the Choose On Change of Field Dimension dialog box. This dialog box allows you to set the level to use as criteria for creating sections or groups on your report. Consider the report designed in the figures. To group data by quarter, you would select level 1 here (see Figure 12.9).

Formatting Your Report with the Layout Tab

The Layout tab gives you some options for formatting your report (see Figure 12.10). OLAP reports look similar to cross-tab reports.

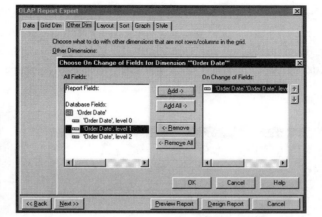

Figure 12.9
Select which level you want to group by. You need to know your data source to know which level to use.

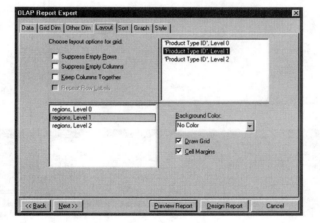

Figure 12.10
Format your grid using the Layout tab options.

Using colors or shading helps with viewing the data in your grid. Experimenting with the options on this tab will help you determine the format that works best with your data, depending on what you want the report to focus on.

Organizing Data with the Sort Tab

The Sort tab functions just like the Sort tab in the other Report Experts. This function is more like grouping rather than real sorting. SCR creates a separate grid for each group, based on the change of field in a dimension (see Figure 12.11). In the report preview you can see that the separate "grids" nest together under larger "groups" (see Figure 12.12). The concepts used in OLAP become easier to understand once you use the tool and see it in action.

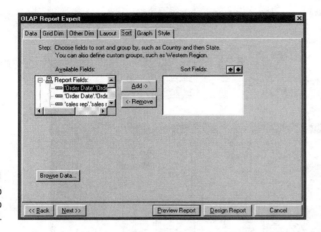

Figure 12.11
Use the Sort tab to group data into their own grids.

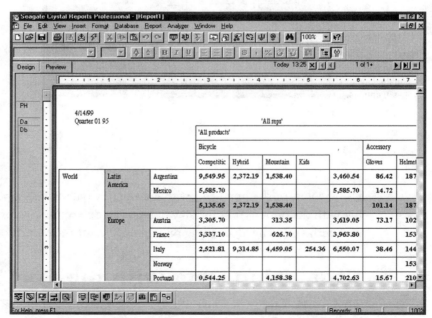

Figure 12.12
OLAP reports have a format resembling a grid or cross-tab.

Showing Data Pictorially with the Graph Tab

You can create a graph for each grid based on the data within it. The Graph tab works exactly the same as in the Standard Report Expert. Refer to Chapter 9 for instructions on graphing.

Giving Your Report Style with the Style Tab

You can select a style for your report from the Style list within the Style Tab. Add a title and any graphic files here as well. The Style tab works exactly the same as the Standard Report Expert.

Click Preview Report to preview your report (refer to Figure 12.12). Like the other Report Experts, you can go back to the OLAP Report Expert to make changes at any time, and all the same rules apply.

Changing the Grid Dimension

By using an OLAP cube as a data source, you can change the grid dimension of an existing report and create an entirely new report with just a few clicks of your mouse. As you'll see, the grid dimension can be changed and a new report generated easily and quickly.

1. From the Crystal Report Designer and with your OLAP report open, click Report, Report Expert to go back to the OLAP Report Expert.

 A warning message appears reminding you that any formatting changes you made directly on the Design or Preview tabs are overwritten when you exit the Expert and apply the style you selected on the Style tab.

2. Using the Grid Dim tab, remove the present dimension from the Rows list, and add another dimension from the Dimensions list (see Figure 12.13). This becomes the new row dimension for the report.

3. Click Preview Report (see Figure 12.14). SCR displays the report using the new grid dimension you specified. Now you have a completely new report from the same data set.

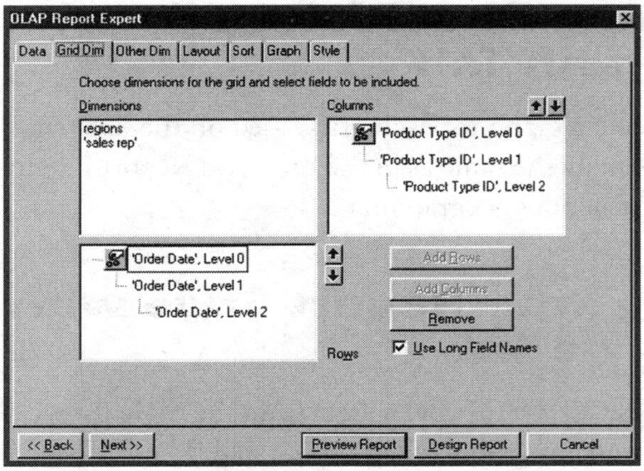

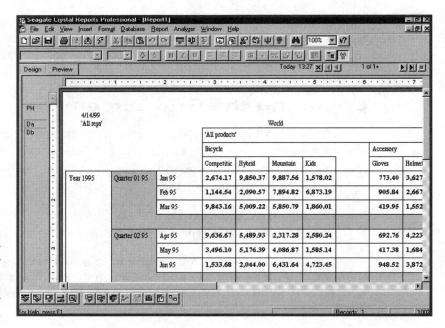

Figure 12.13
Use the Grid Dim tab to change the dimension of your report.

Figure 12.14
Changing the row or column dimension provides many analysis options.

Summary

Reports designed and generated from an OLAP data source allow you to create and manipulate OLAP data. Reporting from large OLAP sources allows you to separate and manipulate manageable pieces of a large cube structure for analysis. One OLAP structure provides the opportunity for many reports to be generated.

Like the standard reports, you can easily update the location of a refreshed OLAP source by clicking Database, Set Location. You can point your report to the refreshed copy of the OLAP cube or structure. You can also use a shortcut menu by right-clicking the cube placeholder on the Design tab of your report.

Cubes are extremely powerful tools that structure data in ways that allow advanced analysis. Seagate Crystal Reports makes cubes easier to digest by giving you the tool to generate reports from them.

PART IV

Using Seagate Crystal Reports with Other Tools

CHAPTER 13

Integrating Seagate Crystal Reports with Other Products

- Integrating with Visual Studio

- Using Activex

- Integrating with Microsoft Office and Other Tools

- Distribution and Deployment Considerations

- Compiling Reports

S eagate Crystal Reports can be integrated into a programming project and resulting application using the Visual Studio family of programming tools. This chapter explores the potential of SCR in this area and is written from the business user's perspective, with the assumption that most readers are not programmers. The goal is to make you more aware of the abilities of Seagate Crystal Reports and then perhaps you can pass the information along to a programmer at your company. If you are a developer, please bear with the references to generic developers.

In this chapter, you'll also learn how to export Crystal Reports to other formats and design a report from files created in the popular spreadsheet program Microsoft Excel. You will learn how to compile reports for distribution, as well as hints and tips for printing and exporting reports with the goal of maintaining all formatting.

Integrating with Visual Studio

Visual Studio is a Microsoft suite of programming tools for developers based on Windows architecture. The most recent release of Visual Studio contains Visual Basic, Visual C++, Visual FoxPro, Visual InterDev, and Visual J++. This suite of tools allows the development team to tackle the design of many applications including Web and database design.

Integrating Seagate Crystal Reports Using Visual Basic

Seagate Crystal Reports works easily with Microsoft Visual Basic. SCR has shipped with Visual Basic for years, and Seagate Software has worked to keep SCR compatible with Visual Basic. The Crystal Reports Print Engine (CRPE32.DLL) can be integrated into your Visual Basic or other programming projects, making the powerful reporting capabilities of Seagate Crystal Reports available to your custom applications. The Print Engine .DLL does the work to preview a report.

 The Crystal Reports Print Engine (CRPE) can be used in ANY programming tool (MS or not) that allows access to API's.

Developers can use the Crystal Reports Designer to design reports and then embed the reports into their own Visual Basic applications. This can be done two ways, either by integrating the Crystal Reports Print Engine and other necessary files into the VB project by writing code to call the Application Programming Interface (API) directly, or by using the Crystal Reports ActiveX control.

The first method, integrating the Print Engine, runs faster than using the ActiveX control, and the total size of the integrated SCR files is a bit smaller. The second method is to include the ActiveX control (also called an OCX control) for SCR in the application project. This control is a handy package containing many default properties already set. It can be dropped into a VB project, a few more properties set, and the application becomes report-enabled. Each method offers an advantage. Using the Print Engine, developers have more control over exactly what files they add to their VB project. With the ActiveX control, they have a neat, easy-to-use package.

 The Crystal Reports Print Engine and associated files can be used in any of the Visual Studio programming tools, the most popular being Visual Basic.

Seagate Crystal Reports includes its own Visual Basic custom control, CRYSTAL.VBX, but use the ActiveX control if possible. It is based on more advanced 32-bit technology than the custom CRYSTAL.VBX. The CRYSTAL.VBX is 16-bit only and contains no new features since version 5.

 Older custom controls were 16-bit and commonly called .VBX files or OLE controls. With the evolution of technology, many of these controls were updated to 32-bit versions with .OCX extensions. These new 32-bit controls are referred to as ActiveX controls. Thus the OLE control listed above would be a 16-bit version with less advanced technology than the OCX or ActiveX controls.

Using ActiveX

ActiveX controls provide plug-in capabilities to programmers, allowing entire application components, in this case the Crystal Reports Print Engine, to be plugged into a Visual Basic project or other custom application. An ActiveX control may be referred to as an OLE control, OCX control, or custom control, but all refer to any control with the .OCX extension.

By adding an ActiveX control to your Visual Basic or other programming project, you create a type of socket where other programs or files can be "plugged in" without having to write any code to connect them. This type of control also allows for information to be passed between the two components as the application runs. You can have a Crystal report built into a custom application that can be refreshed on command. For example, users could simply click a button in the custom application to view a newly refreshed report. The application might pass information to the report, such as a parameter, through the component interface.

In a Visual Basic project the ActiveX control for Seagate Crystal Reports may not be listed. If not listed in the Available Controls list, it can easily be added. When you installed Seagate Crystal Reports, the .OCX file, named CRYSTL16.OCX or CRYSTL32.OCX (for 16- or 32-bit respectively, depending on your installation choice), was added to the Windows\System directory. If using VB 5.0 or 6.0 go to Project, Components. This brings up a list of standard ActiveX Controls. Included in this list may be the Crystal ActiveX Query Viewer, Crystal Report Control, Crystal Reports Design-Time Control, and Crystal Select Expert OLE Module. Select the Crystal Report Control to add to your project and click OK. This adds the control to the general toolbar.

CONTROLS IN THE COMPONENTS LIST

The version of Visual Basic and the version of Crystal Reports you use determine which controls show up in the Components list. Use the Crystal ActiveX Query Viewer for creating and running queries; the Crystal Report Control for the ActiveX control discussed earlier; the Crystal Reports Design-Time Control for a Web tool; and the Crystal Select Expert OLE Module for use with the automation server.

You can access these controls, in addition to the Project Components command, by choosing Projects, Add User Control, or however you normally go to the components or type library lists. If you select Project, References, you see a list of the type libraries for the controls. Here, you could add the components by writing code rather than the plug-in ActiveX control. Every programmer has their own preferred way to access controls and develop their projects—be creative. The online Developer's Help for Seagate Crystal Reports, Visual Basic Help files, Visual Basic Books Online, and Seagate Software's Web site all contain helpful information.

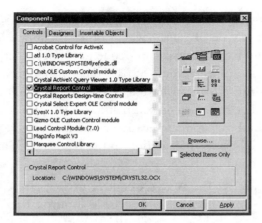

Figure 13.1

The Crystal Reports control can be added to the Available Controls list in Visual Basic.

If the Crystal Reports control does not appear in the Available Controls list box, you need to add it. Locate the file you want to use (such as Windows\System\CRYSTL32.OCX) and click Open. The Crystal Report control now appears in the Available Controls box in Visual Basic, ready to be added to your project (see Figure 13.1).

Setting ActiveX Properties

You can use the Crystal Report control to set object properties at design time or run time. ActiveX properties that can be set include:

- The name of the report
- The destination for the report, such as printer or preview
- The number of copies to print
- Print file information
- Preview window sizing and positioning information
- Selection formula information
- Sorting information
- Other related properties

At run time, reports can be quickly and easily changed by either changing the filter (or selection criteria) for the report with one line of code, or completely changing the SQL statement to retrieve different data or data from a different source. This offers powerful flexibility.

Some properties can only be changed at either design or run time. Refer to the ActiveX Control Properties Index in the Crystal Developer's Help for more information. When setting properties at run time, you need to add entries into your procedure code.

Working with Your Data

Advanced ActiveX components allow you to connect to active data sources. Using the Active Data Driver for Seagate Crystal Reports, you can design reports for your Visual Basic applications that use any of the following data sources:

- Data Access Objects (DAO)
- Remote Data Objects (RDO)
- ActiveX Data Objects (ADO)
- Visual Basic Data Controls
- Crystal Data Objects (CDO)

If developers have access to the database during design time, they can ensure that the proper database drivers and files install with the application. They can also test the report with real data during design.

If the data source is not available at design time, the Active Data Driver supports the use of data definition files. Data definition files are tab-separated text files that define fields in a data source. These definition files allow developers to design their application and run reports built into the application, but they don't hit the actual database and, therefore, don't get any data in the preview of the report. Sample information can be added to the data definition files for the purpose of checking the report, but some restrictions in the functionality of the sample data apply. When the application runs, the reports need to point to the true data source, and the developer needs to ensure that the proper database drivers and connection instructions exist in the program.

ActiveX Report Designer Component

Seagate has introduced a new ActiveX Report Designer Component (RDC) for Visual Basic. The RDC is a standalone Crystal Reports Designer that can be integrated into Visual Basic 5.0 and 6.0 so that developers can design reports from within the Visual Basic Integrated Development Environment

(IDE). In the past, developers needed to go out of Visual Basic and into SCR, design a report, go back into Visual Basic, and run the report. Then go back into SCR to make adjustments to the report, and back to Visual Basic...you get the idea. The Report Designer Component frees developers from having to go back and forth between Visual Basic and Seagate Crystal Reports to design reports. The RDC allows developers to design reports right in Visual Basic. To open the Report Designer Component in Visual Basic:

1. Click Project, Components. Click the Designers tab, and then Crystal Reports 7 and click Apply. Click OK to close the dialog box.

2. Go to Project, Add ActiveX Designer. Crystal Reports 7 appears in the menu list. Click it and the Report Designer Component opens right in Visual Basic (see Figure 13.2).

Developers can design reports using a Report Expert or they can choose the custom report option. They can even import an existing report into their project, all from within Visual Basic. The RDC is 100 percent compatible with existing report files and can read from and to Crystal Reports format (.RPT files). Version 7 of Seagate Crystal Reports includes the RDC. By making reports easier to design from within the familiar Visual Basic interface, including the RDC definitely enhances ease-of-use of Crystal Reports within custom applications.

The Report Designer Component (RDC) ships with version 7 but can also be downloaded for free from the Seagate Software Web site (www.seagatesoftware.com) if you use a version of Seagate Crystal Reports prior to 7.0. If Seagate Crystal Reports 7 does not appear in the Designers tab of the components list, you may have done a custom install and not checked the Report Designer Component. If this is the case, add the file from your CD called CRAXDUI.DLL to your Crystal Reports directory. This version of the Report Design Component has been updated from the copy available on the Web, so if you have the option, use the DLL from your version 7 CD rather than the version you can download from the Seagate Software Web site. On your version 7 CD, Seagate Software has included a Help file just for the RDC, named CRRDC.HLP.

The Crystal ActiveX control and the RDC both provide easy-to-use tools for integrating Crystal Reports into programming projects. The ability to set properties and settings at run time turn a powerful reporting tool into a more

Figure 13.2

The Report Gallery of the Report Designer Component open in Visual Basic.

powerful development tool. This section provides just a hint as to what is possible using SCR with your custom applications. Be sure to seek out the Crystal Developer's Help for your questions.

Integrating with Microsoft Office and Other Tools

Seagate Crystal Reports works with Microsoft Office applications. Once you've designed and run a report in Seagate Crystal Reports, it can be exported to another format or directly to another application. This makes the reports that you create in Seagate Crystal Reports available electronically to people that do not have Seagate Crystal Reports. It also makes the data available in other formats if you choose to manipulate it in an application other than the Crystal Report Designer.

Seagate Crystal Reports can be exported directly to Excel and Word, among other applications and file formats. Additionally, you can export directly to a disk file, an Exchange folder, a Lotus Notes database, or Microsoft Mail (MAPI) destination. The following sections describe each of these export options.

Exporting to Other Applications and File Types

You can easily export Seagate Crystal Reports to Microsoft Office applications and other formats. Once you have a report designed and saved, you can export the report into another format. To export a report:

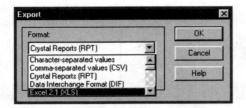

Figure 13.3

You can export
from many
formats into SCR.

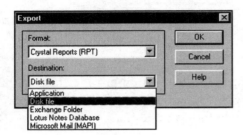

Figure 13.4

Choose from
many destinations
when exporting
a report.

1. Have the report that you want to export open in the Crystal Report Designer.

2. Click File, Print, Export. You can also click the Export toolbar button.

3. Choose the export format and destination you would like to use from the Export dialog box and click OK (see Figures 13.3 and 13.4). Your report now exports to the chosen format.

If you choose an application as your destination, the application you picked automatically opens with your new document open. If you choose a disk file, SCR prompts you to choose where to save your exported file from the Choose Export File dialog box.

The next sections provide specific information regarding a few of the many formats to which you can export.

Exporting to HTML

Reports export very well into the HTML format. You have three choices when exporting to HTML. Which one you choose depends on the type of browser used to view the report.

- If you're using Netscape, select HTML 3.2 (Standard)

- If you're using Microsoft Internet Explorer, select HTML 3.0 (Draft Standard)

- If you're using the new form of HTML, select HTML 3.2 (Extended).

You need to select Disk File from the Destination list when exporting to HTML, and then choose a directory in which to save the file. When you export to HTML, more than one file may be created; therefore, you need to choose a directory or create a new one to put the files into.

 When you save a file in the HTML format, it is saved as DEFAULT.HTM to the directory you specify. You can choose a directory on your Web server or a regular network destination. To view a report in HTML format, open the file using your Web browser.

Exporting to Lotus 1-2-3

To export to a Lotus Notes database, choose Lotus Notes as your destination. Select the Lotus Notes server from the Servers List dialog box that appears next. You then need to click the name of the database to which you want the report exported. Verify the file name and click OK. Take note that you must have version 3.0 or later of the Lotus Notes Windows client. Unfortunately, you can not export to a Lotus Notes OS/2 client.

Exporting the Report Definition

Crystal Reports supports the export of a report definition. This is a text file that explains the definitions of the report, including the selection criteria, formulas used, the definition of each section and all fields within those sections, including their formatting specifications. This file can be opened in any application supporting .TXT files.

Exporting Your Reports to E-mail

SCR offers several ways to export reports to e-mail. You can export directly to an e-mail destination using Microsoft MAPI. Another option would be to export your report to an Exchange Folder on your Exchange Server. Yet another choice would be to export your report to one of your Microsoft Outlook folders via the Exchange Folder destination. And lastly, you can attach any report file to an e-mail message using whichever e-mail client you currently use. Just create your message as usual, and attach the report file as an attachment.

Exporting to a Microsoft Exchange Destination

When exporting from Seagate Crystal Reports, you can choose the Exchange Folder option. By exporting directly to an Exchange folder your report remains in the .RPT format within the Exchange folder you specify. This makes it available for other users who have access to that same Exchange folder. The exported report looks just like an e-mail message, and when you open it, you open SCR to view the report. To export to an Exchange folder:

1. Using the Export dialog box, select Exchange Folder as the destination. Click OK.

2. The Choose Profile dialog box appears, as shown in Figure 13.5. Open the Profile Name list to select an Exchange profile to export to.

If you have access to a Microsoft Exchange Server, you can export your report to a profile on the server.

3. Once you select a profile, the Select Folder dialog box appears and you can select the folder in which you want the report to be saved. Click OK.

If you do not have access to an Exchange Server you can use this export destination to export your report directly to Microsoft Outlook.

1. When the Choose Profile dialog box appears, Microsoft Outlook appears if you have it installed. Click OK. The Select a Folder dialog box opens.

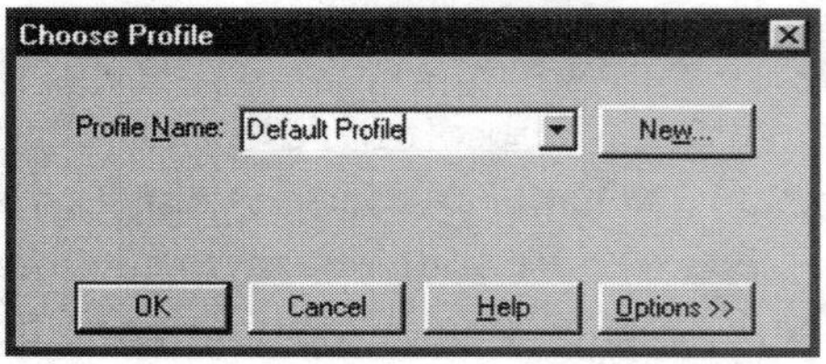

Figure 13.5
Choose the profile you would like to export your report to.

Figure 13.6

Choose the destination of your exported file in Outlook.

2. Choose the folder in Outlook to which you would like to export just as you would choose the folder in your Exchange Profile (see Figure 13.6).

3. Click OK. SCR exports your report to the folder you have specified in Microsoft Outlook. You can now forward this message to any address, and the recipient receives the report along with any text that you add to the message.

Creating a Report from a Spreadsheet

A popular feature of Seagate Crystal Reports is the ability to use an Excel spreadsheet as a data source for reports. You need to save your spreadsheet in a special way, set it up as an ODBC data source, and then design a report from it using the Crystal Report Designer.

Saving Your Spreadsheet with a Named Data Range

These steps walk you through setting up your Excel file with a Named Data Range that you can use as a data source for a report. Be sure to first open the Excel file you want to report from. To save an existing speadsheet or workbook in Excel with a Named Data Range:

1. In the spreadsheet, select all of the cells you want to use as your data source. Be sure to include the column headings, which Seagate Crystal Reports interprets as field names. Also, include an extra blank row after the last row of the range. This allows you to later insert new records in the range without having to redefine the data range.

2. Click Insert, Name, Define. This opens the Define Name dialog box, as shown in Figure 13.7.

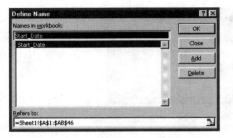

Figure 13.7

Define and name
the range of data
you want to use in
your report with
the Define Name
dialog box.

3. The name of your first column heading appears in the Define Name dialog box. Click Add, which adds that first and only name to the list. Click OK. This is now the name of your data range.

4. Click File, Save As. Enter a name for your new file and click OK. This new file can now serve as your data source.

5. Close the file, and exit Excel.

Setting Up Your Spreadsheet as an ODBC Data Source

You now need to install and set up an ODBC driver for Excel (something you only have to do once), and then create an ODBC pointer to your Excel data source. To do this, use the ODBC Administrator, which ships with Seagate Crystal Reports. You can find it in the Seagate Crystal Reports program group. To set up Excel data as an ODBC data source:

1. On the User DSN tab of the ODBC Administrator, select Excel Files and click Add (see Figure 13.8). The Create New Data Source dialog box opens (see Figure 13.9).

2. Select the Microsoft Excel Driver (*.xls) and click the Finish button. The ODBC Microsoft Excel Setup dialog box opens (see Figure 13.10).

3. In this dialog box, you need to type a name for your data source, which shows up as the name in the Log On Server dialog box in the Crystal Report Designer. You can optionally enter a description.

4. Click Select Workbook and select the file you saved earlier in Excel as your data source. Close both the Select Workbook and Excel Setup dialog boxes. Then close the ODBC Administrator.

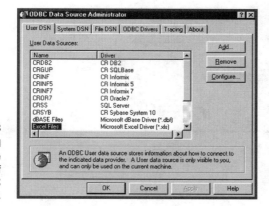

Figure 13.8

Select Excel Files from the User DSN tab of the ODBC Administrator.

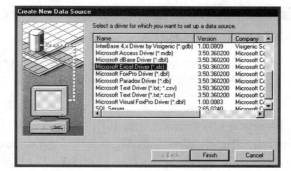

Figure 13.9

Select a driver from the Create New Data Source dialog box.

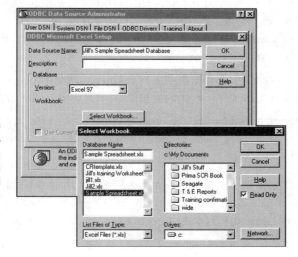

Figure 13.10

Name your new data source using the ODBC Microsoft Excel Setup dialog box.

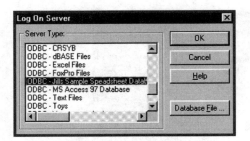

Figure 13.11

Choose the data source you created in Excel for your report.

Using Your New Data Source for Designing a Report

Now you are ready to design a report using your Excel data source! Open the Crystal Report Designer and use the following steps to start a new custom report:

1. Start a new report and click Custom1. from the Report Gallery. When the dialog box expands, click the SQL\ODBC data source button. The Log On Server dialog box opens (see Figure 13.11).

2. Scroll down to find and select the name you entered as the Database Name in the ODBC Administrator (it will be in the format "ODBC – <name of your excel file>"). Click OK. You have now chosen your Excel file as the data source for your report.

3. The Choose SQL Table dialog box appears, with the name of the data range you created listed as a table. Select it and click OK.

4. The Design tab of Seagate Crystal Reports opens for you to design your report. The named data range in your Excel spreadsheet is your data source for this report.

Designing a report from an Excel spreadsheet involves several steps to set up the spreadsheet as a data source, but provides the ability to use the powerful functionality of Seagate Crystal Reports to run reports against data contained in Excel files.

Distribution and Deployment Considerations

When you export a report and save it in a new format, Excel for example, it has an .xls file extension and all the properties and functionality of an Excel file. In addition to exporting a report to a different format for distribution, Seagate Crystal Reports has another option called Compiled Reports. By compiling a report in Seagate Crystal Reports, you create a mini-program that allows other people who do not have Seagate Crystal Reports installed to view the report in the its native SCR format (.RPT file).

Compiling Reports

Seagate Crystal Reports contains an Expert to help you compile a report for distribution to those who do not have Seagate Crystal Reports software on their PC. SCR evaluates the report you want to compile and asks several questions in the Compile Report dialog box that you need to address.

To compile your report you must have the report open in the Crystal Report Designer, and you must be sure you have saved it. To compile a report:

1. Click Report, Compile Report. You could also use the Compile Report button found on the supplemental toolbar.

2. In the Compile Report dialog box, SCR enters a default path and file name for executable file it creates. It uses the same directory path where you saved the .RPT file, as well as the same file name, only with the extension .EXE. If you want to change the path or file name, click Browse.

3. Creating a program group for your compiled reports makes them easy to find, so be sure to click Yes under Create Program Item for the Report. Seagate Crystal Reports automatically names the program group Seagate Crystal Reports, though you can change this if you wish (see Figure 13.12). The program group is added to your Start, Programs menu.

4. Choose whether or not to distribute the report immediately after compiling, and then click OK. SCR compiles the report and may open a program group window with an icon for the newly compiled report.

Figure 13.12

Use the Compile Report dialog box to specify the name, program group, and whether you want to distribute the compiled report.

If you selected Yes under Distribute the Report After, the Report Distribution Expert opens. See the next section for instructions on completing this set of steps.

You can create a desktop shortcut icon for the compiled report. When you double-click the icon, you can view or print the report without opening the Crystal Report Designer.

Using the Report Distribution Expert

The Report Distribution Expert works with compiled reports so that you can distribute reports to others who don't have Seagate Crystal Reports software installed. You have the option to open the Report Distribution Expert when you compile the report, or you can open the Distribution Expert by clicking the Report, Report Distribution Expert command.

If you do not compile a report first but just use the Distribution Expert, Seagate Crystal Reports does not compile the report to create the .EXE file or a program group item. In most cases, you should compile and distribute in one step.

The Report Distribution Expert contains several tabs that you need to address (see Figure 13.13). To distribute one or more reports:

1. On the Options tab, add or remove reports to be distributed. You can distribute more than one report at a time (refer to Figure 13.13).

2. You have the option to include database files used by the report, and also the option to include DLL's required for exporting the report. If you do not include these files and distribute without them, the compiled report cannot be refreshed or exported.

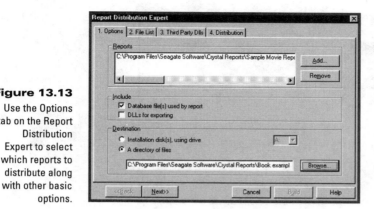

Figure 13.13

Use the Options tab on the Report Distribution Expert to select which reports to distribute along with other basic options.

3. You must set a destination for your Distributed Report, either to a floppy or hard disk. You can set the path using the Browse button.

4. Go to the File List tab (see Figure 13.14). SCR takes a minute or two to analyze the report for dependent files. Once this task completes, a list of all the files that Seagate Crystal Reports packages with your report appears in the File List. You can add or delete files here depending on what the report needs to function.

5. The Third Party DLLs tab allows you to add DLLs that might be necessary for the report to run, like ODBC drivers or files specific to your database not included in Seagate Crystal Reports (see Figure 13.15).

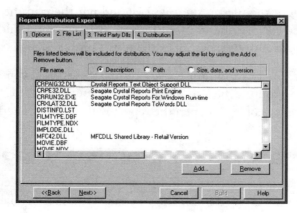

Figure 13.14

The File List tab shows the files that SCR deems necessary for the report to run once distributed to another machine.

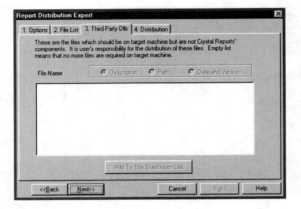

Figure 13.15

Use the Third Party DLLs tab to add any DLLs that might be necessary for running the report on another machine.

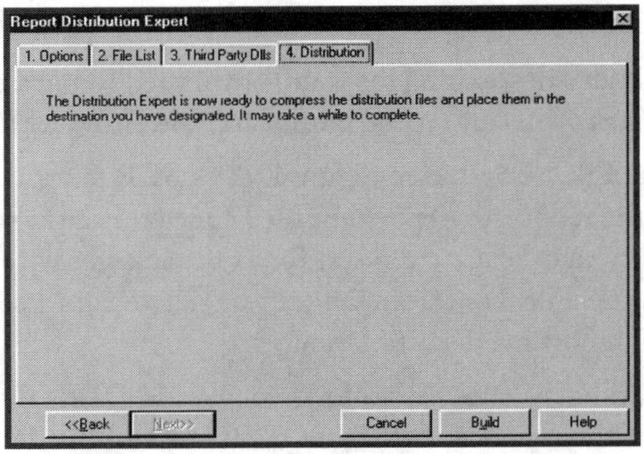

Figure 13.16

The Distribution tab entertains you as you wait for your report to compress and get ready for distribution.

6. The Distribution tab simply lets you know that SCR is ready to compress all of the files in the File List and put them in the directory you specified for distribution (see Figure 13.16). Click Build and the Report Distribution Expert does the rest. This takes a few minutes.

Once the Report Distribution Expert completes its task, you can distribute the compiled group of files to a machine without Seagate Crystal Reports software. Other people can open the report with limited functionality.

Working with a Compiled Report

To open the compiled report, simply double-click the compiled report desktop icon, program group item, or the executable file name. A dialog box opens

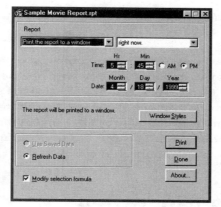

Figure 13.17

You can set options for viewing your compiled report from this dialog box.

with the name of your compiled report across the top and several options for viewing the compiled report (see Figure 13.17). To set options for the compiled report:

1. Choose from three print options: Print the report to a window, export the report, or print the report to a printer (refer to Figure 13.17). You can also choose to print the report at a set later date and time by selecting an item from the list at the top right or using the Time and Date fields.

2. You have two options: to Use Saved Data, or to Refresh Data. If you refresh data you need to be sure that the report has access to its data source.

3. Click the Window Styles button to open another dialog box that gives you options governing the report preview window (see Figure 13.18).

Figure 13.18

Choose which options to include in the preview of your compiled report.

4. Click the <u>P</u>rint button to print the report immediately. If you set the report to print at a future date and time, click <u>D</u>one.

SCR creates and uses three files in the compiling of a report. The report file (.RPT); an executable (.EXE) file with the same name as your report, and a CRF file (.CRF), which contains all the configuration information for the compiled report. When you distribute your report, the directory you specify also contains the DLL and other files needed to run the report, including a SETUP.EXE file that the user needs to set up and run the Compiled report on their PC.

Exporting Considerations

When designing reports in Crystal Reports, keep in mind how you plan to distribute reports throughout your organization. A few questions to ask yourself include:

- Who will I need to send the reports to? Will I be sending hard copies or electronic copies? Will the receiver have Crystal Reports or will I need to send compiled reports?

- How often will I be distributing a certain report? Daily, weekly, monthly?

- What will the report be used for? Daily/weekly business decisions? Tracking information? Will the report be used for invoicing?

- Will a certain report be used on the Web, for example, by salespeople or at a major project presentation being giving at a conference?

The above list gives a sampling of potential uses for reports that you design in Seagate Crystal Reports. How you export or distribute them depends on who they need to go to and how to achieve the best presentation quality report within the constraints of your business.

For example, if you run weekly reports that keep track of the movement of inventory, a basic report with little complicated formatting might be best. But if you want to compare the movement of inventory over months or among products, you need a more sophisticated report. If you need to export the report to co-workers who do not have Seagate Crystal Reports and you plan to export to Word, you may want to use less conditional formatting, such as conditionally changing the font colors, because formatting does not export as well. If you need the export to look as true to the original Crystal report as possible, you may want to export to the HTML format and instruct your co-workers to view the report using their Web browser. If you need to export your report for download into another data source for future manipulation in a spreadsheet, Excel would be a good option but, like with Word, some of the conditional formatting might not stay true to color.

Experiment with exporting your reports to different formats. Much of how your exported reports look depends on the print driver itself. If the print driver on one machine differs from the machine where the report was designed—or it's an older version—your report might not look right when printed. Some fields might not be aligned correctly or might be missing altogether. To fix this problem, install the most recently updated drivers for your printer. If fields get cut off even after installing the updated printer drivers, increase the size of the fields on your report by expanding the objects. This way they are more apt to fully print even if one printer driver uses a wider font size than the driver on the designer's machine.

If you have problems with pagination or how your report looks and fits on the page, here are a few hints:

- Set your own margins when designing a report. If you use the default, and then the machine you print from has a different default setting, you may cut off information or your report may not be properly formatted.

- Printed reports most closely match previewed reports when you set your video driver resolution to 640×480 pixels. If you design a report using 800×600 resolution, you may encounter formatting changes that you did not anticipate.

- Always leave Free Form Placement turned on. This helps ensure that your formatting stays true to whatever machine you open your report on.

 Free Form Placement is on by default. Change this option globally on the Layout tab of the Options dialog box (click File, Options). Or change this option per section of a report using the Section Expert.

Summary

This chapter covered a variety of tasks. Seagate Crystal Reports works quite well with Visual Basic, offering the power and functionality of the Seagate Crystal Reports tool to developers for integration in their own applications.

A Crystal report can be exported into many different formats to meet your needs. Exporting is straightforward, and with the formatting hints in the last section you may find that exporting meets any needs you may have beyond those available in SCR. Experiment with exporting to find which formats work best for you and your company.

CHAPTER 14

Integrating Seagate Crystal Reports with the Internet

The Internet provides a very easy and cost-effective way to distribute information to people and businesses locally, nationally, and internationally. Integrating the capabilities of Seagate Crystal Reports with the speed and ease of Internet communication affords you a powerful information distribution strategy. You will learn about the options available for placing reports on the Web, the architecture of the Web Report Server, and how to install and configure the product.

In this chapter, the generic term *Web server* refers to a computer that distributes and handles requests for HTML information viewed in a Web browser. The Seagate *Web Report Server* component distributes reports over the Web (through a Web server). The two terms sound similar, but they refer to two different components.

In order to install the Crystal Web Report Server you must be using the Professional version of Seagate Crystal Reports.

Web-related Features of Seagate Crystal Reports

Seagate Crystal Reports has several key features that help business users take advantage of Internet opportunities. These features include Thin Wire Architecture, Smart Navigation, and Smart Viewers.

Improved Performance with Thin Wire Architecture

Thin wire architecture refers to the Crystal Web Report Server capability to send only the pages requested (called *Page On Demand*)—instead of the entire file—to a Web browser. This helps reduce network traffic and increases the speed with which the client sees the report when viewed over the Web.

Quick Searches with Smart Navigation

Smart Navigation is the ability to jump to a specific section or group on a report instead of having to move one page at a time. This is very important in a Web browser environment because it allows you to navigate through a large report and focus in on the particular area of interest quickly and efficiently. Smart Navigation populates a Group Tree on the left side of the window with branches that signify groups on the report. This Group Tree operates the same as the Group Tree in the Crystal Report Designer. Web administrators can control the Group Tree and other functions using the Web Reports Server Configuration utility, described later in this chapter.

Keep in mind that by generating a Group Tree the Web Report Server must make a complete pass through the report before returning the first page. This can tie up resources and slow performance somewhat. The default setting generates a Group Tree, but you can change this default.

Smart Viewers

Smart Viewers allow the Web browser to read a report in SCR's native .RPT format (important because the formatting of a report does not change when read in the .RPT format). Smart Viewers display reports in the same manner as the runtime Preview window (in which a compiled report appears).

The Crystal Web Report Server checks for the type of browser requesting the report and sends the appropriate Smart Viewer to the client to allow proper viewing of the report. The three types of Smart Viewers include ActiveX, Java, and HTML:

- **Smart Viewer for ActiveX.** An ActiveX control that can be placed in an HTML page and viewed through any Web browser that supports ActiveX, such as Microsoft Internet Explorer version 3.02 and later. If you use Internet Explorer, ActiveX is the default Smart Viewer.

- **Smart Viewer for Java.** A Java applet that can be placed in an HTML page and viewed through any Web browser that supports Java, such as Netscape Navigator and Communicator. If you use Netscape, Java is the default Smart Viewer.

- **Smart Viewer for HTML.** Not actually a component that can be configured, but the Crystal Web Report Server converts the existing report format into HTML a 3.2 format.

The ActiveX and Java viewers provide the most functionality. The Smart Viewer for HTML does not allow Smart Navigation, drill down on charts and maps, drill down on subreports, or exporting, because the report has already been exported to the HTML format.

Interacting with Reports on the Web

SCR offers three ways to interact with reports on the Web: Static, Dynamic, and Ad Hoc.

- **Static.** A static report is a snapshot of data at the time the report was run, placed on the Web. This data never changes and is not interactive. To update the information, a new report must be re-generated and then placed on the Web server.

- **Dynamic.** A dynamic report uses the Crystal Web Report Server to allow users to interact with and refresh reports against the data source. You can set up parameters to allow users to change record selection and, thus, the results of the report.

- **Ad Hoc.** Ad hoc reports can be quickly built over the Web using Seagate Query, described in Chapter 11. This tool allows you to build reports over the Web, and then open them for further refinement in the Crystal Report Designer, if necessary.

Working with Reports on the Web

You can provide Crystal reports on a Web site in two ways: Active Server Pages or the Crystal Web Report Server. Active Server Pages offer more power and functionality through scripting, whereas the Crystal Web Report Server offers ease of setup and simplicity at the cost of some functionality.

 Most of the discussion in this chapter focuses on the Web Report Server because the scope of this book does not encompass the scripting required by Active Server Pages.

Active Server Pages and Automation Server

Active Server Pages work in conjunction with the Crystal Print Engine Automation Server to allow developers to create scripts and applications that change the functionality of Web sites used to access reports. With the Automation Server, developers can configure the presentation of reports in the Web browser. However, using the Automation Server and Active Server Pages requires extensive programming and familiarity with scripting languages such as VBScript or JavaScript. For additional information on the Automation Server see the Crystal Reports Developer's Help file.

Active Server Pages can only be used with Microsoft's Internet Information Server (IIS).

The Seagate Crystal Reports CD includes many examples of this type of scripting, in addition to examples installed on a sample Web site using the Crystal Web Report Server.

Crystal Web Report Server

The Crystal Web Report Server offers a second way to work with reports. It is very easy to install and configure and available immediately to process report requests. To make a report available to the Web browser, you simply move the .RPT file to a directory on your Web server and create a standard HTML link on a Web page. The Web Report Server does allow some interaction at the time users run the report (such as entering parameters, altering record selection, and executing stored procedures) but these functions are not as powerful as those available in the Automation Server discussed earlier.

Crystal Web Report Server works best for smaller departments and accommodates about 30 concurrent users. Many factors impact performance over the Web, including RAM, report size, server utilization, intranet traffic, and database performance. For support of a larger number of concurrent users, look into Seagate Info (see Chapter 15).

Architecture and Components of the Web Report Server

The following steps loosely define the process Seagate has implemented for generating and displaying reports in a browser via the Crystal Web Report Server:

1. Users, via the Web client, make a request for a report. The Web server then passes the request to the Crystal Web Report Server.

2. If the report already exists in the temporary cache and does not need to be refreshed against the database, the Web Report Server sends the page back to the browser.

3. If the page does not exist or needs to be refreshed, the Crystal Web Report Server sends a request to process the report and create a page.

4. Once the report runs and is placed in the temporary cache, the Web server returns the page to the browser.

Though this process includes many technical steps, it is important to get a good overall picture before diving into the technical side. In the next section, the components involved in producing reports for the Web are briefly discussed. For additional information, contact Seagate Software technical support (see Appendix B) or refer to the Web Guide (see "Additional Help and Documentation" at the end of this chapter).

Web Server Extensions (ISAPI/NSAPI vs. CGI)

The Crystal Web Report Server works with two main types of Web servers: ISAPI/NSAPI and CGI. ISAPI refers to the application programming interface (API) for Microsoft's IIS, and NSAPI refers to the API for Netscape's Web server. The Crystal Web Report Server serves as an extension to one of these Web servers, adding functionality used to view Crystal reports. When working in conjunction with an ISAPI/NSAPI type of Web server, Crystal installs the file CRWEB.DLL.

CGI refers to the Common Gateway Interface, standard on Web servers. Seagate Crystal Reports 7 is the first version to support compatibility with CGI Web servers. When working in conjunction with a CGI type of Web server, SCR installs the file CRWEB.EXE.

In short, the Crystal Web Report Server complies with most Web servers available today. Though you need to install the correct Crystal Web Report Server file for your type of Web server (ISAPI/NSAPI or CGI), SCR's installation process makes this easy by detecting the type of Web server being used.

Crystal Web Report Server Components

Two components comprise the Seagate Web Server: The Crystal Web Page Server, which handles the report, and the Crystal Web Image Server, which handles the graphics and charts.

Seagate Crystal Web Page Server

The Crystal Web Page Server handles requests for a report, generates the output, and returns that output to the Web server. It also manages report processing, allowing multiple requests for a report at the same time. This makes reports available faster when the report has been previously processed and still sits in the temporary cache.

The Web Page Server creates reports in either HTML or EPF. It does so by using the correct .RPT file, running the report against the data source, and saving the report file.

 Crystal Report Designer uses the Print Engine to process reports. The Print Engine is the underlying foundation that many components rely on. It is necessary for the Crystal Reports Designer, Seagate Query, the Automation Server with Active Server Pages, compiled reports, and using Visual Basic or C++ to work with reports.

Output Generated by the Web Page Server

The Web Page Server generates two types of output: HTML or Encapsulated Page File (EPF). If the client browser requests the page in an HTML format, then the Web Page Server generates HTML pages containing Crystal Images, as interpreted by the Seagate Crystal Web Image Server.

If the browser requests the report from a Java or ActiveX viewer, then the Web Page Server generates EPF pages. Seagate developed EPF based on the industry-standard Encapsulated Postscript format (EPS). Pages in the EPF format can handle complex design instructions, thereby displaying information more accurately and more cleanly than HTML. Because this is a proprietary format, EPF only works with ActiveX and Java Smart Viewers.

Seagate Crystal Web Image Server

When a report must be returned in HTML format, the Web page Server renders the graphics, maps, charts, and OLE objects as Crystal Image (.CRI) files. When the Web Report Server encounters a Crystal Image inside an HTML page, it asks the Crystal Image Server to translate it into a format that can be displayed by a Web browser.

If you use Windows NT, for best perfomance run both the Web Page Server and Web Image Server as NT services. Give each of these services administrative privileges so that this account has access to all resources on the network. Make sure to set up the service to start automatically, and specify This Account when you assign privileges.

Installing the Crystal Web Report Server

Seagate Software has made it quick and easy to install the Crystal Web Report Server and its components. Before you start the installation process, you'll need to stop your Web server. In Windows NT you do this via the Control Panel, Services option. In Windows 98, use the Personal Web Manager to stop the server. Then start the installation process and follow the prompts until you get to the Installation Options dialog box (see Figure 14.1).

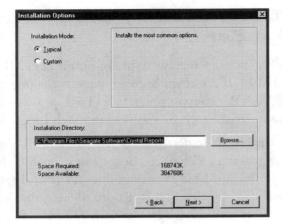

Figure 14.1

Choose the Custom installation mode on the Installation Options dialog box.

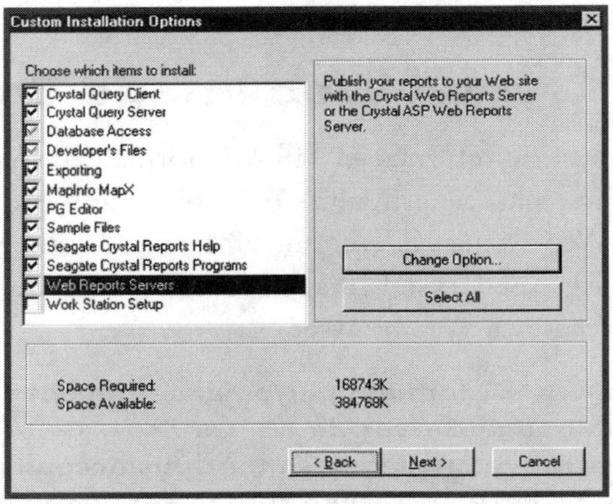

Figure 14.2

Make sure you include the Web Server components in the custom installation.

1. On the Installation Options dialog box, click Custom and then Next. The Custom Installation Options dialog box opens (see Figure 14.2).

2. Select Web Reports Servers from the list of components to install, and then click Next. Seagate Crystal Reports checks your system to determine which Crystal Web Report Server components need to be installed. The next window shows you your choices (Microsoft, Netscape, or CGI), as shown in Figure 14.3).

3. Select the server you wish to install. The installation continues as usual. Follow the instructions to finish the installation.

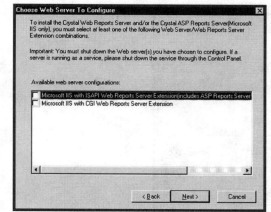

Figure 14.3

The installation program makes Web Report Server choices automatically available depending on your Web server software.

4. Finally, restart your computer before continuing, to allow the changes to take effect.

Firewalls can prevent ActiveX and Java Smart Viewers from being installed properly. If you have problems with your Smart Viewer, check to see if you have a firewall installed. You can also use the Smart Viewer for HTML instead of the Smart Viewer for Java or ActiveX, since HTML is the lowest common denominator.

Configuring the Web Report Server

You can configure the Crystal Web Report Server with the Web Configuration utility, called Web Reports Server Configuration, found in the Seagate Crystal Reports program group. In the following sections, which are organized according to the five tabs found in the Web Configuration utility, the important settings you may wish to alter for your installation of the Web Report Server are discussed.

Page Server Tab

The Page Server tab allows you to change settings for the Web Page Server (see Figure 14.4). The Server Port number must match the port specified for .RPT files on the Server Mappings tab. By default, SCR sets the port number to 2000. If you change the number here, be sure to also change it on the Server Mappings tab.

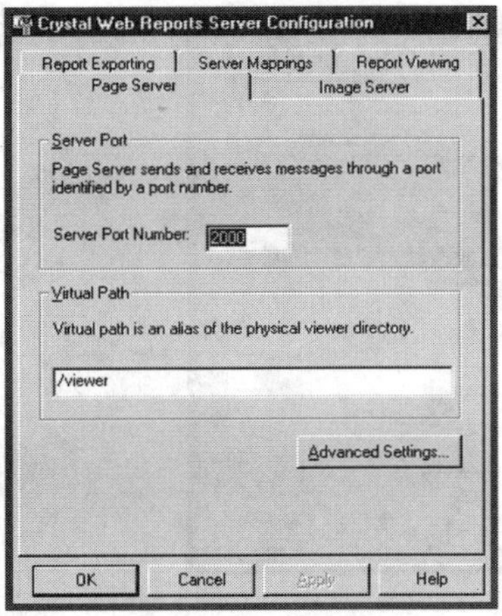

Figure 14.4

Options to change
the port number
and virtual path
in the Page
Server tab.

The Virtual Path specifies the location of the ActiveX and Java Smart Viewer files. The default location is C:\Program Files\Seagate Software\viewers. You can set up the alias referred to on this tab using your Web server administration software.

The Advanced Settings button opens a dialog box that allows you to set the maximum number of threads, jobs, and idle times (see Figure 14.5). These settings are important because they allow you to fine-tune the Page Server for its best performance.

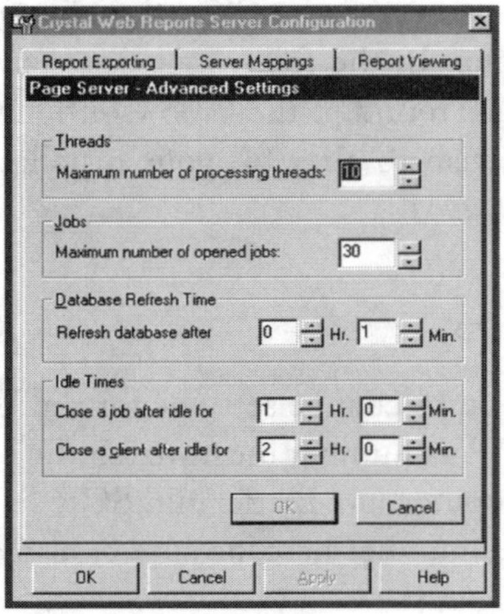

Figure 14.5

Advanced
settings to control
performance on
the Web Report
Server. To
increase
performance in
most cases,
reduce the
number of jobs so
that the server
needs fewer
resources.

The Page Server is a multi-threaded application in version 7 of Seagate Crystal Reports. It uses threads to process requests that the Page Server makes, and each thread in use consumes computer resources. Therefore, you may want to alter the maximum number of threads according to the amount of resources available on the machine running the Crystal Web Report Server. The maximum number of jobs tells the Page Server how many reports it can process at once. You can lower the maximum number of jobs to control the resources on the machine and troubleshoot performance problems.

The Database Refresh Time setting controls how long an already generated report page can sit in the temporary cache before it expires and must be refreshed against the database. This important setting can minimize the impact that clients have by refreshing reports against the database server. The higher the refresh time, the fewer hits to the database. But, if the data changes often and it's important for users to see the most current information, then you might want to lower the refresh time setting.

Image Server Tab

The Image Server tab controls the settings for the Image Server component (see Figure 14.6). Like the Page Server tab, the server port number here must match the number on the Server Mappings tab for .CRI files. The default port for the Image Server is 2001. The maximum number of threads allows you to fine-tune the amount of resources that can be used for processing

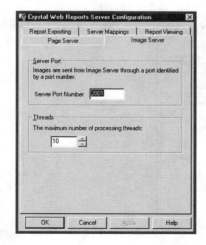

Figure 14.6

Image Server port settings must match the Page Server settings.

image requests. If you change this setting, consider the amount of resources on the Web Report Server computer as well as what other applications or services demand resources on the same machine.

Report Exporting Tab

The Report Exporting tab controls whether to allow a Smart Viewer to export reports to other formats and, if so, which formats (see Figure 14.7). Choices include Seagate Crystal Reports (.RPT), Rich Text Format (.RTF), Microsoft Word (.DOC), and Microsoft Excel (.XLS) formats. You can turn off this option if you want to control the output of the data so it doesn't leave your system through an export.

Report Viewing Tab

The Report Viewing tab allows you to control the options available for manipulating a report in a Web browser (see Figure 14.8). Settings that can be modified include drilling down on reports, displaying the Group Tree, and zooming in and out. It is also important to note that you can prevent a user from refreshing the data (thus hitting the database). You can change these settings to improve performance on the client.

In the Group Tree area, you can also turn off the Group Tree or set the maximum number of groups that can be generated in the tree. This setting can

Figure 14.7

Report Exporting tab options make exporting formats available to the client.

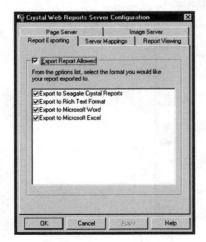

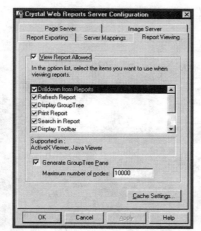

Figure 14.8
Change options in the Report Viewing tab to increase performance on the client by turning off some options.

increase performance, but may limit usefulness of the Group Tree if all groups on the report are not displayed.

Click the Cache Settings button to change the size and location of the cache directory (see Figure 14.9). In general, you should try to change this setting to less than 2GB. SCR cleans up the temporary cache files at the interval specified in this dialog box. By making this time longer, you allow SCR to use the same pages already generated, preventing additional hits to the database to refresh a report.

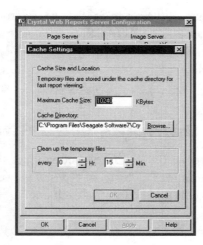

Figure 14.9
Tune Web Report Server performance by changing cleanup time and cache size in Cache settings.

Figure 14.10

Sample Web page when you choose Web Samples and Utilities Page.

Samples and Exercises

The Seagate Crystal Reports 7 CD contains a number of sample Web pages and sample applications from which to learn (see Figure 14.10). Click Web Samples and Utilities Page in the Seagate Crystal Reports program group to open the samples and utilities Web page.

As you look over the choices, you'll see the Seagate Query tool (which was covered in Chapter 11), examples of Active Server Pages for developers, and Web Report Server samples. By this point you've already installed the Seagate Query, so clicking this link takes you to the Seagate Crystal Query Client Web page.

Report Server Samples Web Site

Be sure to take the time to explore the Report Server Samples site (see Figure 14.11). It offers a demonstration of the different types of viewers so that you can get familiar with the options and features of each one.

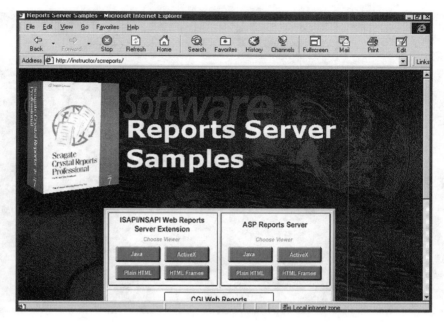

Figure 14.11

Choose these buttons to see sample reports on the Report Server Web site in the corresponding formats and viewers.

When using a Smart Viewer, you can then choose from several sample reports, which are the same regardless of the type of Smart Viewer you choose. The purpose of these demonstration reports is to allow you to get familiar with the different functions each of the Smart Viewers allows. Feel free to open reports, close them, export data, change reports, and change Smart Viewers. If you use a Microsoft IIS Web server with Active Server Pages installed, you can explore the ASP Reports Server viewers as well.

 Take notice especially of the differences in functionality between HTML and either Java or ActiveX.

Developer Active Server Page Samples

If you run Microsoft IIS and have Active Server Pages installed on the Web server, you can experiment with the Developer Active Server Pages Web site (see Figure 14.12). The purpose of this site is to demonstrate the powerful functionality available when using scripts to control how reports display on your Web site. The examples allow you to customize your Smart Viewer (by

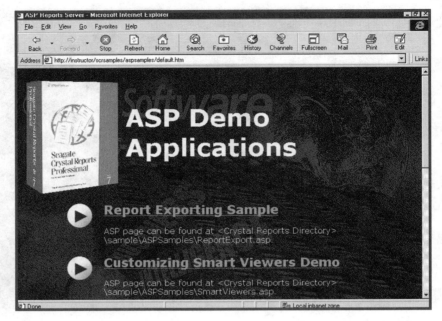

Figure 14.12

You can find sample reports and scripts using Active Server Pages on this Web site.

turning buttons and functions on or off), use record selection, and export a report to a different file format.

Additional Help and Documentation

There are a number of places to find help on Web-related issues and questions; you just need to know where to look. Seagate has scattered print and online documentation covering reporting on the Web among many different files and locations. Use Table 14.1 as an index or reference to this useful information.

To find Help (.HLP), Adobe Acrobat (.PDF), and HTML (.HTM or .HTML) files, you can use My Computer or the Explorer, and then double-click the file in order to open it within the related application (such as your Web browser or the Adobe Acrobat Reader).

Table 14.1 Finding Additional Help and Documentation

CATEGORY	ITEM	LOCATION	DESCRIPTION
Seagate Crystal Reports 7 CD	Web Guide (see Figure 14.13)	HTML: \Docs\Webguide\ click_me.htm	Contains version 6 information but is basically the same for version 7
		Adobe Acrobat: \Docs\ Webguide.pdf	
Online Help	Developer's Help	DEVELOPERS.HLP	Useful information about Automation Server, Active Server Pages, and the Web architecture of Seagate Crystal Reports
	ReadMe File	README.HLP	Contains information on Report Server settings and registry keys settings
	Other Help Files	\Seagate Software \Crystal Reports *.HLP	Numerous other Help files cover topics such as charting, mapping, Crystal Dictionaries, and more
Seagate Software Web Site	Technical Reference	www.seagate software.com– TECHREF.PDF	Useful in understanding technical options
	Automation Server and Web Reporting white papers	www.seagate software.com/ prod-bi-techsupp/ whitepapers/scr_ technical_papers_ index.asp	Additional information about the Web Report and Automation Servers

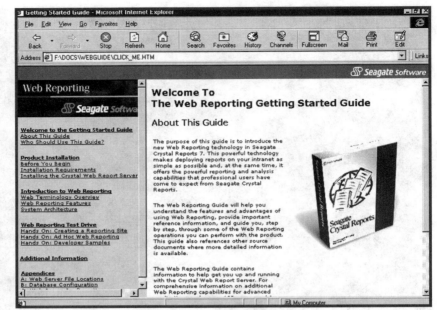

Figure 14.13

The Web Guide provides additional assistance in using Seagate Crystal Reports with the Web.

Summary

This chapter focused on the features and benefits of using the Web to distribute information. The components of the Automation Server and the Web Report Server were discussed, and you were led through an installation and configuration of the Web Report Server. The sample site that automatically installs on your Web server was also explored.

The Internet will continue to dominate the strategies of distributed companies who want information quickly. Seagate Crystal Reports can help organizations achieve their information distribution goals.

CHAPTER 15

The Benefits of Seagate Info

- What Is Seagate Info?

- Dividing the Work with Three-Tier Architecture

- Info Servers

- Extended Architecture Components

- Migrating from Crystal Reports to Seagate Info

S eagate Software markets Seagate Info as a completely different product than Seagate Crystal Reports. However, Seagate Info encompasses the components of Seagate Crystal Reports, thus the connection to this book. If you design reports using Seagate Crystal Reports and your company has either deployed or is thinking about deploying Seagate Info, this chapter is for you.

This chapter provides some basic information about the features and major functions and components of Seagate Info. Keep in mind that Seagate Info is a powerful system that encompasses much more than can be fully described here.

If your company has already deployed Seagate Info, this chapter will help you understand the complete reporting system, which in turn will help you determine the best ways to develop and create reports within that system. If you currently work with Seagate Crystal Reports only, this chapter provides an overview of what Seagate Info offers in addition to Seagate Crystal Reports. This is meant to help you be aware of Seagate Info and its basic capabilities, so that you can determine whether an upgrade to Seagate Info might be something to consider for your company.

What Is Seagate Info?

Seagate Info 7 is the newest release of what was previously known as Seagate Crystal Info. Seagate Info takes Seagate Crystal Reports a step further by adding a user-friendly client interface—for refreshing, viewing, scheduling, printing and exporting reports—with powerful back-end components—for managing security, report distribution, scheduled refreshes, posting reports on the Web, and more. Security can be set for individual users or any size group of users. These individuals and groups can access and share reports, queries, programs, and cube objects from an easy-to-use desktop or Web environment.

Seagate Info gives end users the ability to schedule reports and queries—created with the Crystal Report Designer or Seagate Query—to run anytime, day or night, even if they've turned off their individual client workstation. Reports, queries, OLAP cubes, and other reporting objects can be generated once and shared among users, saving valuable time and resources. Dedicated machines house the scheduling (Automated Processing Scheduler) and processing (Info Servers) components of the system, linked together via a communication backbone called the Sentinel, which rides on top of your current network protocol. By implementing Seagate Info, your business can take advantage of three-tier architecture to design, schedule, process, and analyze data.

Dividing the Work with Three-Tier Architecture

Seagate Info organizes its components into three tiers. Three-tier architecture is a method of designing applications that distributes processing to multiple machines. The purpose of such architecture is to allow more work to be done more quickly by more users, by designating specific machines (components) to do certain jobs.

Seagate Crystal Reports employs a two-tier architecture—you have Seagate Crystal Reports installed on your PC (tier one), and you connect to a data source (tier two). Your PC does the majority of the work in this system, collecting data from a source and then processing and formatting it on your PC with the Seagate Crystal Reports software.

Seagate Info's three-tier architecture involves an extra, middle tier of components (see Figure 15.1). This middle tier serves to schedule and process reports. You still use the Info Report Designer (same as the Crystal Report Designer in Seagate Crystal Reports) to design reports. Seagate Info just gives you the ability to transfer scheduling and processing of that report to middle tier components, freeing your PC. In Seagate Info, the Info Desktop makes up the first tier; the second tier contains the Automated Processing Scheduler and Info Server components; the third tier contains your data source. Adding a middle tier of components means that the scheduling and processing of reports moves off the end users' workstation to a designated server machine, or several machines (running the Automated Processing Scheduler and/or Info Servers). This frees up the client workstation to attend to other tasks.

Components of Seagate Info within the Three-Tier Architecture

Seagate Info has many components that help make it a flexible system for managing reporting across your business. Each of the three tiers of Seagate

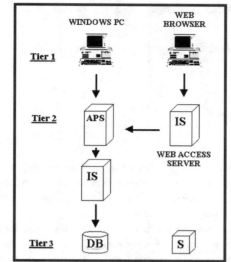

Figure 15.1

The Seagate Info three-tier architecture allows a business to have different machines taking care of different jobs over its network.

Info contains several types of components. Which components you use depends on your current system and your company's needs.

Info Desktops

When interacting with Seagate Info, you first encounter an Info Desktop, the first tier of the system. All client interaction with Seagate Info starts with the Info Desktop. There are several desktops to choose from:

- Info Desktop for Windows
- Info WebAccess Desktop for HTML
- Info WebAccess Desktop for Java
- Info Desktop for Outlook
- Offline Info Desktop

All Info Desktops require a user ID and password, except for the Offline Desktop (see Figure 15.2). Once logged on to Seagate Info, you can view and access all the folders to which you have security rights.

Figure 15.2

When you open the Info Desktop, the user ID and password you enter determines what information and options you can access.

An administrator uses the Info Administrator application, a component of Seagate Info, to set up each user and assign an initial password (which users can later personalize from within the Info Desktop). The administrator also sets up each user's security rights within the system, determining which folders and options can be accessed. Also note that, after initial setup, the name of the Automated Processing Scheduler machine shows up in the logon dialog box automatically.

All of the Info Desktops look similar to an e-mail or file manager type of interface, as shown in Figure 15.3. Each folder may contain report, query or cube objects, or even other programs. Like a report displayed on the Design

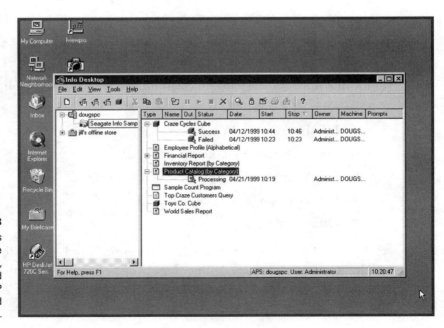

Figure 15.3

Different icons that indicate the type of object, such as standard reports, OLAP reports, and queries are used.

tab of the Info Report Designer, these objects contain no data. Rather, they are templates for collecting, calculating, and formatting the data that makes up a report.

In the right-hand pane of the Info Desktop, top-level items represent reports without data—like the Design tab in the Info Report Designer. Second-level items represent *instances* of the report refreshed with real data—like the Preview tab in the Info or Crystal Report Designer.

The Info Desktop you use is determined by your functionality needs and the way in which Seagate Info is implemented at your company. As mentioned, you can choose from the Info Desktop for Windows, two different WebAccess Desktops, the Outlook Desktop, or the Offline Desktop. You must be using the Info Desktop for Windows in order to have the Info Report Designer available to you. Seagate Query is available using all of the Info Desktops, except the Offline Desktop. Refer to the sidebar in this chapter for a brief description of the WebAccess Desktops. The Info Desktop for Outlook simply creates the Info Desktop within your Microsoft Outlook interface, so that those who already use and are familiar with Outlook can use it easily. Adding offline folders to any Info Desktop—making instances stored to those folders available when not logged on to Seagate Info—creates the Offline Desktop.

 The Seagate Info package includes the software for *all* the Info Desktops, including the WebAccess Server mentioned in the WebAccess Desktops sidebar. Your company can choose which components will best meet its needs.

The Info Desktops have several functions. Using Info Desktops, users manage folders, objects, and instances. Like in most e-mail programs, *folders* help organize a large number of items (in this case, reports) into related groupings. *Object* refers to items that can be initiated for processing, such as a report, OLAP cube, or query. And, *instance* refers to the returned result set of a processed object, for example, a report with information from the database. Double-click an instance to open the appropriate component for viewing and analyzing instances.

- Info Analyzer or Info Viewer displays reports
- Info Worksheet displays OLAP cubes
- Info Analyzer or Info Viewer displays query result sets

WEBACCESS DESKTOPS

Seagate Info allows you to access the Automated Processing Scheduler from a Web browser. To do so, an Info WebAccess Server must be installed and set up on your organization's Web server. Once the server has been set up, you can access your Info Desktop through the Internet without any additional Seagate Info software on your PC. Though you do not need any software to access an Info Desktop in this way, you do need a user ID and password. You cannot access the Info Report Designer from the WebAccess Info Desktops, but all other functionality is similar, including access to Seagate Query.

You log on to your company's WebAccess Server via your browser by entering the URL address for the server. You have a choice as to which Info Desktop you would like to use (Java or HTML); your choice depends on your browser, system components, and setup. Once logged on, you can interact with the Automated Processing Scheduler—just like with the Info Desktop for Windows—to schedule, view, and analyze reports. Refer to your Seagate Info documentation for more information regarding each type of Info Desktop.

From the Info Desktop, users can schedule objects to process at any time, date, or series of dates. For example, a user in the Accounting department might schedule a credit card reconciliation report to automatically run once a month.

The Info Desktops serve as the gateway to several other tools. Which Info Desktop you use determines the available tools. The Info Desktop for Windows includes the following four designers:

- Info Report Designer
- Seagate Query
- Info SQL Designer
- Info Cube Designer

The WebAccess and Outlook Desktops all provide access to Seagate Query. This allows users to design ad hoc queries over the Web. Refer to both Chapter 11 on Seagate Query, and your Seagate Info documentation for more information regarding the tools available from each type of Info Desktop. Remember, if you use Seagate Info to design reports, you must connect to the system using the Info Desktop for Windows.

Automated Processing Scheduler

The Automated Processing Scheduler (APS) component of Seagate Info serves as the security guard for the system. The APS is part of tier two. Every user *must* log on to an APS through an Info Desktop in order to use any component of the system, except the Offline Desktop. The APS enforces all of the security rights and roles of each individual user and delegates work to Info Servers. The APS stores each user's Info Desktop information in the System Database, such as information about the objects that have been scheduled and processed and the status of instances.

Through the Info Administrator component, administrators control what each user has access to see and do. These rights include whether particular users may design and/or schedule reports, programs, queries or cubes, or whether they may add and delete folders and objects from their Info Desktop. These rights are set up in the Info Administrator, saved in the System Database, and enforced by the APS.

Info Servers

Seagate Info has several types of Info Servers for different processing needs. Info Servers are also members of tier two, along with the APS. Info Servers act as the workhorses of the system, processing all job requests sent to them from the APS. Since Info Servers do the processing rather than the client machine (your PC), report processing does not tie up the client machine nor require the client machine to be on. This architecture allows you to schedule your reports to process in the middle of the night when network traffic is lowest, or during the week when you happen to be on vacation!

You can specify which Info Server you want your object to process on, depending on the type of object, your location, database connectivity, or workload. Seagate Info makes several types of Info Servers available depending on what type of object you want to process. For example, reports process on an Info Report Server, cubes on an Info OLAP Server, and queries on the Info Query

Server. Your system may also contain more than one of any specific type of Info Server. For example, there may be two Info Report Servers, one for processing HR reports and the other for processing financial reports. Because work is divided between many machines for processing one machine does not get bogged down with too many work requests.

Each one of the Info Servers has specific installation requirements and functions, which meet the growing and changing needs of all kinds of businesses. All of the Info Servers meet slightly different needs. Companies with fewer users need fewer Info Servers. Large organizations benefit from using more Info Servers. Administrators of a system evaluate the needs of the entire organization and set up the appropriate Info Servers for use.

 Info Servers do not need to be huge dedicated server machines. Client workstations can be set to run as Info Servers during off-hours to take advantage of the second tier.

Sentinel

The Sentinel is the communication backbone of the Seagate Info system. The Sentinel rides on top of the existing network protocol allowing the Info Desktops, APS, and Info Servers to communicate with one another. Seagate Info supports four network protocols:

- Netware IPX/SPX
- NetBEUI
- TCP/IP
- CIMP (Crystal Info Messaging Protocol)

 You don't need to worry about the Sentinel or even turn it on; it starts automatically when you open your Info Desktop.

Your Database or Data Source

You may have one or many databases, data sources, or data warehouses from which you must collect data in order to meet your reporting needs. The data source is considered tier three in the Seagate Info architecture, but is neither shipped with, nor part of the software.

As mentioned previously in this chapter, you connect to your data from Seagate Crystal Reports when designing your reports using two-tier architecture. If using Seagate Info, you must be sure that the Info Server being used has access to the data source via your network.

Extended Architecture Components

Seagate Info has several other components that manage and add functionality to this three-tier system. These components include the Info Administrator, System Database, and the designers—the Info Report Designer, Seagate Query, Info SQL Designer, Info Cube Designer, and Info View Designer.

Info Administrator

The Info Administrator component of Seagate Info manages the entire system. Administrators use the Info Administrator to define users and user groups, assign rights, and manage passwords within the system. All of the information set in the Info Administrator resides in the System Database.

The Info Administrator also manages information about the Info Servers, such as how they are defined and their availability. Administrators can set up calendars and templates here, configure files and generic events, and define many other system options.

Info System Database

Do not confuse the Info System Database with your production database (the database containing information you're reporting on). The System Database stores all of the user security, folders, settings, and job requests associated with an APS and all related Info Desktops.

The Seagate Info installation places this MS Access database on your APS machine. You may use Microsoft SQL Server, Oracle, Informix, or Sybase as your System Database instead of MS Access, the only requirement being that you must connect to the Info System Database via ODBC.

Info Report Designer

 Seagate Info includes the Info Report Designer, which is basically the same as the Crystal Report Designer included with Seagate Crystal Reports. From the Info Desktop for Windows, you can open the Info Report Designer and take advantage of its full functionality.

Seagate Query

 Seagate Info also includes Seagate Query. You can use this newly designed query tool just as you learned in Chapter 11 of this book. Access Seagate Query with either its toolbar button or the Tools, Seagate Query command. Seagate Query is available from every type of Info Desktop except the Offline Desktop.

Info SQL Designer

 The Info SQL Designer is the same as in Seagate Crystal Reports. See Chapter 10 for information on this topic. Open the Info SQL Designer using its toolbar button or the Tools, Info SQL Designer command. This designer is only available using the Info Desktop for Windows.

Info Cube Designer

 Seagate Info contains a tool for designing OLAP cubes. Chapter 12 covers creating reports based on an OLAP cube. However, this book does not cover the Info Cube Designer, which is a component of Seagate Info only, not of Seagate Crystal Reports.

Info View Designer

Use the Info View Designer to create a custom view of your data source. The Info View Designer replaces the Crystal Dictionaries component of Seagate Crystal Reports. The Info View Designer is similar to Crystal Dictionaries with the added feature of column and row security. Like a Crystal Dictionary, an Info View can simplify a database for business users who may not have an extensive understanding of their organization's data structure. The Info View Designer allows the database expert to give end users a metaphorical pair of glasses through which to view the database. What end users see appears much easier to interpret and report from. Open the Info View Designer from the Seagate Info program group. It cannot be accessed via the Info Desktop.

 Chapter 10 discusses Crystal Dictionaries. With knowledge of that tool, you can decide if the Info View Designer might be a useful tool for your business.

Migrating from Crystal Reports to Seagate Info

Both Seagate Crystal Reports and Seagate Info are excellent products and, depending on your needs, one or the other might be best for you. There are several reasons why you might want to consider moving from Seagate Crystal Reports to Seagate Info. Seagate Info gives you the ability to schedule and share report objects with co-workers by taking advantage of the Info Desktops. Also, the ability to off-load the processing of jobs to other components within the three-tier architecture can be quite an advantage.

Seagate Info centralizes and manages your business's reporting. Rather than having individuals designing and running similar reports—which could result in duplication of valuable effort—one person or a group may design reports that other designated employees can access whenever they want. The Info Desktops enable a virtually unlimited number of users to access and share the same reports when they need them, while maintaining a secure environment.

Summary

Seagate Info provides an excellent environment to manage data. Compatible with almost any database, network, and intranet system, Seagate Info can help organize your data and meet your reporting needs. The powerful Info Report Designer teamed up with the three-tier architecture of Seagate Info provides answers to your business questions with powerful report, query, and cube tools in an efficient, scaleable, and straightforward environment.

The reporting needs of your organization dictate whether Seagate Info might be a more appropriate tool. Seagate Crystal Reports alone facilitates report design and per-user deployment and processing. Seagate Info supports full management of reporting. It allows the use of several middle tier components that increase processing power, along with the functional Info Desktops that facilitate report sharing and distribution over Windows and Web environments.

Though this chapter has given you an overview of Seagate Info, it is by no means a comprehensive representation of what Seagate Info has to offer. For more information, refer to your Seagate Software Sales Representative or the Seagate Software Web site.

CHAPTER 16

Managing Report Development Projects

- Planning a Report

- Becoming Familiar with Your Data

- Interviewing Your Customer

- Building a Report Step-by-Step

- Documenting and Saving Your Report

In this chapter, you'll learn how to get started in approaching a report project. One of the first questions people ask when faced with a real world report is "Where do I start?" The approach here begins with simple items first, and then progresses to more advanced items on the report. This philosophy of report design makes report writing easier and less stressful.

Planning a Report

It is very important to plan your project before you start writing reports. Before you even open the software, you should complete a number of actions.

Becoming Familiar with Your Data

You build your reports from data, so it makes sense for you to be familiar with the structure, fields, relationships, and location of that data. First, find out who the DBA (database administrator) is, and whether he or she is available to help with questions during your project. For example, you can ask the DBA where to locate the tables and fields for the report. Often the DBA can help with linking tables or creating views in the database.

Views are a collection of tables and fields that the DBA turns into a virtual table so that the report writer only needs one view to complete the report. Like dictionaries, views can simplify report writing by handling all the table linking, freeing the report writer from having to do so.

The DBA may also provide you with a printed data model or relationship diagram to help with the report writing process. It's helpful to see your data represented visually when linking tables.

Interviewing Your Customer

To understand how to successfully build a report, you must gather important information, such as which fields to use and calculations to include. Can your customer—the person or group who will ultimately use the report—provide you with a "mock" report with the columns and groups already diagrammed? If not, you'll need to create this mock report diagram with your customer. Include information like fields, formulas, groups, sorts, graphs, subtotals, record selection, and parameters. Paper and pencil often make the best tools for sketching the basic layout of the report. You should also review other reports that the organization uses to see how the reports have used logos, colors, and other graphics.

If you need to make a change to the design of an existing report, whom do you need to ask? Find out who approves changes in the report design process.

Will the reports most often be printed or viewed online? If printed, will black and white or color printers be used? If the reports will print to a black and white printer, be careful about what, if any, colors you use on the report (for text, graphs, maps, or other graphics). The colors may look great when you preview the report onscreen, but may print too faintly to be easily read on paper. Try using pattern fills instead of colors.

Will the reports be exported to HTML (for the Web) or to another program (such as Microsoft Excel)? Knowing the destination helps with design because fields can be made wider to accommodate the export issues. To distribute to the Web, use the Smart Viewers for ActiveX and Java, covered in Chapter 14. These viewers retain the .RPT format and eliminate export issues.

Can you verify the data in the new report against an existing report or database? Can you look at an existing report to see the formulas used in it? If so, duplication of these calculations will be much easier.

Which fonts need to be on the report? What look does the organization use when it comes to fonts? Use common Windows fonts, like Arial and Times New Roman, so that font substitution doesn't occur. If a font doesn't exist on a client machine, Windows substitutes another font in its place. This can potentially change the formatting and look of the report dramatically.

How will you determine record selection? What formulas, if any, do you need before starting the report? Record selection is an important item to add to the report quickly because it reduces the number of records returned to the report. This makes testing the report much quicker and keeps the database server more efficient because it doesn't need to return the entire database.

Creating a Template with Common Graphics and Fonts

After the interview process, create a template with the common elements for the reports. Include items such as logos, colors, boxes and lines, shading, and so forth. Keep it simple so that you don't need to delete many items before building each report.

Consider including information about you (the report writer), your company, and the report itself in the Summary Info window. You open Summary Info by selecting it from the File menu. On the Summary tab, you can enter your name, your company, the title of the report, a description of the report, keywords, and a subject to help when searching for a report using the Reports At A Glance program. You can also review some interesting statistics about your report on the Statistics tab, such as creation date and amount of editing time.

You might also have the template include Special Fields such as Print Date/Time, Data Date/Time, File Path/Name, or Page Number in the Page Header or Page Footer sections. Use a small font size to keep this helpful, but not critical, information out of the spotlight. When looking at a printed document these fields can show information such as when the report ran, how old the report data is, and where to find the report.

If you're working with a team of report developers, you may want to investigate using a version control product (such as Microsoft Visual SourceSafe) to allow only one developer at a time to check out and work on a report. In any case, make sure you save your report with different file names from time to time so that you can go back to an older version if you accidentally "break" your report.

Also, report files sometimes get corrupted for unknown reasons. It's a relief to have copies in case a particular file won't open or work. Please note that Seagate Crystal Reports does not have an auto save feature, so you'll want to save frequently and to different file names from time to time.

When you've completed the template report, use it to start the reports in your project. To access your template, choose Another Report from the Report Gallery and point to your template report. This way, you won't accidentally overwrite the template.

As you can see, a lot of questions need answering before you can start. Overall, you want to have a good idea of what tables and fields you need and how to get help with the database if you need it. Generally, a database expert will be available to you. If you don't know where the data needs to come from, ask someone for help. You may not know that you've incorrectly linked tables, and then have trouble figuring out the problem if your report does not look right or contain the right data.

Building a Report Step-by-Step

Now that you have a template to work with, you can start building an individual report. Complete the basics of the report first and then add more advanced options like formulas, parameters, subreports, cross-tabs, graphs, and maps. Using this method, you can see results as you go:

1. Add tables to report and link. If you use a view, query, or dictionary, linking becomes less of an issue.

2. Add fields to the report. Use the information from the interview and mock report to add the columns and data to the report.

3. Define the Record Selection to limit the number of records to be returned. Add parameters for record selection, if necessary. Sometimes these formulas are difficult, however, so feel free to skip them now and add them later. But, including some record selection criteria early limits the amount of work your machine does when processing the report in the next step.

4. Preview the report to see what it looks like to this point. At this time, resize and rearrange fields as necessary. Make sure that the column headings read the way you want. You should probably wait a few more steps before doing any further formatting. But, make sure you save your report frequently!

5. Set up groups defined in the interview and on the mock report. Check the sorting on the groups (Ascending, Descending, Original, or Specified Order). Make sure to check for second and third level sorts. At this point your report should really begin taking shape. If your report does not look like the mock report, then recheck the groups, record selection, and fields on the report. This is an important checkpoint because grouping is critical to making the report look correct.

6. Add summaries and subtotals to all groups that need them. Also, add text to explain what the numbers indicate.

7. Format objects (such as fields) so that they display data in the format needed for the report (such as currency or date). Make modifications to fonts, colors, borders, and other format options in order to call attention to an important field. Save your report.

8. Look at the report on the Preview tab and take a few minutes to be sure that your report is taking the shape you want. You may want to offset the groups, format all the column headings the same way, get rid of decimals, and so forth. At this point, you may want to add any conditional formatting to use on fields on the report.

9. Add formulas to build calculated fields. Formulas often stump report developers—even experienced report developers. Don't stop the report development process to work on a tough formula. You can use double slashes (//) to comment out sections in a formula or add comments to document your formula. This is useful when troubleshooting a formula (to test specific sections or lines). If you encounter a tough formula and get stumped, comment out the entire formula and leave it on the report. The Formula Editor ignores anything to the right of the double slashes. This enables you to keep the formula on the report and still allows the report to process (without getting errors). Save your report.

10. Add other advanced items such as parameters, subreports, cross-tabs, graphs, and maps. This, of course, depends on your specific report.

11. Do any section formatting or section conditional formatting. You may need or want to manipulate the sections containing a graph, or spend some time with a subreport.

 You will find that previewing your report often helps you format it the way you like.

12. Test data for correct results. Verify your formulas, record selection, groups, and summaries against a legacy report or the database itself. Though often time-consuming, this step is very important for ensuring the accuracy of the data on your report.

13. Clean up the report and get the formatting perfect. If you plan to export to another program, experiment with the export. You may want to try other export formats to see if the results change. Try Excel 2.0, 3.0, 4.0, and so forth to see how those versions format the report. You can also try exporting to Lotus 1-2-3 and importing into Excel. All of these formats are compatible with Excel but they give differing results. Save your report.

14. Publish the report.

Generally by Step 7 the report really starts taking shape. Do as much without formulas or conditional formatting as possible because formulas can be complicated. It's important to get the look of the report early on so you have the structure in place before you start adding specific special items.

It's easiest to work on the formulas towards the end of the report development process for two main reasons. First, formulas can sometimes be frustrating if you are trying something totally new. Don't hold up your report design because you cannot get one formula. Second, formulas usually don't add much to the structure of the report. Thus, if you get the basic structure and format set, you can later focus on just the formula problem and not feel anxious about not accomplishing anything yet.

Formulas, parameters, subreports, graphs, and maps are usually important to the report itself, but not to the structure of the data in the report. Get some success before taking on the more difficult portions of the report! You often use the Formula Editor in formatting as well, but wait till you have the structure of the report intact before creating conditional formulas. Formulas often manipulate or possibly replace database fields. With the format of your report set, you can easily replace database fields with formula fields.

When adding subreports, cross-tabs, graphs, and maps to reports, simply add the extra sections needed and format accordingly. Of course, you can modify existing sections in order to accommodate insertion of a graph or other large object, but it is easier if you have the basic format set before inserting additional large objects.

 When adding subreports to a report, you may find it easier to complete only basic formatting before you insert the subreport. This way you can format both the main report and subreport at the same time so they match.

Documenting and Saving Your Report

Make sure that you save your report frequently! Seagate Crystal Reports has no auto save function, so you need to do it yourself.

Another good tip is to export the report choosing the Report Definition format (covered in Chapter 13). This creates a text file that documents your fields, formatting, record selection, formulas, groups, and other items on the report. By having the definition of your report documented separately from the report itself, you can print this document and save it in a binder for reference. For example, if you design a slick formula that you might use in other reports, you can save the formula in a Report Definition file and keep it by your desk. This way you don't need to find the report file and open it to see the formula. This feature is hidden away but a real time saver for those of us who write reports.

 There are now third party software products that accomplish this documentation task as well.

Summary

Although there is no right or wrong way to design a report, a list of steps helps when faced with designing a report. In this chapter, you learned one approach that is helpful in making quick, measurable progress towards the final report. Remember to save your report frequently and as different file names so you'll have "old" versions to look at if you introduce a change when fixing another problem. As you continue writing reports, you'll continually learn more about the process. Like success in any endeavor, it is a journey, not a destination. Good luck!

PART V

Appendixes

Setting Up an ODBC Data Source

C hapter 3 introduced ODBC (Open Database Connectivity) and discussed creating a report from an ODBC data source. This appendix examines how to set up this data connection and what to look for if you have problems.

What Is ODBC?

According to Microsoft Corporation, ODBC is "a programming interface that enables applications to access data in database management systems that use Structured Query Language (SQL) as a data access standard." ODBC allows programs to send data back and forth to many different types of databases, without having specific drivers written to form a bridge. With ODBC, a single application can work on a variety of database platforms.

So why doesn't everyone use ODBC? Perhaps because using ODBC is rather complex to set up and can be slow in performance. Software vendors write native drivers specifically for connecting to a particular database, usually requiring no special setup instructions. Because native drivers specifically connect the application and database, they usually perform faster and take advantage of specific "bells and whistles" offered by the database.

Unfortunately native drivers exist for only the most popular software packages and database standards on the market—that's a majority of the marketplace, but not the entire marketplace. Thus, many companies use the universal standard of ODBC.

Creating an ODBC Data Source

Since a lot of different programs use ODBC, many packages include it in their setup process. Seagate Crystal Reports automatically installs ODBC version 3.5 on your system. Version 3.5, in addition to the ODBC Administrator application, includes many of the more common ODBC drivers for Excel, Dbase, Access, Text, Oracle, Sybase, SQL Server, Informix, and DB2. This discussion will focus on the 32-bit version of ODBC rather than the 16-bit (Windows 3.x) version.

Checking for or Installing a Driver

The first step in the process of creating an ODBC data source involves installing the ODBC driver provided by the software manufacturer. This is the tough part about using ODBC. The setup for each driver differs and no universal "how to" guide exists. Before you decide to add a driver, however, you should check if it has already been installed on your computer.

1. Open the ODBC Administrator by clicking the ODBC icon in the Control Panel or choosing the ODBC Administrator command from the Seagate Crystal Reports program group.

2. Click the ODBC Drivers tab. This tab displays information about each installed driver, including the version, company who wrote the driver, file name, and file date (see Figure A.1).

Checking first for a driver on the ODBC Drivers tab can save you unnecessary work, as well as prevent unintentional changes to your system.

If the ODBC driver you require does not appear on the ODBC Drivers tab, it needs to be installed. Refer to the driver's documentation for installation instructions. You may want to seek assistance from your IT department or a database administrator.

Figure A.1
Look at the ODBC Drivers tab to see which drivers have already been installed on your system.

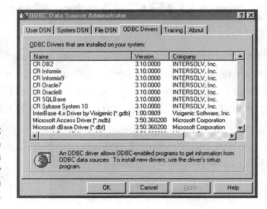

Adding a DSN

Now that you know the right driver is available, you can build a DSN. A DSN is a bit like the path names you use to point to files on your computer. The DSN points to the database. ODBC Administrator lets you set up three types of DSNs: User, System, and File. The User DSN is available only to the current user. A System DSN is available to all users on a machine (different profiles or log on names), including NT services. A File DSN is a file-based data source that can be shared by people with the same drivers. System DSNs are especially useful because they can be used by others and by your system automatically (see Figure A.2).

Generally, you need to configure an ODBC connection with information such as a user name, password, server, and file location. The format of the dialog boxes varies depending on the driver, but the following steps cover the basic things that must be set up for the ODBC connection to work.

1. Choose ODBC Administrator from the Control Panel or the Seagate Crystal Reports program group.

2. Click the System DSN tab, and then click Add. The Create New Data Source dialog box opens (see Figure A.3).

3. Select the driver required to connect to your database, and then click Finish.

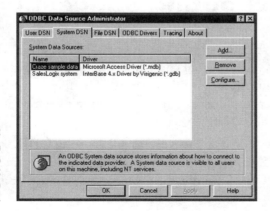

Figure A.2

Use the System DSN tab to set up an ODBC connection to your database.

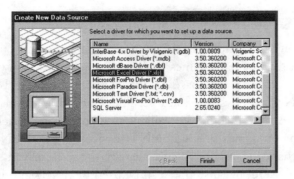

Figure A.3

When setting up a
new ODBC DSN,
the setup wizard
shows all
the drivers
available to
create the DSN.

4. Most drivers now open a dialog box or a wizard (a series of dialog boxes) that prompt you to provide information such as server, user name, password, and file location. You may need to refer to the instructions in the driver's documentation to complete the dialog box or wizard.

5. Save the connection and then test it by trying to log on to your database through Seagate Crystal Reports or a data connection utility that may be included with the driver.

To create a sample data source, refer to "Creating a Report from a Spreadsheet" in Chapter 11. It walks you through setting up an Excel spreadsheet as a data source for a report using the ODBC Administrator to install the proper ODBC driver.

Troubleshooting Suggestions

One of the first steps in troubleshooting an ODBC error is checking the versions of ODBC files on your computer. To do this, open the About tab in the ODBC Administrator (see Figure A.4). The files listed here should all have matching version numbers. If the version numbers do not match, you may need to reinstall ODBC.

Seagate has a very good document on troubleshooting ODBC problems. You can find it in the Knowledge Base on their Web site. The name of the article is "How to Fix ODBC 3.0 Problems—Summary." Search for article number C2001040.

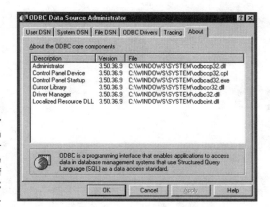

Figure A.4

Check the version number of your ODBC files in the About tab of the ODBC Administrator.

How to Get Help

T his Appendix outlines the best ways to find help with your questions about Seagate Crystal Reports.

Types of Help Available

You can get help from several different sources, including your computer, the Internet, phone support, and certified trainers and consultants.

Online Help

The easiest way to get assistance is to check out the online Help on your own machine. The main Seagate Crystal Reports Help file serves as a gateway to other online documentation installed with Seagate Crystal Reports 7.

When you choose Seagate Crystal Reports Help from the Help menu in the Crystal Report Designer, you open only the main Help file.

A little known fact is that Seagate Crystal Reports actually comes with more than 10 additional Help files. The main Help file for the Crystal Report Designer is CRW.HLP. To open another Help file, open the File menu in the Help window and click Open. An Open dialog box appears, displaying the other Help files available to you (see Figure B.1). Also, take a look in the Seagate Crystal Reports program group, from which you can access many of these Help files.

The following list summarizes many of the Help files and what each one covers. Note, however, that depending on the components installed on your machine, you may not have all these Help files, or you may have Help files in addition to the ones listed here.

- **CRMAP.** Mapping
- **CRDIT.** Document Import Tool
- **CRRDC.** Report Designer Component for Visual Basic
- **CRSQL.** Crystal SQL Designer
- **CRW.** Crystal Report Designer (default Help file)
- **CRWEB.** Web Reports Server

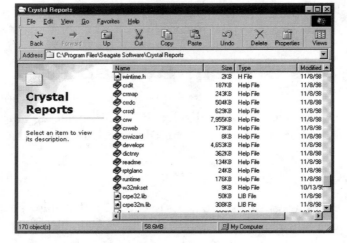

Seagate Crystal
Reports has many
Help files
available to you if
you know where
to look.

- **CRWIZARD.** Application Wizard for MS Development
- **DEVELOPER.** Application Development
- **DICTNRY.** Crystal Dictionaries
- **README.** Overview of topics and issues in version 7
- **RPTGLANCE.** Reports at a Glance application
- **RUNTIME.** Runtime, international, and compiled reports requirements
- **W32MKSET.** Btrieve setup utility

Using System Information

If you experience unusual problems when working with Seagate Crystal Reports, built-in utilities help you see what is going on with your computer. Click the <u>H</u>elp menu and choose <u>A</u>bout Seagate Crystal Reports (see Figure B.2).

The About dialog box displays your version of Seagate Crystal Reports along with your registration number (which is very important for technical support). You also see helpful information on how to contact Seagate Software via their Web site, e-mail, fax, and telephone. At the bottom of the dialog box you'll see two buttons: More Info and System Info. These are the utilities you're looking for.

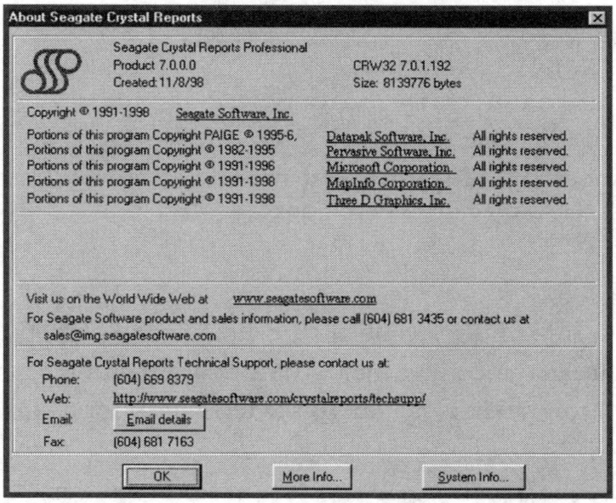

Figure B.2

About Seagate Crystal Reports lists information about your program.

Click More Info to show files currently loaded into your computer's memory (see Figure B.3). This information helps when searching for the cause of a problem. If you call in for technical support, you may be asked to look here to help the technician identify the source of the problem.

The dialog box categorizes files by the following:

- Dynamic Link Libraries (DLL)
- Drivers (DRV)

Figure B.3

Use the Loaded Modules dialog box to find different files loaded on your system.

- Executables (EXE)
- Fonts (FON)
- Others

You can look at the files with information about their path (location on hard drive), version number, or date.

Click <u>S</u>ystem Info to display information about your computer, such as its operating system, amount of free memory, video driver, printer driver, and network. Again, this information is helpful to the technician for technical support.

Getting Help at Seagate Software's Web Site

Seagate Software has a Web site at www.seagatesoftware.com/crystalreports/ that provides product information, technical support, access to the Knowledge Base of past technical support incidents, white papers, downloadable files and updates, and technical newsletters (see Figure B.4).

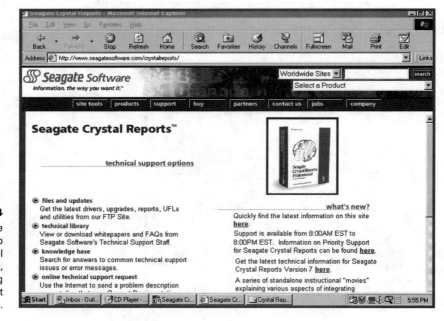

Figure B.4
Seagate Software has a good Web site with useful information, including technical support and white papers.

The white papers provide a very rich source of common questions and answers, as well as how-to guides on many subjects. Some of the documents that you have been referred to earlier in this book come from Seagate Software's Web site.

The Knowledge Base is a Web-based method to search existing technical support questions and answers. The search engine takes some getting used to (by default it searches for any occurrence of any word you type in), but with patience, it can be a good tool for getting help on a variety of subjects.

The Technical Newsletter (via e-mail) is an automated method for news bulletins and hints that can be sent to you each month. It's a good idea to subscribe to this free service.

Requesting Technical Support by E-mail

In addition to getting help at Seagate Software's Web site, you can send a blank e-mail to Seagate Software's technical support group (at support@webacd.seagatesoftware.com) and the system automatically sends you a form on which to submit your request. The turnaround for an average response is 24 to 48 hours. Although not as fast as a telephone call, e-mail support offers an easy and painless way to get help for questions that aren't critical today.

Using the Telephone for Technical Support

You can choose from two types of available telephone support: free and prepaid. Seagate Software offers free support to anyone with a registered product. The only cost is for long distance charges (to Vancouver, BC, Canada). The technical support phone number is 604-669-8379. Technical Support also accepts faxes at 604-681-7163.

The second type of support is Priority Support, which has an annual fee. There are three major advantages to using the Priority Support plan. First, when you call Technical Support, you are moved to the front of the line (but still behind other Priority Support callers ahead of you), thereby reducing your wait times. Second, you get an 800 toll free number to use (no long distance charges), so you can call in as often as necessary. Finally, Priority Support members get extended hours to call (hours vary by plan purchased). If you are responsible for supporting Seagate Crystal Reports in your organization, the conveniences of Priority Support are highly recommended. For more information about Priority Support, contact Seagate Software at 800-877-2340.

Making the Most of Certified Trainers and Consultants

The Professional Services Organization at Seagate Software launched a Certified Training program in 1995 and a Certified Consultants program in 1998. Certification requires prescreening, classroom training, and a difficult exam (which usually takes at least 30 hours to complete) with a score of at least 85% required to pass. Certified Trainers and Certified Consultants have differing backgrounds and experience and can help you with your Seagate Crystal Report questions and projects.

It is important that you ask for a Certified Trainer or a Certified Consultant, because often times uncertified trainers or consultants charge the same prices for a vastly different product. To get the most for your money, make sure that you're getting a Certified Trainer or Certified Consultant who has proven themselves to Seagate Software and is authorized to use official materials. The following is a list of the different types of Certified Training available:

- Onsite (or private) training
- Public training conducted at a Certified Training center and offered throughout the world every week
- Computer Based Training (CBT)
- Custom Computer Based Training specific to your company and needs
- Custom Courseware and Training from a Certified Trainer

For more information on training, contact Seagate Software at 800-877-2340, or contact The BridgeBuilder Company at 800-222-7731 (www.bridgebuilder.com) for additional information on custom courseware and computer-based training.

3-tier architecture. Seagate Info uses three levels of components, each of which completes different processes. With this architecture, the client machine offloads the scheduling and processing of reports to a designated server machine, and the database resides on a third machine.

Absolute formatting. The default formatting for any field or object that you set using File, Options or the Format Editor.

Active Server Page (ASP). A technology that allows developers to create scripts and applications to change the functionality of a Web site by creating a dynamic page that can be viewed from the most popular Web browsers. ASPs must be used with Microsoft's Internet Information Server (IIS) version 3.0 or higher.

ActiveX controls. Controls that allow programmers to plug in DLLs, in this case the Crystal Reports Print Engine (CRPE32.DLL), to a custom application or Visual Basic project.

Aggregate function. A special command, provided with the database, that gives a single result based on an entire set of records in a table.

Automated Processing Scheduler (APS). This middle-tier component of the Seagate Info system serves as the security guard for the system. The APS records information regarding jobs, which the Info Desktop accesses.

Automation Server. An in-process automation server based on the Component Object Model (COM), allowing developers to configure the way reports appear in a Web browser.

Common Gateway Interface (CGI). A standard communication interface for Web servers. Version 7 of Seagate Crystal Reports is compatible with CGI Web servers.

Conditional formatting. A way of changing formatting dynamically, depending on certain conditions, using the Highlighting Expert or a conditional formula.

Crystal Chart. A component accessible from within the Crystal Report Designer that allows the user to design custom charts.

Crystal Dictionary. A structured, customizable view of data in a database. Dictionaries help users unfamiliar with database terminology and structures create reports from a clearly understandable view.

Crystal Image Server. Component responsible for translating Crystal Image (.CRI) files into a format that can be displayed in a Web browser.

Crystal formula language. A script language provided with Crystal Report Designer that allows users to write formulas.

Crystal Query Client. A component similar to the Crystal Report Designer that allows users to build ad hoc reports over the Web. The tool saves the query files in the .RPT format, allowing the files to be opened in the Crystal Report Designer. A user can also open reports created in the Crystal Report Designer in the Crystal Query client as well.

Crystal Query Server. Component that allows the Crystal Query Client to connect and process query requests. The Query Server allows the administrator to configure and modify settings that can control the amount of work that the server does.

Crystal Report Designer. The "main" component of Seagate Crystal Reports; this is where reports are designed and previewed.

Crystal Web Reports Server. Provides the configuration application for control over how reports are delivered and accessed over the Web. The Crystal Web Report Server allows some interaction at the time the report runs, such as using parameters, record selection, and stored procedures.

Custom report. An option for designing reports where a Report Expert is *not* used and all functionality of the report is added from the menu and toolbars.

Data file. A type of connection from Seagate Crystal Reports to a database that uses a native driver between SCR and the database to which you are connecting.

Data source. Your source of data. This may be a database, data warehouse, query, dictionary, and so forth.

Datatype. The definition of a field or variable in terms of the kind of data the field or variable holds. Datatypes include number, string, datetime, Boolean, binary, and currency values. Each database provides support for some or all of these types, or variations of them.

Design tab. The tab in which you design a report. It contains five sections by default, and more sections can be added at any time.

Dimensions. The major entities, factors, or components of an OLAP data set. Dimensions are used when designing cubes to define the data that is to be included in the cube.

Document import tool. A report conversion tool that can be used to convert ASCII text reports into Seagate Crystal Reports. Access the tool from the Report Gallery.

Equal join. See *join types*.

Fields. Any field you insert onto a report: database fields, special fields, formula fields, parameter fields, running total fields, summary fields, and so forth.

Foreign key. In a database table, a foreign key is the field or combination of fields that refer to the primary key in another table.

Format Editor. A dialog box that provides tabs according to the type of field being formatted. Any field or text object can be formatted using this Editor.

Formula. Expressions written by the report designer to manipulate data or the appearance or behavior of an object on the report.

Formula Editor. SCR's tool for writing formulas. The Formula Editor contains three "trees" from which you can select fields, functions, and operators to add to your formula.

Functions. Special commands provided by SCR for writing formulas. They are generally used to retrieve a value or to format a field.

Grand totals. Summary totals for an entire report. These totals print in the Report Footer section of a report.

Grid Object method. The OLAP method Seagate Crystal Reports uses to create reports from cubes. With this method, three or more dimensions can be included in a single grid object, and that object can be formatted and pivoted to meet your analysis needs.

Group Tree. Also referred to as Smart Navigation, this is a navigation tool for moving through a report. The Group Tree lists all of the groups on a report. When you click a group name the Preview tab displays that group wherever it occurs in the report.

Grouping. A way to organize and summarize related information in a report. For example, in a report that lists employees, you might group employees by department.

Hierarchies. The multiple levels of an OLAP dimension. The relationship between these levels has many different names depending on your OLAP tool, such as levels, children, parents, or descendants.

Highlighting Expert. A tool that allows you to conditionally format a number or currency field with border, font, and background attributes, instead of having to write a conditional formula.

Info Desktop. A Seagate Info component where all client interaction with Seagate Info is based. This interface requires a logon password. Through the Info Desktop, the user can access the Crystal Report Designer.

Info Servers. This middle-tier component of the Seagate Info system serves as the workhorse of the system, processing job requests. There are several specific kinds of Info Servers, each processing a specific type of job.

ISAPI. The Microsoft Internet Information Server application programming interface.

Join Types

> **Equal join**. This join refers to the link between two tables in a report. An equal join type is the default for ODBC and SQL connections to a database. This join type pulls all records onto a report that have a matching value in both tables. Also referred to as an inner join.

> **Left outer join**. This join type is the only join available for the data file connection. Referring to the link between two tables in a report, the left outer join includes all records from the left table, and any matching records from the right table.

> **Right outer join**. A join type that includes all records from the right table, and matches only from the left table.

Left outer join. See *join types*.

Linking. See *join types*.

NSAPI. The Netscape application programming interface.

ODBC. Open Database Connectivity is a standardized communication tool for use between software programs and databases. It allows a software program to work with a wide variety of database types.

ODBC Administrator. This tool is not really part of Seagate Crystal Reports but ships and installs with your software. Microsoft provides this tool so that you have access to many ODBC drivers that help you connect Seagate Crystal Reports to many databases and other programs.

OLAP. Online Analytical Processing is a technology for creating multidimensional structures for use in data analysis. These structures are usually referred to as cubes or hypercubes.

Operators. Special commands provided by SCR for writing formulas. Operators are generally used to compare objects.

Page controls. Arrow key controls on the upper right corner of the Preview tab that allow you to navigate through a report.

Parameter. In Crystal Report Designer, parameters provide a means for requesting and capturing values from the user.

Preview tab. This tab is where you can see what a report will look like if you print it. It contains records from your database and the exact formatting indicated on the Design tab.

Primary key. In a database table, the field or combination of fields that make a record unique. Not all tables have a primary key.

Query. A means to extract a subset of data from a data source. The query captures a snapshot in time of select data. SCR has both the SQL Designer and Seagate Query tools for designing queries.

Query Explorer. A tool used to select tables and fields in Crystal Query Client.

Query tab. Similar to the Design tab, but found in Crystal Query Client.

Record. A unit of related information in a database. A record might contain many fields pertaining to the customer: customer name, account number, order numbers, order dates, address, phone, and so forth.

Record selection. A means of filtering the records that you want to appear on a report from all of the records in your database.

Report Designer Component (RDC). A standalone Crystal Reports Designer that can be integrated into Visual Basic 5.0 and 6.0 so that the developer can design reports from within the Visual Basic IDE.

Report Expert. A wizard or interactive template that walks you through designing a specific type of report by prompting you for information to be included in the report.

Report tab. Similar to the Preview tab, but found in Crystal Query Client.

Right outer join. See *join types*.

Seagate Info 7. The newest release of Seagate Software's Seagate Info. Seagate Info uses the Crystal Report Designer, but includes numerous other components that handle the scheduling and processing of jobs, user security, and more.

Shortcut menu. The floating menu that appears when you right-click a field or object. The menu lists commands specifically available for that object.

Smart Linking. A tool that performs table linking automatically. Smart Linking looks at the data in the tables you have included for your report and links fields together that meet linking criteria.

Smart Navigation. A technology allowing the ability to jump to a specific group on a report instead of having to move one page at a time.

Smart Viewers. Controls that allow Web browsers to read a report in the native .RPT format (important because the formatting of a report does not change when read in the .RPT format).

Special fields. Page numbers, dates, file path, selection criteria, and other fields you can add to a report to provide extra helpful information.

SQL. Structured Query Language is the industry standard database language. By using this standard language SCR accesses information from any source which supports SQL (which is almost every source available).

Stored procedure. In some databases, a set of stored SQL statements that can be executed as a command with or without passed-in parameters to perform database table maintenance, record selection, or other data manipulation functions. SCR can use stored procedures to access information.

Tables. A database structure that organizes data. Tables must be linked together via a common field using the Visual Linking Expert for both tables' data to be available for a report.

Text objects. Objects you can add anywhere on a report that serve as mini-word processors where you can add text, combine text with fields, or combine fields.

Thin wire architecture. The capability of the Crystal Web Server to send only the pages requested (referred to as Page On Demand) to a Web browser instead of the entire file.

Top N/Sort Group Expert. Allows groups to be sorted based on summary calculations of data contained within the groups.

Totals. Subtotals and summaries added to reports. These totals automatically print in the Group Footer section of the group they summarize.

Visual Linking Expert. A tool for manually or automatically linking tables. This is where the join type can be changed and tables and databases added and removed from a report.

XTREME.MDB. Sample Microsoft Access database shipped with Seagate Crystal Reports software and used throughout the book for examples.

INDEX

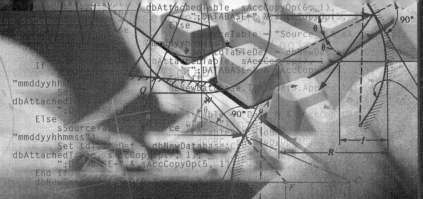

A Revolutionary Approach To Teaching Programming

PRIMA TECH'S

HANDS ON

Series

PRIMA TECH presents a new approach to teaching programming. Rather than focusing solely on language syntax, HANDS ON books allow you to learn the language by creating useful, practical applications. You'll progress through a series of projects that gradually become more complex, allowing you to apply and build upon each accomplished project. This method teaches programmers the way they prefer to be taught—by *doing!*

CALL NOW to order (800) 632-8676 ext. 4444

A Division of Prima Publishing
www.prima-tech.com

Prima Publishing is a trademark of Prima Communications, Inc.
All other product and company names are trademarks of their respective companies.

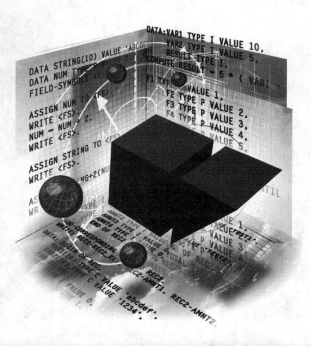

Learning Microsoft® Office 2000 is a breeze with PRIMA TECH's bestselling *fast & easy*™ guides

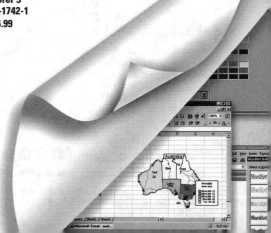